Shepherd Wars & Sheep Attacks

William Thompson Jr.

Copywrite 2007/Copywrite2008
by *William Thompson, Jr.*
PUBLISHED BY

Write Everlasting Tips,

Publishing company

Unless otherwise indicated, all Scripture quotations are from the King James Version of the Bible.

ISBN-0-9755994-2-9
ISBN-9780975599426

Printed in the United States of America

To contact the author,write
W E T Publishing Co.
7525 Arbor Hill Dr.
Fort Worth, Texas 76120

Contents

Introduction...VI

Dedication...X

1. *Sold On Separation!............................. 11

2. Battling The "GOD" Complex!.............. 37

3. Thy Rod and Thy Staff!...................... 67

4. Sheep Led Shepherds............................ . 91

5. Now Who Will Care For The Sheep? 105

6. Doubters & Haters!................................ 129

7. Sheep Gone Wild!................................ 149

8. Sheep Bites 179

9. Leg Of Lamb.. 195

10. Undressed & Unprotected.................... 221

11. For The Cau$e of CASH................. 239

12. Divided instead of Divine.................... 277

13. Grace in the Battle!*............................ 303

14. In Your Face...................................... 341

Conclusion -

    The Big Guns In The Battle*.   377

Dedication

To *Truth*, which is the

Written, Infallible, WORD OF God; Hope, Faith and Trust in the Lord;

Finally:

TO Mrs. Sharon R. Thompson,

And to all of the Thompson-etts;

Antonio, Misty, Aaron, and William III

I Love You All

Sheppard Wars & Sheep Attacks

✢ Introduction: ✢

A comprehensive focus; of the inner struggles of the Body of Christ at large; from the perspective of a dedicated churchman who has lent his own personal experiences with God and the body of Christ. This work is not intended to be just another sketch of the historical aspect of the delineated accounts in the past ripples among the establishment of denominational segregated alliances, whereas, people are catagorically placed among the likeness of their own peers, whether they be spiritual or humanistically religious.

I have lived all of my life in the church, only to realize that the struggle doesn't appear to be relenting with the passing of time and the bulging existence of educated people who are now docked in the pews of the church; you'd think that people would be smarter now? Rather, the wars among the churches appear to be visciously gaining momentum as time progresses onward through the declining ages of humanity.

The fight among the organized denominations and the people of the selected groups, is on right now in the present atmosphere of the places of worship, world wide. There are those among the brethren, who hold each other by the throats; and sometimes that is literally the case! People are mercilessly being held hostage to their past lifestyles, being denied the benefitted revelation of their change through faith in God, forgiveness of their sins by God, their peers, and ultimately self.

It is not always easy to work with others who are indeed the personnel of the clergy and the local church body.

It is religiously acceptable, to encounter attacks from other religious outsiders who refuse to embrace Jesus Christ as the only begotten of God. You sort of expect them to fight for the right to introduce their own unsubstantiated opinions about what they believe people should know about God, and how we should worship.

The word of God says that; "If the gospel be hidden, it is hidden to those who are lost." They are Truly Lost! But, one of the major causes of the rifts among the churches, lies within the fact that many people feel that it is acceptable if those meandering nomads; who could never ever find their way to the truth without the word of God, be favorably entitled to vocally express their own disconnected opinions in our houses of worship.

Opposers to Christianity, are determined to expatiate their cause for anyone that is willing to listen. While those who have chosen the church of God, through Jesus Christ our Lord, fight against the unacceptable opinions of Christian detractors, on the inside of the church, at large;

They feel that they are running with the only truth there is to be received. Though religiously deceived; according to the Holy Bible, they are ignorantly blinded, and totally confused relative to the actual truth of the gospel of God.

The actual balance of the informative weight of the written matter of the wars of the Christian churches has plundered the total platform base of the scale. Everyone should step on the scale to be weighed in the balance, as the scale will not only reveal my own wieght, but your's as well. Your weight measurement, never has to be the same as mine, the reading on the scale is truth!

Just as many people avoid stepping on the scale to weigh themselves, likewise, people also avoid the biblical scale of truth, citing the actuality of the imbalanced behavior of both the leaders and the laymen of the churches, who have kept the fight going for decades.

To those who have been caught up in these wars, perhaps you were never taught that we are all on the same team. There is just no sound reason that we should ever be found battling each other as we have done for decades, ignoring the commandments of God without fear or any reverence to the word of our God.

Christ won't be stepping down to referee and to ring the bell of the last round to declare the winner of all church's battles. Fighting should already have been put to an end by the time that Jesus cracks the sky.

Christ, is coming soon! I want you to come and go with me to meet Him in the air, when He shall appear! I expect, that you want me to be there with you on such a glorious occasion, to be raptured up to be with the Lord forever!

God wants us to quit standing off against each other, and embrace one another as blood-washed brothers and sisters in the true fight against sin, and Satan.

I've been ordained to simply speak out, from the inside of the struggle, sharing with you from the inwardly defining position, as a lifetime member of the church, to reveal for some, and to discuss with others.

I hope that you are saved and strong enough to share the blessing that you are about to receive for the sake of the body of Christ, and the inner health of the church.

You will be blessed beyond your wildest imagination, to encourage the people of the church to get along like the bible says that we are to get along.

All that could be said has not been said intentionally, for the purpose of preserving the integrity of the true sheep of His pastures. Many still need to come into the fellowship of the Sheepfolds. Nothing in this book has been written for the purpose of destroying the reputation of the fellowship of the body of Christ.

Sheppard Wars & Sheep Attacks; should be a reading reward like no other book that you will have ever read. You just might need to put on the armor of God, preferably the helmet of salvation, and for sure the shield of faith, in an effort to come out on the other end at the exit of this reading exposition, better than you were when you entered.

The blessing of the Lord be with you now!

About The Author

William (Bill) Thompson Jr.

Has been in the ministry of preaching the gospel since Feb. 7,1982, and has engaged in studies and training of the bible. He has been in the church all of his natural life and has the experience of a true churchman that lends the passion for which he ministers the gospel of God. He is an ordained ministering elder of the Church since June 1998, by the age of 3 years he had already began to express a passion to play the piano and to preach the Gospel. Born March 12, 1961 in El'paso, Texas, to the union of the late Rev. William Thompson Sr. & Rev. Daisy Y. Mclawler-Thompson; the family later relocated to Fort Worth, Texas where he grew up in the church singing in the choir and learned to study his own bible. He attended the Fort Worth Independant School District and graduated from P. L. Dunbar Sr. High, class of 79'. He attended Tarrant County Junior Colledge, Dallas Theological Seminary, and Vogue Bueaty Colledge. His uncle; the Late Apostle Russell Thompson, laid his hand on him at the age of 11, from that point on he knew that there was more for him in the Lord. He moved to the next level in an effort to get to that which he desired most of the Lord.

He is a talented instumentalist, and has composed many songs. Pastor Thompson has crossed the lines of denominational influences as a friend and brother, enabling himself to become identified as a child of God and not Just a Baptist, a Methodist, a Pentecostal, or for that matter, just another member of the Church Of God In Christ! He has ministered in music for ministries in the DFW Metro-plex, and OKC, OK. He has traveled with evangelist, and has been the guest musician for many revivals, musicals, weddings, conferences, recordings and etc. He founded and established the Spoken Word Center, School of Prophetic Excellence 2004. Pastor Thompson hails from an extensive linage of dedicated ministers. He's a decendant of the Late; Reverend Vol William McLawler of Louisville, Kentucky; and of the first generation Church of God In Christ. By the grace of God and divine providence, he found his way back to the grass roots of his own spiritual inheritance. His endeavor is to serve the people of the Lord everywhere that will receive of the awesome gift of the Holy Ghost to which he has been endowed. He is known and respected as a "True Prophet" of God. Pastor Thompson has been married to Sharon Renee for 25 years and is the father of four children.

For We Wrestle Not......Eph. 6:12

WRESTLING.   Catch as Catch Can Style.

One

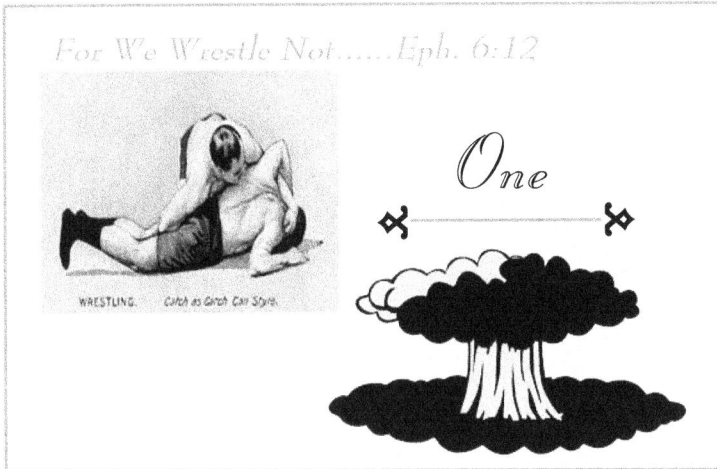

*Sold On Separation!

Come now let us reason together, saith the Lord: though your sins be as scarlet, they shall be as white as snow; though they be red like crimson, they shall be as wool. If ye be willing and obedient, ye shall eat the good of the land: But if ye refuse and rebel, ye shall be devoured with the sword: for the mouth of the Lord hath spoken it.   Isaiah 1:18-20

Their heart is divided; now shall they be found faulty: he shall break down their altars, he shall spoil their images.   Hosea 10:2

God is faithful, by whom ye were called unto the fellowship of his son Jesus Christ our Lord. Now I beseech you, brethren, by the name of our Lord Jesus Christ, that ye all speak the same thing, and that there be no divisions among you; but that ye be perfectly joined together in the same mind and in the same judgment. Is Christ divided?

I Corinthians 1:10-11, 13A

And let us consider one another to provoke unto love and unto good works: Not forsaking the assembling of ourselves together as the manner of some is; but

Signs of Opposition Established through Denominational Persuasions?

*I*t's been a very painful realization for what should be a unified body of Christ, to face the fact that within the many diverse bible teaching institutions, most organized, denominationally structured churches, underneath the umbrella of Christianity, all refuse to come together as one body established by Jesus Christ, for fear of losing power and authority as the head of the flock, and the leader of the pack.

Christianity teaches us that Heaven is our final destiny, after we have completely finished our purposeful stay here on earth. Likewise, we also preach the same fact that Jesus Christ is Lord; and that He is the only way to salvation in God through faith and repentance.

In one way or another, all Christian churches have similar resemblances in the order of which worship services are practiced, globally. The highlight of our services is normally preaching the gospel, and extending an invitation to discipleship in Christ, in effort to allow the Holy Spirit to move in our presence!

Our churches are comprised of leadership at the helm to establish and to maintain order, even though we are past the point of recognizing that the structure and the people in the churches are out of order. Leaders are comprised of those that went as a result of the call of God, and those who chose to come forward to take the stern of the ship as a career pastor, having never been commissioned to go, but on their own, for any unspecified number of reasons chose pastoring the church as a means for financial income, whether they are truly respected as the leaders or not, both leadership types are in place.

Let me begin by acknowledging the fact that there are many great leaders in the churches, who are truly focused on the word of God and the salvation of man. They are very passionate to the cause of Christ and will not be swayed nor encouraged to compromise the message of the gospel, neither their positions as Christian leaders, all on the strength of their calling.

In defense of the office of the pastor; there are pastors that can be found around the denominational spectrums everywhere, who are living examples of the sermons that they preach. Though being few in number, and dwarfed in between the vast number of religious impostures; they are not that far from reality, as many would have you to believe.

They are often the leaders who are overlooked, overworked and under-paid. The true leaders are usually the pastors that the average people choose to walk away from the easiest, it appears? Perhaps they are too focused on the real purpose of the church for some people. THEY ARE OFTEN ACCUSED OF BEING TOO SERIOUS!

WITH THIS ALL BEING SAID;*****

It's the leaders that refuse to come together to bring the people into oneness. As the ages close, the people seem to exist within a deeper wedge, relative to their religious perceptions about God and the true purpose of the church.

People have concepts of religion that they have been taught throughout the years, but they do not exemplify spiritual relationships with God, as required in the word of God. While the denominational arguments progressively rage onward in the presence of the churches, too many people are literally dying, having never exemplified any connection to the resurrected power of Christ, in their lives.

On any given Sunday morning, when driving by many churches of all denominations, we see parking lots that are filled to capacity with cars driven from far and near, and church auditoriums that appear to be swelling, pushing the walls outward, for more people to get in.

These days the people are encouraged to develop relationships with the buildings, while being excused from walking upright as a visible child of God. However, on the very same Sunday mornings, there are sporting arenas and restaurants, as well as job corporations, with crowds of people that actually dwarf the attendance of any one of the churches.

Some people will defend the cause of their church, who are totally illiterate to the actual cause of Christ? They have not yet come to the understanding of the true purpose of the visible church in this world.

The church is not a business organization, like we are being more vigorously challenged to embrace the church as being. THE CHURCH IS AN "ORGANISM." It's alive and breathing and producing living offspring in the spirit of the Lord. We are to be recognized as the family of God, forever; we are the children of the Lord! Not, vacationers visiting the household of faith, or spectators who are only gullible to see if there is any reality to the power of the church.

What would the church be, if on the front of the buildings of the churches everywhere, the signs only read; "THE CHURCH?" The average churchmen are enraged at the thought of the signs of their own denominations being worded to reflect only the church, as God has chosen and not the dominating structure of their own religious choosing. My reference is not to the Church of Christ organization; it's to the body of Christ; worldwide.

In my own opinion; the denominational structure of the churches would definitely be the only way to go if the bible read that God had established a particular place in Heaven for every individual denominational structure. But it doesn't! The bible states that there is only one Heaven for the church of God to be received into.

As a matter of the fact, the bible states there is only ONE LORD; ONE FAITH; ONE BAPTISM. Only in the carnal minds of sinful man, do we get many ideas, out of the one truthful reality of God. Somehow, I believe that we as people feel that God is impressed with our intellectual abilities to segregate ourselves into multiples of diverse religious idioms outside of the oneness of God, call it church and still claim to be within the singleness of the spirit and truth of the scripture.

No matter how crazy our ideas might be, we feel that just because we are able to seat a group of people to influence the religious patterns of thought in their minds, we seem to be confident that God will also be governed by what we believe about Him?

Are we really that crazy? Or, are we so carried away with the struggle to be the number one church on top of the denominational spectrum when the Lord Jesus returns to rapture the church out of the world? Whatever the true answer is, we are definitely sold on the idealism of separation in the churches.

The actuality of separatism exists within all inner racial boundaries in the country of the USA, whereas we are already separated according to the color of our skin, and our economical and social status. In many of the neighborhoods that are now mixed raced, the people of those neighborhoods are not necessarily living together as a unified people of the same country. The average American; has been conditioned to accept separation as the proper order.

Sold; and Selling It

At a very early age, I begin to have such invigorating debates relative to which church denomination was actually the right church organization to be a part of. I have been sent to Hell; *(told that I was going to hell),* by members of other denominations opposite from the one that I was a part of, simply because I would not change and become a part of the other denomination, of their own choosing. I had been taught in a Sunday school class that people of other denominations were going to hell because they would not come on board with the denomination that we were in.

We used to hear Sunday morning messages from the pulpits on a regular basis, relative to the fact that the church we were sitting in, at the time of the sermon being preached, was indeed the right church and the only church to be a part of. We were taught that the people of the other churches did not have God in their lives, and that they were enemies to the cause of Christ.

Although I later learned that we all have similar ways

of worship in the Christian churches, we were taught that just because the other churches opposite of our denomination did not worship in the exact same manner of which we did, that they were not worshipping God the way that they were supposed to?

The completeness of worship, is not totally rapped up in the manner of which we go about doing whatever we do, worship is not to be ascertained as if to be any particular practice or formidible routine to be carried out in the congregation of the people, rather it is totally engulfed within the respect of who it is that we bestow the reverence of our worship, which in my opinion according to the Holy Bible, had better be God through Jesus Christ!

Only what God has indeed done for us through the sacrifice of His only begotten son; Jesus Christ; gives us the rights of true worship, not the structure of our own denominational rites. The organized, regulated practices of your church does not have the power to establish for the entire world, what does or does not constitute true worship, as long as the people have the right object of worship in order, which is Christ, according to the word of God.

I have discovered that many people are sold out to the idea of separation on Sunday mornings and every other day of the week, relative to the churches. As it relates to witnessing to other people in the communities, the structured idea of the witness' denomination is actually what is being illustrated to the people being witnessed unto, rather than Christ.

People are trained to be marketers for their denominations and spokesmen for their own ideas of worship which is in error to the cause of the true purpose of the church, while they should be transformed into being Disciples of Christ.

The arguments, disputing which denominations should be respected as the right organized structure for the church to worship under, have been debated for so long that no one seems to have the courage to tell the leaders who participate with these unnecessary orders of business, that they are wrong for presenting a structured idea and not Christ.

The rules and the regulations for the structure of the church, are already established in the bible, the problem is that not every leader wants to take the time to search the scripture to know them, or they don't feel that it is necessary to admonish the people to live by the bible's standards on a daily basis. Everything must have rules and regulations to govern the behavior of the persons involved. Not everything; goes!

The scriptoral regulations, are as the fence around the perimeter that aligns the circumference of the grazing pasture. The fence is the only way to ensure that the sheep are abiding within the boundaries of the assigned pasture. Likewise, the only way to know that we are abiding within the installed boundaries of the church is through the written word of God.

Nothing, and no one else has the power to define or to establish the fact that we are truly operating as the church other than the Holy Bible. Many leaders, have taken it upon themselves to be little gods in the eyes of the people of the churches, they fail to realize themselves, that they will have to answer to the Lord in the judgment for purposely leading the people astray.

Traditional Hostages!

*M*any people who profess to being non-violent, will wrestle you down to the ground for making a statement about their church of choice! Some of the religiously astute members of the Christian church, will have a tendency to totally lose the focus of their salvation, in the midst of discussions about the fact that we are dangerously separated when we ought to be worshipping the Lord together.

It's a laughing matter to most people, whenever we discuss the matter of being so divided on Sunday mornings. We have been separated for so long, that most have literally come to believe that we are on opposite sides of the very same "one-sided" purpose of the church, which when closely examined, the idea is crazy and rather twisted!* Christ is one-sided; unlike a two-sided coin!

Most everyone is singing; "My Church is Better Than Your Church." We have begun hearing messages that suggest, that it is actually God's divine will that we are separated. People have been brainwashed so, to the point, that they have developed identifiable traits in their religious and/or spiritual demeanor, relative to the churches that they attend.

People from certain churches, talk a certain way that is even unmistakably identifiable to the personality of their leaders. Those, who lose sight of the fact that their focus is supposed to be on the Lord, soon alter their own behavior for the purpose of fitting in to the in-crowd of the ministry to which they are attending.

It is often these types of adaptable traits that are worn overtly in the demeanor of the people that is often substituted as being the recognizable characteristic of what is supposed to be the spirit of God. It is erroneous to believe that any particular religious behavior relative to a group of people; depicts true Christianity, and the righteousness of God. Unless we live according to the written word of God, our lifestyles are totally unacceptable to God.

We as people, love being accepted by the upper classmen of any particular society, to the point that we are prone to forsake our own gifts and callings, while some will even go as far as to purposefully deny their own anointed spiritual endowments, for the purpose of pleasing the in-crowd, if not for the sake of pleasing the leader.

If you ever wanted to know how to detect whenever a person of the church has truly bought into the concept of separation, now you know a few of the signs to look for characteristically in the demeanor of certain people who are determined that they are not going to be left out of the inner loop in the church.

Be ye not unequally yoked together with unbelievers: for what fellowship hath righteousness with unrighteousness? And what communion hath light with darkness? And what accord hath Christ with Belial? Or what part hath he that believeth with an infidel? And what agreement hath the temple of God with idols? For ye are the temple of the living God; as God hath said, I will dwell in them, and walk in them; and I will be their God, and they will be my people. Wherefore come out from among them, and

II Corinthians 6: 14-17

In some way or another, we seem to have missed the message that this scripture has spoken to the church. Separatism, is evidently the breeding grounds for accusatory spirits among the people of the church, because we are consistently finding irreconcilible differences between each other, on the basis of accusing one another of being more sinful and ungodly than we are ourselves. Many believe that they are better spiritual examples than the other people of their surroundings, and other churches.

It is no wonder across the board, that we as people of the body of Christ don't believe in one another any better than we do? For this reason, we find ourselves always praying or at least willing to pray for sinners and the ungodly, over and above praying for one another. We have to come up with something or another to make us feel noble, because I believe that deep within the souls of all of us, we know that separating ourselves from one another, for sure, is not the righteousness of Christ, or the plan of God for the church!

Separatism also opens the door for demonic activity! Because, in an effort to be secluded and separated from the people of God, you will have to maintain a judgmental spirit of self-righteousness, that enables you to see the need to put distance between yourself and other people of the body of Christ, as a result of the pride that has set up in your own heart, flowing through your spirit.

Unreasonable Distance!

*I*t is actually obvious that we are not thinking of the Lord whenever we mistreat one another, or else we would entreat one another in the love of God. There is absolutely no way that we could be thinking soberly when we make decisions to distance ourselves from the people of the Lord, with no determination to forgive one another, or to make an attempt to come together with those individuals who have offended us.

Many of the organizations were either broken or established over financial disputes. It doesn't take a rocket scientist to figure out why so many of the biblical standards for the church have been compromised.

Many of these leaders are not even concerned with the spiritual welfare of the people of the church, as much as they are determined to take the positions that they are right, to ensure they have the premesis that enables them to keep the people thinking separation. These churches seem to believe that people will come in contact with their spirituality one day, whenever God gets ready for them to make the discovery.

They have become unreasonably intoxicated with fitting in with the more sociably accepted leaders of the community; those leaders who appear to have forgotten that they belong to the church and not to the secular society, or to humanistic ideology.

Instead of the separation of the church and the state, many of these churches have begun to compete with the state and the local government for publicity of the social commonwealth of their surrounding communities. Church leaders are becoming publicity seekers more and more; they refuse to dodge the lenses of the media's camera in the midst of any social uprising in the community.

The church, was never ordained of God to be an after the fact type of an entity, coming to the aid of the fallen individuals, or to the rescue of those individuals who have endangered their livelihood through wayward living? But, the sole purpose of the church is to show people how to avoid getting into the many snares and entrapments, to the pitfalls of sinful deception that come as a result of selfish and unrestrained living on the edges of life.

Some churches, prefer the "SUPER-CHURCH" dispositions around the community. They prefer to be the ones to call on when a person may get into some type of trouble. The projection of this particular attitude forces them to feel that they have out classed their fellow-churchmen, to the point of citing the need for separation. They may feel that when another church is not capable of supplying the very same assistance to the community as they themselves, that there is no need to maintain fellowship with them.

It is unreasonable to feel that your church is better than any other church in the surrounding communities simply because you may have a greater ability based on the number of people in the congregation. The number of the people to hear a sermon on any Sunday morning may not even reflect your true purpose for being in the community.

Many say they believe that they are doing what the Lord requires for the church to be doing, when simultaneously, they are neglegent to deliver the uncompromised message of the gospel of Jesus Christ.

Leaders, that are determined to stay the course of preaching the messages of faith and salvation, cause friction to these self motivated entities that are styled as churches. They see many people helped as a result of their own organized muscle, but not many of the people that they give help to are seldom ever transformed by the renewing of their minds to reflect the presence of the living God.

Most people, whenever they come to the church, they only want assistance with the established lifestyles that are dragging them under the ground in the first place! They don't want the help that would show them the way to alter the present circumstantial outcomes that they are experiencing on a consistent basis.

Whenever people want real spiritual help, they usually don't call on these types of churches, because they know that most of these places don't offer any real spiritual guidance. People know when they are out of control and they know when they have fooled others around them into believing that all they need is the like common assistance that they could probably receive in the welfare lines, if they have the patience to wait in them.

It is dangerous for the church to allow the parishioners to inflate it's ego, relative to the exaggerated evaluation of the help that's been given to them. Other churches, that you have probably never heard of are doing more than you could have ever done, because they are in a better position to do so, even more so than your church, with the least bit of a strain. And no need for the assistance to be publicized throughout the community.

While these churches expend unnecessary energy making sure the community knows that they are assisting the needing people, they are also often stealing the glory that only belongs to the Lord!

WHAT'S MOST IMPORTANT?

Should the church help people live more comfortably here on the earth, or should we still be striving to help the lost people find their way to Jesus Christ; so that their hurts might indeed be healed and that they will be enabled to pull themselves up from the ground where they might have found them self, before coming to the church?

YOUR ANSWER :

OH YES! I'M A CHRISTIAN!

While the different denominations; of the so-called Christian umbrella, argue about which parts of the bible to believe and which parts of the bible are of no essence to us as Christians, in these late generations, too many people have been allowed to shortcut their way through the church right into the pit of hell!

People clap a certain way or they behave in a particular manner or they only associate with people of their denomination. Some are forbidden to even marry outside of their own denomination, or to date and form friendships without their inner-circles of religious identity.

Everything that has absolutely nothing to do with Christianity is taught and enforced, as mandates for belonging to many of these so-called Christian churches. Since we are all professing to be Christians, there should be extreme similarities in all of us, the same way that sheep look like sheep no matter of the species, and they have similar characteristics in behavior. They simply act alike and eat grass alike, and they all live in the pasture and the hills.

Holiness, is what is already established according to the bible, and it doesn't change relative to which denomination an individual may choose to attend. Many people are taught to ignore the teachings of the bible, that may not be taught within their teaching circles and are discounted as even being important to the people of God. What one group calls sin according to the bible, another group excuses it completely and they suggest to the people that it doesn't take all of that!

I don't think that we, of the Christian church; ought to ever be caught arguing about what is actually holiness and what is sinfulness, when we still have the very same BIBLE that we referred to in order to be saved! The bible is right all by itself, still; and it is absolutely unintelligent for all of us who claim to be Christians, to read from the very same bible and to view the very same passages of the scripture, and refuse oneness of understanding that would allow us to be likeminded as a Christian, leaving people only to turn to their own intellects for an interpretation of the scripture.

Only the devil could ever suggest that the people of

the church conduct themselves in such separating manners, such as fighting over the teachings of the bible, driving such irreparable wedges in our abilities to settle our differences and to come together to be the whole body of Christ.

It may in fact have been the devil, who threw the first punch on the leaders of the churches stirring up the fight among them, but if you really look on the inside of these church wars, you would soon discover that the devil has thrown his punch, and have long since then, left the scene of the crime. The devil has left the building! There are people fighting now who are both layman and leaders, that don't even have a real clue as pertaining to what the fighting is all about.

I would usually cross over into other denominations; NOT OTHER RELIGIONS; for different services or musicals, and even to minister to the people. I was sometimes reprimanded and criticized for mixing with what my church at the time considered to be, those sinners! Jesus Helped Me, even though I was blinded for quite a while by the indoctrination of the church, that I chose to attend! I later learned that I really did not aspire to sending people to Hell, as I had been taught, I realized that my calling was to keep all people from going to Hell!

Now that I have matured, of course I am able to recognize the differences in the teachings that are in fact totally to the left of what the bible teaches us, on all sides of the spectrum. I had to step back in order to see where we were all going wrong!

Many years ago I walked into a particular church, and the pastor who is now deceased, was on the floor ministering. In the middle of his message for the evening, he spotted me after I had been there for only a short while, and immediately changed his message, and began to preach against my hairstyle. The men who were members of the church there wore the crew cuts and fades even before they became as popular as they are today.

I walked into the church sporting a hairstyle, that was to my shoulder in length. So of course, I was going to attract attention that I'm sure that pastor quickly made up in his mind to cancle.

That was the only real explanation that I could come up with, as I quickly went back out the door. I got into my automobile and went to church somewhere else that Sunday evening, that did not focus on me upon my entrance into their worship service.

Do you have any idea of the number of the souls that have been lost, as a result of the onslaught of the denominational determination to keep the people separated and secluded, in the religious mentalities of the parishioners, which has caused many people to throw up both hands and to decide that it is not worth it, at all, to attend church?

Is there anyone, who cares that there are people in HELL that would not have been there, had the church come together to take the world for the Lord? I really want to know if there is anyone who cares about lost souls?

I'm not talking about indoctrinating people, molding them into coorporate denominational clones that just keep the debates going on, where the new comers to the denomination are awarded and applauded for pulling others into the ongoing inner-wars of the Christian church.

It's Obvious That They Bought It!

*M*ake no mistake about it; I am not the only person to realize that there needs to be some changes made relative to the fact that the churches are too separated. But, many of the organization heads are like taskmasters over their own religious slaves. YOU DON'T GET CHANGE, UNTIL YOU MAKE CHANGE!

Many of the local leaders are aware of the need to bring the body of Christ into oneness, but they are held hostage to their commitments to uphold the traditions of the organization, whether they are beneficial to the cause of Christianity or not.

Some leaders are not as progressive as they ought to be, even when the people of their own congregations are begging for a change that would even have a much greater benefit to their community, than it would even have on their local congregation.

However, many of the local leaders of the churches wouldn't dare to even dream of making changes that would cause their Bishops, Moderators, or Overseers to become enraged for even suggesting that there be change, possibly putting their own positions as leaders in jeopardy.

Leaders that are placed, as a result of their own religious careers and their scholastic achievements, are even more so hostages to the traditional order of their churches, mainly because they may not even have a true calling or a relationship with God. Many often lack the spiritual authority, which is the anointing, to move the presence of the Lord into the atmosphere of their separated churches, in which the spirit of the Lord is actually what brings down the needed change.

They enter their positions of leadership with a vow to uphold the traditions of separation many times even before having a thorough knowledge of what it is they are truly vowing to uphold.

Many of the leaders, after being placed into the positions of leadership in the churches find that they do not totally agree with the established religious order of the denominational structure, relative to the fact that it ensures separation, yet they remain hostage to the order by choice. You can never really know what it is that you are actually getting into until after you will have been in the situation for a while.

The denominational Generals in charge; appear to be set in place to keep the traditional order of separation a reality. As if you have never heard it before, change starts from the top and it trickles down to all others underneath the helm of the leadership. Whenever the weather changes in our present <u>external</u> atmosphere, it is the roof tops of our houses and the tops of our heads, that realize the changes first, simply because the change comes down from above.

We become hostages to the present atmosphere for only as long as the weather conditions remain as they are, but as soon as the conditions are changed above us, we become aware of a different order in the atmosphere relative to the conditions of the weather, although we may have already witnessed similar circumstantial weather conditions, to the likes of what we are presently experiencing as the changed order in the atmosphere.

The one condition unstated in the previous paragraph, that must be gleaned from the information above, is the fact that the changes in the atmosphere are only temporary and at best they are often very short spanned, from day to day. This is also true of the churches, that are plagued with powerful negative influence that denominations have on the people that have chosen to fellowship their tenure, as a member of the church of Jesus Christ.

Separation, is the reality of the existence of the churches worldwide, but, the continuation of that religious behavior will not be the beneficial sustenance, of the future climate of the church. Separation, has begun to gangrene at the foot of all of the standing platforms of the local churches, and in the bending of the joints of the denominational legs, whereas we are approaching the TIME OF AMPUTATION!

The Surgeon General and Chief Captain of the churches, have ordered a fix to the problem! But, health needs for the church, must be administered through the hearing of spiritual ears. The problem is that not many of the leaders have an ear to hear what the spirit is saying to the church, which causes many limbs and branches of the church at large not to heal.

Yet if any man suffer as a Christian, let him not be ashamed; but let him glorify God on this behalf. For the time is come that judgment must begin at the house of God: and if it first begin at us, what shall the end be of them that obey not the gospel of God? And if the righteous scarcely be saved, where shall the sinner and the ungodly appear? Wherefore let them that suffer according to the will of God commit to the keeping of their souls to him in well doing, as unto a faithful creator.   I Peter 4: 16-19

Separation Brings Divorce!

Separation, stinks of unforgiveness to me, simply because it has lasted for so long among the top leaders, of many churches. Those persons that are historically astute and thoroughly enlightened relative to the denominational wars, are rather skilled at supplying what they feel are the reasonable justifications for being separated from the other denominations?

I have been given historical lessons on the divided stance of church organizations and their determination to remain segregated; usually the historians can go on for a while discussing the past and how it is that the need for churches to be separated, was, and is still necessary.

The past Generals in the battle of separation, are all resting in their graves, but, yet still ruling and controlling the order of the churches from their graves. They were so convinced of the need to be separated, that they passed on the detrimental determination of separatism to the upcoming leaders, for the purpose of keeping them in touch with the early establishment of the church's arguments!

The reasons that they argued, died with them! The money they all argued over, is all gone now! The buildings that they thought were of the greatest monumental construction, relative to their own denominations identity, have all either been destroyed, demolished, abandoned, renovated or totally reconstructed. Whereas, not even the buildings of the past are the same.

The old age building structures served the purpose of highlighting the fact for us, that buildings don't make the churches; the people do! Jesus Christ never came to the earth to save the life of buildings; rather He came for the saving of the souls of mankind. AND BY THE WAY; HE WON'T BE COMING BACK FOR YOUR BUILDINGS!

Rather than the churches fighting over finances, real-estate, and politics; the emphasis should be placed on the fact that there is too much separation among the people of the body of Christ. We must be out of our natural minds, if we think for one moment that God is going to allow all of the attitudes of separation into Heaven, only to allow segregation to destroy the unity of the heavenly body all over again, alike Lucifer!

These separated people need to research the account of the devil causing a separation in Heaven. Perhaps too many of the people of the churches don't really believe the scripture concerning the fall of Satan? Satan has deceived the minds of the people, so severely, that they have become sympathetic to the lying cause of Satan's expurgation.

God is the same, He has not changed to this very day; He is very serious about the welfare of the church; as we are the sons of God; He loves us beyond our comprehension. Don't ever forget the fact that God gave His only precious Lamb; for a perfect sacrifice to save us from the destruction that Satan had brought to mankind, in the Garden of Eden.

Alike the separated churches of today, who don't seem to realize the fact that they are in agreement with Satan's agenda, as the different organizations refuse to come together, which is the underminding scheme of the devil to try and frustrate the God given purpose of the church in the earth. Adam and Eve in the garden; whenever they came into agreement with Satan, by way of the serpent, immediately they REALIZED separation from God!

God divorced Satan from the presence of His glory, when he brought about separation among the host of Heaven, before the beginning of the creative process of the entire universal cosmos. Divorce, has a permanent sting like death, in that the separation can be relentlessly painful to those persons of whom either case scenario might involve.

My friend, the devil was separated, and divorced simultaneously, at the very same time of his fall from heaven. As we know according to the scripture, the devil never had another chance to repeat the devastation against the heavenly host.

God, on the other hand, had already given mankind another chance when Jesus went to the cross of Calvary, for the sins of the world. We were already threatening permanent separation and divorce from God, but by His Grace and mercy we received a chance that we did not even deserve. Through Jesus Christ, God allowed us to reunite together with Him in a marriage commitment.

In representation of all mankind, Adam had already broken the heart of God, but God never broke a sweat for the simple fact that He already had a plan to redeem man.

What more can He do for us, that we might get the message, that we should have gotten, a long time ago? He laid the foundation and opened up the way for us, what more can He do? It's time for us to take the locks off of the doorways to the halls of separation, to allow togetherness to enter into the fellowship of the churches.

On the day of Pentecost according to Acts 2: 4; it has been made very clear to us that the Holy Ghost did not fall from Heaven upon mankind, as was prophesied and promised by Jesus Christ until they were all together in one place with one mind and with one accord. The main requirement was that they were to be together, in unity, in the love of God, and in praise.

We have been hearing of the Lord's return to the earth, to rapture the church out of the world, but, I am convinced that the Lord is giving the church a chance to come together as the one body of Christ, that it is originally established and ordained to be. The Lord is not coming back for just a leg or an arm or maybe for just an upper torso of the body of Christ, like at a crime scene!

I don't believe that the Lord is coming back for a church that looks like the fragmented body of a soldier on the battlefield that had been blown to pieces by a grenade or a missile. Soldiers and veterans of the war, in the armed forces can vividly imagine exactly what I am talking about; they have the picture, as did the prophet Ezekiel.(chapter 37)

Together we can bring the change that will please the Lord, to the point that He will come and get us out of the turmoil and the downright disapproval that we experience so often from the people of the world, that need us so desperately to help them find their way to the savior. Evidently, it is not yet the time for the Lord to return for the church, but don't get too relaxed just because the Lord hasn't come yet and forget the fact that He is coming!

It's time for an international recall on separation at all the four corners of the earth. We have got to make a move on the fact that we are dangerously separated, before the people get the idea that the church, as we know of the church in the world, is not working for the purpose in which it was established. Should the world take such a position against the church, they are going to establish their own church in the world, and I guarantee you, for sure, that it won't work for the saving of the souls of man.

You might think that people are complaining now and that people are out of control in the church; just wait until the world makes an attempt to establish its own church without the aid of the Holy Spirit of God to keep us in the will of God. The world has been sitting on ready to get rid of the written word of God and to take the bible out of the hands of the believers.

Don't we believe that we are helping their argument by being so separated and segregated?

The most segregated time in our country, is during the Sunday morning worship hour. Only a few churches have lowered the dividing petitions that kept other people from all nationalities and races from coming into the oneness of the body of Christ.

Will you be next?

For We Wrestle Not......Eph. 6:12

Two

WRESTLING.   Catch as Catch Can Style.

Battling
The "~~GOD~~" Complex!

Because that, when they knew God, they glorified Him not as God, neither were thankful; but became vain in their imaginations, and their foolish heart was darkened. Professing themselves to be wise, they became fools, and changed the glory of the uncorruptible God into an image made like to corruptible man, and to birds, and four-footed beast, and creeping things. Wherefore God also gave them up to uncleanness through the lusts of their own hearts, to dishonor their own bodies between themselves:

Romans 1: 21-24

Author's definition:

When leaders presume to take on the identity of a god: Require worshipful reverence as of a god in the congregation of the people; They have an Authoritative manner of controlling headship; Spiritually manipulating people to obey them; Neglecting to be identified as a called and ordained leader of the one and only true and living God.

It's Never Been My Struggle!

*I*t is very difficult to worship God; desiring to be a god at the very same time! Ask Satan; what it was like being Lucifer; when his primary purpose was to lead all the host of Heaven in worship? Something went wrong in the spirit of Lucifer that caused him to want to be the object of his own worship. He no longer wanted to worship God in the beauty of holiness, he wanted to be worshipped!

I'm convinced, that any leader that can still find the gall to attempt to require the people to reverence them as a supreme being, doesn't really believe the scriptural account of the fall of Satan and a third part of the host of Heaven.

There is far too many leaders in the pulpits of the churches, preaching every Sunday, to crowds in excess of thousands, both saved and unsaved; but they don't really believe the bible that they are preaching from, no matter what version or biblical translation they prefer to use!

I thank God that I learned at a very early age, that the

word of God is first of all for me to receive and to apply to my own life, before I would ever consider sharing the word or preaching the word of God to anyone else. I was taught, although I did not always adhere to my teaching; that my life would be the only bible that would be read by many people who surround me on a daily basis.

Rejection of me as a person, and the fight from the inside of the church against my ministry, had been so powerfully waged against me for so long, that I actually convinced myself that no one even cared about me or even cared about whatever I did? This deception was believed, until I did things that did not reflect the word of God, that was truly flowing inside of me.

The same people who rejected me from the beginning; and I quote, they said; "HE WON'T EVER BE NOTHING!", I'd like to believe now that many of those past leaders had little-god complexes, in that they felt they were capable of changing my calling and my understanding about receiving my calling to the Office of The Prophet, and they thought that I would allow them to thwart my purpose, further denying me of my destiny.

Either one of two things took place with me concerning my detractors, as a result of them watching me over the years; people made a big deal out of every mistake that I ever made and every sin that I had ever committed, further driving a nail in the coffins made of the negative prophecies against my life; Or they chose to believe in me as a man of God as they should have, as many others sought spiritual counsel from me and were inspired to make it through many challenges, as a result of my ministry to them.

It was indeed extremely hurtful, that people in the church

rejected me, even though God had begun to use me greatly, they treated me as if I were a stepchild of God's, or a son of Satan; though they had known me for quite some time. I was even more determined, greatly, to hold on to the unchanging hand of the Lord and to never let go of it, knowing that God is always right, and He's righteous concerning me!

People can push an individual to unimaginable limit, even over the edge of reasoning when they are allowed to do so. Perhaps from reading just these few paragraphs, it may have become clear to you, that I allowed the attitudes of rejection in the spirits of others, to be seated in my spirit! I also allowed their opinions of me to consistently walk through my mind, for a while!

If I were going to allow anything to cause me to feel more special than normal, as a result of the mistreatment from my former churchmen, it would have been the idea of being a victim to the negative attacks of the people of the church against me, and certainly not any ability that would have allowed me to exalt myself, feeling like the people ought to respect me as a god; judging the very capable, and spiritually connected ministry that they had received from me.

I always expected that the ministers that I trained under, would have been very proud to witness the spiritual maturation of my life progress to a level of stability to walk with the body of Christ, which would also allow me to stand with them in conviction. To my surprise, they were the exact opposite to what I had always expected, often criticizing me for being determined not to be just another person hanging around the church, with no other ability than to knock the dust out of a broom, only after someone else had used it to sweep! They never preferred for me to have been the one that swept the floor.

I expected they would be proud of the anointed ability to dissect the word of God, and to break open the word of truth, for the people that would be the up and coming witnesses in the body of Christ. I had a desire to teach others the way that I had been taught, however, by the time I came along to begin teaching, the Lord began to endow me with fresh revelations of the same word of God that I had always heard over the pulpits in the churches.

From the very beginning of my ministry, I was encouraged to develop the like convictions of the Apostle Paul;

And my speech and my preaching was not with enticing words of man's wisdom, but in demonstration of the spirit and of power:

I Corinthians 2: 4

I never had a drive in me to excite people from the pulpits, to make them feel good, or to get them to pat me on the back telling me that I had done a good job in the pulpit, especially if the message should fall short of being centered on the gospel of Christ. I had been a witness to this behavior in and throughout the church for a very long time. On some occasions, the people stated that they did not even understand the message the speaker was trying to convey to the church.

They Wanted to be God to Me!

I never had a mind to be a blur in the minds of the people of the church, neither did I have a mind to back away from the spiritual development and progression in the Lord, simply because it would upset someone else in the ministry, mainly the leaders.

The leaders always told us, to know who we are in the Lord, but the very moment I discovered who I am in the Lord, I seem to have sent them into a spiritual shock; you would be surprised of the number of the ministers and the leaders of the churches who were determined to convince me that that could not possibly be who the Lord says that I am!

These were the leaders whose bible studies and prayer meetings, I had attended and possibly their Sunday school classes over the years. I had attended their weekly training sessions on Sunday evenings and countless revivals. These were leaders that had even spoke into my life, saying to me that one day the Lord would use me greatly.

I saw these leaders weekly, as it should be quite evident that they should have known me well? As long as I stayed on one of the instruments or in the choir-stand; they seemed to be ok with that. They often spoke well of my music ministry whenever I ministered to the church, but of course, for only as long as they were in charge and at the helm of the ministry. Often times, I was regarded as one of the better musicians in the churches; according to the leaders?

It was not until the time that my ministry began to blossom and I began to move in the spirit of God and in the office of the Prophet, that most of the leaders seem to reveal to me, that they really had a problem with me. Many of these same leaders have acknowledged that indeed God has called me to the office of the Prophet and have stated to me that they believe that I am a SEER! That erases the idea of being a self proclaimed Prophet! I would be terrified to stand before the people of the Lord self endowed with personal agendas. I fear God!

II Peter 1: 19-21

I often wondered, how they might have reacted had I begun chanting Occult ritualistic chants and casting spells, burning candles, using black cat bones, turning Tarot cards and gazing into crystal balls? I wonder if the fight would be the same?

I don't believe that they wanted me to take their teaching as seriously as I did? Perhaps they lacked confidence in their own teaching and never expected that anyone would emerge, as a forefront spokesperson in the ministry of God.

Most of the young guys that I came up with in the church went on to backslide and leave the church. Some of the guys that I actually admired in the church while back in my youth, later developed drug and alcohol dependencies of which in the eyes of judges and very unforgiving members of the churches, erased any possibilities of them being used of the Lord, ever!

Some of them ended up in the penitentiary, some are sleeping in their graves, while others who are now in churches, are spiritually stagnated, as if they were never taught anything at all. Their levels of spirituality is pathetic for persons who were supposedly raised in the Pentecostal church.

When I think about it; perhaps the life that the other guys are living, is the life that some of the leaders had pictured for me? However, I don't apologize to anyone for what the Lord has indeed done in my life. Because of the anointing, I am a major benefit to the body of Christ, of which I believe was the Lord's purpose in the first place. I don't even believe that my family expected for me to make it to the place in the Lord that I did; but I made it!

I was invited to minister for an acquaintance of mine, and during that service, the Lord used me greatly. I ministered prophetically to just about everyone in the house; by their own admissions, the word given to the people was accurately, right on the target! The people acknowledged that they knew that it was the Lord speaking through me, and they also wanted me to know that they received my ministry.

The pastor, knew for sure that I had no knowledge of his own personal affairs, but I ministered to him as if I had been sitting in the same seat with him, during the situations that the Lord revealed to me, concerning him. Even after being ministered unto himself, still he publicly disregarded me as a prophet of God, saying to the people of his congregation, that there are no more prophets in the world!

I didn't argue with him in the presence of the people of his congregation and neither did I debate the issue with him afterwards. He was so intimidated with my ministry and the accuracy of the prophetic gift working in me that he did not even bother to bless me for speaking to his congregation! I have discovered that being a true prophet of the Lord causes problems for many other ministers who are not likewise, as equally endowed with the call to the Prophetic office.

Were it not for the fact that I knew that the Lord and I were the only ones present to hear Him speak to me telling me who I am, I'm sure that I would have rejected the word of the Lord as a result of their rejection. Those who are not true in their own calling have a problem with others being true. They seem to prefer that you would be as unconnected with the spirit of the Lord as they are.

People know when there is a very special endowment of the anointing upon the life of an individual, although they will do everything possible to discredit the anointing, in the presence of the people of the church. However, it is the responsibility of those who have been endowed to direct the people to worship the Lord Jesus Christ and to never allow the glory of the Lord to be touched by anyone!

Make no mistake about it; I know who I am in the Lord and where all of my help comes from. I'd be a fool, to begin thinking that I am my own source of information all of a sudden, and further more, to request that others respect me for knowing things that I could not have known otherwise, without the Lord telling me first. I thank God, that I realized that God alone made me all by Him self; He is God! God made you too; whether you desire to acknowledge the fact or not!

Most people that were hurt early on in the church as I was myself, many of them turned away from the Lord to occultism and to other dark spiritual practices as a method and a means of dealing with their pain. A vast number of the people who were hurt, chose to leave the Christian church altogether, vowing never to ever return even to mentioning the name of Jesus; as their savior.

What is actually more frightening and dangerous to the cause of Christ, is the fact that many of the victimized persons stayed on the inside of the church waiting on the opportunities to one day emerge to lead and to rule, styling themselves as a spiritual authority, although they have never been delivered and healed from the pain of their past hurt. These persons are very dangerous to the evaluated reputation of the church and are mentally disrupting to the mental focus of many potential followers of the teachings of Christ.

Bunkers That They Call Pulpits!

*O*nce, I went to help a church in their music ministry. While being there, one of the things that I noticed was that the pastor used the pulpit to fuel the wars that he had been having with a few other ministers for about a decade or two. He would say things from the pulpit, to the members of the congregation encouraging them to stay away from the ministers that he was warring with.

In an effort to get the people to stay away from the churches of his enemies, he would speak very negatively about their teaching and preaching, suggesting that they were in error to the word of God. He didn't have a problem telling the people that there was something sinfully wicked and wrong with the other pastors, that they didn't need to be exposed to. These were not the exact words used, but, it is the exact meaning for the words that were spoken over the pulpit.

I never really knew what to say about the behavior of the different pastors that would stand in the pulpit of the churches and verbally throw rocks and hurl railing accusations at the other pastors of the different denominations, and even of different churches other than their own in the very same denomination.

Some were bold enough to say, that if you quote me as saying that I said a certain thing from the pulpit, I will emphatically deny it all of the way. Some even said; "I will tell the people that you are lying on me, you're nothing but a ball faced liar!"

It's a drastic thing, that the pulpit has been used to fire shots at others that have been styled as the enemy, even though we are all on the same team in the Christian churches. Just because they did not like certain people, was no reason to attempt to destroy that other ministers' character, by blasting their reputation in the pulpit.

Some things that were otherwise unknown to the majority of the people in the church's congregation, were publicly spoken. How did you think that certain, very private issues about a particular person, was revealed to the people of the church without that individual in question telling the information?

I'll tell you how it all happened; the shots were fired from the bunkers! Many of the leaders are so entrenched and deeply embedded behind the pulpit, that they think that they are at liberty to do and to say whatever they please, regardless of the damage that may be caused as a result. When certain persons of the clergy step behind the pulpit, they become altogether a totally different person, like Clark Kent when he steps into the phone booth?.....

BUNKER–A DUGOUT AREA BUILT OVER WITH STEEL AND CONCRETE, LOGS, EARTH, ETC., TO BE USED AS A DEFENSIVE POSITION IN BATTLE. BUNKERS ARE OFTEN BUILT INTO HILLS OR OTHER NATURAL BARRIERS.

Bunkers are usually built to withstand rapid gunfire and blasts from grenades and the likes of other bomb shell type assault weapons from the enemy. In other words, the bunker is a place for a soldier to hide while being able to launch counter-offensive assaults on the enemy, while still in hiding.

Many pulpits have been turned into nothing more than battlefield bunkers! The analogy of being a soldier in the army of the Lord has been taken to the left; way too far out of context, to the point that it doesn't appear that we are conscious of who the real enemy is any longer. We have been encouraged to take up battle against each other, of which diminishes the perception of the church down to the size of nothing more than a clique or a gang.

I am apologetic, that you were taught that I, and people like me, who were not members of your denomination, were to be regarded and further treated as your enemy. What if certain species of fish, were of the opinion that all other species of fish, did not belong in the ocean or the sea because they were not of the same species, as they themselves? Suppose they further determined that the other fish deserved to be ousted from the water?

If you think for one moment that the other fish would comply with the desires of the other fish, or if they even cared, then you have slipped from reality. No one has to ever ask a fish whether or not they belong in the water? As a matter of the fact, if you just drop a net or a line in the water you will discover what fish feel about being in the water. Upon being pulled from the water, all fish and aquatic animals fight hard to be permanently returned to their natural habitat.

Likewise, ALL Christians; belong in Jesus Christ. There are no provisions to be both out and in simultaneously at the very same time. Here is what I mean about being out, but in, at the same time. Christian Scientist and Metaphysicists, which are so closely related that you would have to know the distinct differences between the two; at any rate the two are at odds with the teachings of the King James Versions of the scriptural accounts of the life and times of Jesus Christ, though they claim to be Christian?

These two, conflicting claimants of the Christian religion, seek to disprove the truth of the scriptures. Their greatest efforts are to show the common people of the society that the teachings of Jesus Christ are over exaggerated, and therefore unreliable. Such teachings; seek to take away the power of the blood of Jesus; which SAVES THE WORLD FROM SIN!

> *But without faith it is impossible to please him: for he that cometh to God must believe that he is, and that he is a rewarder of them that diligently seek him.*
>
> Hebrews 11: 6

Just because some egotistical person is standing in the pulpit claiming to be more that just a man of God, that doesn't mean that God has given them the equal right to be transformed into a god. Jesus Christ; is God, who came as a man in the flesh and dwelt among us! [ST. JOHN 1:14.]

No man or woman on the face of the earth is able to say WHO CAN OR CANNOT BE A PART OF THE BODY OF CHRIST, OR WHO IS OR IS NOT TRULY A CHRISTIAN, BASED ON THEIR DENOMINATION IN THE CHRISTIAN CHURCH, that they are a part of.

Those who have truly been washed in the blood of Jesus Christ; and have repented of their sins, and have turned away from their sinful ways; and are living in the newness of life in Christ, filled with the Holy Ghost and walking in the spirit of the Lord daily, are fully a Christian, and are of the body of Christ world wide, with GOD'S consenting approval!

It is time-out, for all of the unreasonable pointless and unnecessary oppositions to members of the body, simply because they have not agreed with any particular denominational rule or mandate. So what; somebody didn't do things the same way that you did to be saved? Most likely, you may have forgotten the fact that it is what Jesus did on the cross that enables salvation in the earth, and not ever was it your denomination or what ever you might have been required to do as a requirement of your church's denomination, before you were allowed to feel as though you might have been saved.

You might need to go back and check the scripture, as you may not have been saved? You may have met the criteria for membership in a certain denominational church, but unless you believed like the bible says for every believer to believe, you may have missed out on truly being forgiven of your sins.

You cannot be a part of another religion outside of Christianity, and still be a Christian! However, Christianity is not a religion; it is a life of righteousness in Christ Jesus; through the shed blood on the cross.

> *And when I passed by thee, and saw thee polluted in thine own blood, I said unto thee when thou wast in thy blood, Live; yea, I said unto thee when thou wast in thy blood, Live.* Ezekiel 16: 6

If there was no blood, there could be no life, as nothing that is alive and breathing on this earth, could live without blood running through its veins. You can be sure that your pastor is not God, because he still has his own blood in his own veins. Remember that Jesus Christ shed his blood for all humanity, so that we might have LIFE; in him! Yet; He Got Up From The Grave, ALIVE; and is now alive forever more! You must believe and receive the Lord Jesus Christ and the sacrifice that He made on the cross of Calvary. THAT'S CALLED CHRISTIANITY!

Many people have been deceived into believing that they are active members of Christianity, when all of their actions and their practices say otherwise. You cannot possibly be a Christian and have major problems believing and accepting the King James Version of the bible.

People claim to be Christians all of the time, but only the same way that other people claim to be married who have never even uttered a marriage vow even in a wedding rehearsal. They just decided to move in together and to set up house as if they have made the commitment before God, their families, and their witnesses. There has never been a commitment made to confirm a realistic status into Christianity. They never even came to the alter to confess before the Lord!

Americans believe, that just because they verbally confess, without any spiritual transformation, that they are indeed Christians, because they might attend a Christ centered church which teaches that we are Christians, they believe that only through what they have said out their own mouths, the criteria for being a Christian has been met. Just because you might sit in the pews of the church on Sunday for an hour or two, that doesn't make you a Christian!

Here's my point in fact; whenever a person exalts themself to the status of being god in the eyes of other people, they intentionally fail to lead the people to Jesus Christ; spiritually, so that they are made alive in the spirit. As a result, the same people are usually led right through the church and then to the grave headed straight for the pit of hell. This is so, because the people have allowed a man,to determine for them, whether they are truly saved or not.

But the hour cometh, and now is, when the true worshippers shall worship the Father in spirit and in truth: for the Father seeketh such to worship him. God is a spirit: and they that worship him must worship him in spirit and in truth. St. John 4: 23-24

Wor-Shepherd? Or WORSHIPPING?

*Y*ou cannot worship God in spirit and in truth; when you are loyally reverent to a leader that is a fake, a fraud, or even untrue, relative to the calling of God that may not even be upon their life, to lead the people of God. Any leader, that has not been authenticated by the calling of God initially, they are going to lead you into error simply because, they are out of touch with the divine order of God, as it relates to leading the people of God, in the churches of God.

Many leaders have gotten to be so controlling, demanding the undivided attention of the people of their congregations, that people have fallen away from actually worshipping God, and have begun exaulting their leaders instead.

I'm not talking about obedient people who serve their leaders because they truly respect them, and acknowledge them as God-fearing leaders, that walk circumspectly to the call of God on their lives. It's right to give respect and to support the man or the woman of God, and their ministries in everyway possible, for the benefit of the Kingdom of God.

For the sake of not being able to mention all of the ways that a ministry should be supported, I will conclude by saying that whatever my hands find to do, that will be a benefit to the pastor and to the membership base of the ministry, I am about getting it done.

I believe in undergirding the shepherd and the leaders financially, emotionally, and by all means spiritually, supporting the vision of the ministry, prayerfully.

Perhaps you have been to churches that quench the spirit

of the Lord in the worship services, and interfere with the move of the spirit of the Lord because they have a printed program? The spirit of the Lord has a tendency to increase in the atmosphere and to rise in elevation, as the people give reverence to the presence of the Lord. It is God's purpose that we worship Him only, and that we never give worship to another.

I have witnessed pastors who were seated sometimes with their legs crossed in the pulpit, rise from their seats to put a halt to activities in the worship service that would take all of the focus off of themselves. Many times this has been done to suppress what has been referred to as, EMOTIONALISM. I have heard some leaders say that they did not want the people to get too emotional.

As people begin to raise their hands in worship and stand on their feet to reverence the presence of the Lord, that may have been ushered in through another person that might not have been a member of that church, the pastors would immediately stop the music from playing, stop the choir from singing, instruct the people to stop clapping their hands and even tell the entire congregation if they deemed it necessary, to sit down and to come back to the order of the house..............

IS YOUR ORDER; GOD'S ORDER?

In situations like these, whereas the shepherd seemed to reject the idea of spiritual worship in the church, but, were rather preferrable to the rites of ritualistic order-forms in the religious worship of the church, I have seen that the people obeyed the orders of the leadership like mechanically trained soldiers in the cartoon's armed forces.

Here's what I mean! The people say; "Amen" only when they are told to say; "Amen"; they only clap their hands when instructed to do so; whatever they are told to say during worship is all that they are going to say. It doesn't matter what the scripture has to say about worship, if the leadership of the ministry is opposed to what the scripture has to say indeed about worshipping the Lord in the sanctuary, the followers are also usually opposed.

People stand, for their pastors to enter into the sanctuary of the churches with their entourage, while they are encouraged to sit while the presence of the Lord comes in and further determined to sit on the moving of the spirit, in the house of God.

Just because certain churches are embracing the move of God in the sanctuary, don't get the idea that all churches are likewise embracing the move of God. Many, are still convinced that it doesn't take all of that to worship? Just what it is that they are worshipping when they enter the sanctuary is quite far from my understanding, when they are clearly not in the spirit.

As I have mentioned earlier, the highlight of the Christian church is the delivery of the word of God. I have been to a lot of churches, whereas the message delivered to the people is so elementary and lacking in substance, that my spirit groaned within me, for lack of not being fed. There is no way that I could have been the only person in the house that felt as I did, but you would never know it relative to the response from the people in attendance.

The people were screaming and shouting so loud that you could hardly even hear what was being said from the pulpit, if you were not accustomed to hearing above that volume level of noise. I have used a term whenever I talk about what I will refer to as a dead message; "SOUND GOOD, BUT, SAYING NOTHING."

My only point is that some people have gotten so carried away with their leaders, that it really doesn't matter if the message lacks substance, they are excited about the fact that it's their pastor, who is speaking at the time.

SHEPHERD WORSHIP; is very dangerous to the body of Christ, in that the wrong image of the body has been released upon the on-looking, unsaved, society of our surrounding communities.

The wrong person leading, will often have the right combination to lead the people all the way away from the presence of the Lord; and away from the truthful reality of salvation in Christ Jesus.

While struggling once in my own ministry, I had a very good friend and a fellow pastor to say to me that; "If God is in it, there is no struggle!" How wrong that statement is; simply because God in His infinite wisdom, He knows what it takes to make a determined leader that has been called, a Good Shepherd.

Certain experiences that we have, while on the way to the top (if you will allow me), are the defining circumstances that enables us to know that God is able to bring us out of anything, and the experiences are what enable us to properly conduct ourselves wisely, once we have successfully settled into our ministry!

Such idealism, in my own opinion, is the reason that we have so many spiritual weaklings at the top of the churches. How do we expect that the people who follow our ministries would develop and become strong Christians, when the leaders are bailing out at the first signs of trouble? Don't ever forget the fact that Job's friends were also determined in their own hearts, that he had somehow failed God, leaving him to suffer almost to the point of death.

In the end, it was God, Himself; that rebuked the friends of Job, because they had falsely evaluated Job's plight, in that they were sure that God was not with Job in the trials that he was going through. On the contrary, God was definitely in the midst of the trials with Job, else Satan would have torn Job to pieces!

Just because a person may be charismatic in their speaking abilities and have acquired a few college degrees, doesn't mean that they might be more skilled at leading the people of God, and it certainly never warrants a reason for worshipping them. Many of today's leaders have not even died to the will of themselves, as of yet, and God knows that they certainly didn't die on the cross of Calvary!

So you are in more danger than you might think if you feel that your shepherd is worthy of your worship? No matter what we may do as shepherds to insure the spiritual assurance of the people of the church, we are never going to be the reason for the church's existence or for the people in the church, therefore no one should ever be found bestowing the worship that only belong to the Lord, upon us!

Self-Exaltation!*

$\mathcal{O}$ur problem as people of the Christian church, is that we don't live close enough to the word of God, while we are determined to walk this Christian walk of faith and victory. The only way to lose sight of the Lord in our daily walk, is to neglect to study the scripture daily. Contrary to what most of the people of the church have been taught, the spirit must also be fed daily and not just once or twice a week.

This my friend is the reason that we have Christian radio and television broadcast, that allow for multiples of ministries to air the word of God over the airways to the body of Christ. There are also, many different forms of media literature that are available for the believer to read and to enhance their biblical knowledge.

However, as result of the God complex, many of the leaders forbid their followers to tune in and listen to the word of God on radio or television, by way of talking negatively against them over the pulpits. But, I will cite the fact that such admonishment is primarily for the purpose of being able to hold on to the membership base, and to alleviate any possibility of losing control of the people to any of the mass media ministries.

The flip side of the coin in this case scenario is to see the exaltation of the pastors themselves to the same, equal, or an even greater status as the ministries on the air. Competition here in the DFW Metroplex area, in Texas, is at an all time high. You would be totally surprised at the lengths that some pastors will go to compete with another pastor or church in the area. I believe the terminology of kicking a person while they are down, may have originated here in the metroplex?

Efforts to bring the pastors together for any one function in this area, has fallen short over and over again. The war among the shepherds, is evidently more important than anything else that is relative to the church. It's hard to come together with others when in fact you are determined to be greater than everyone else that you might know or may be aware of.

There are a lot of things taking place within the brotherhood of the pastors that may or may not be public knowledge, which is extremely destructive to the spiritual welfare of the church styled as the body of Christ; worldwide. The leaders make moves on each other the same way that players move the pieces on a Chess board. They move on each other's reputations and business affairs that they are associated with, and their membership base to insure that the other pastor is kept in a position that is always going to be submissive to their own. *Check Mate!*

Warring to be the best and number one among the pastors can and will eventually bring about a since of self-exaltation! The spirited testosterone levels of the leaders keeps them fighting for the right to be the most popular among the people, and the best recognized as a successful motivator, builder, and civic leader.

Check Mate!

Whenever people appear to be progressing, they feel that they have the right to take the credit for the change in the lives of the people. Sometimes they will go all of the way and publicly announce that they are the ones that helped certain people to make it from where they were, to where they are right now. The bigger a leader may become in their own eyes, they also forget the fact that the people belong to the Lord, and that they do not have ownership of the people, simply because the people are members in their churches.

In closing this chapter, it is necessary that I let you know that this particular discussion of leaders with a "GOD COMPLEX" is not a brand new topic of interest for those of us who are in the body of Christ. To be very honest with you; success can be dangerous and very detrimental for many people who have the influence to lead the people of the Lord.

What is even more detrimental, is whenever people under

the leadership of certain leaders, become successful themselves, their new success seems to trigger the hidden switch of pride on the inside of the leader, that might have been tucked away from the visibility of any of the followers. It is understandable for any leader to be excited, when one of the persons they had been vigorously targeting, pushing them to reach their potential, actually succeeds.

Often times, we as the leaders are working contiguously behind the scenes, to encourage the growth and the development of individuals whom we may have cited as gifted and called to the ministry of God. However, we must never forget the fact that we can only stir up what is already on the inside of an individual. If they don't have it; you can't put it on the inside of them no matter how hard you try!

Most shepherds, have the experience of dealing with these kinds of people, we wished that we could literally open the skull from their brain and pour in whatever it is that they need to be successful in the Lord, but we can't do that!

Whenever someone has been motivated to be who and what they are, it's exciting to witness them begin to walk in their purpose. To see people whose lives have been truly changed, to the point that they have altered their lifestyle to reflect the word of God, signifying that they have believed in their own change, this can cause a shepherd to blow, like a whistling smoke stack with excitement.

A Lesson To Be Remembered!

*I*n the book of Daniel; the 4th chapter to be exact; the king had a disturbing dream, a dream by the way that was so perplexing, that none of his own wise men could interpret the meaning of the dream for him, so he called for the Prophet Daniel to interpret the dream. Read the story sometimes!

King Nebuchadnezzar; became a bit too overly excited at the success of beautiful Babylon. One day he looked out over the city from the palace where he was living in the midst of the kingdom from his own high place and took all of the credit and the glory for the existence and the progress of the great city. He even took credit for the people in the kingdom, as if he were their god.

The King had forgotten the dream that Daniel interpreted for him, in that it described how the Lord would strip the kingdom out of his own hands. He forsook the warning from the Lord to humble himself; instead he lifted up himself in pride, and suffered the mighty wrath of God. God threw him down on the ground with beast and the creeping things that God had earlier told mankind, by way of Adam, to have dominion over, to subdue and to conquer.

Through an interpretation of the scripture, it is to be understood that the King remained in the humbling experience for a period of seven years. Seven is God's number of completeness; when God starts dealing with you for being out of order in the body of Christ, as a leader, He will finish dealing with you no matter who prays for you! Amen!

King Nebuchadnezzar's condition remained until God decided to change the condition. The king went out of his mind, his hair grew out over his entire body like that of a wild beast; relative to the pictures that we have seen via the television, of the would be legendary "Bigfoot"; roaming through the jungle.

His nails grew out on his hands and feet like bird claws, which tell us that he was in a predicament for a while, because it definitely takes time for the nails to grow like that. If we don't frequently clip our nails now, even in these present times, they soon grow out of control, which is also unsatisfactory to the health codes of our society.

His hands became useless to him, in that he would not be capable of touching anyone in the province of his own kingdom without damaging them.

On the other hand, God always has a gentle touch when dealing with us while we are submitted to him. His hands are never rendered incapable of touching us, wherever we might need his hand touch.

King Nebuchadnezzar, fell to his hands and knees and was made to crawl like a four footed beast. He also behaved himself like a beast, he began to eat grass! This picture certainly reveals in my opinion, a man that had gone mad and was completely out of his own sober mind.

We often hear sermons about the demoniac at the coast of the Gaderenes; who lived among the tombs and cut himself with sharp stones, no chains or fetters could restrain him. But it is quite seldom that someone will talk about King Nebuchadnezzar; simply because of the story's representation relative to leaders who go out of control and forget that God, is God.

We are to look to God, as leaders and to remain under the controlled auspices of the Holy Ghost; while we lead the people of God. We can never become the God that we are supposed to fully rely upon, we never will be God! Let me encourage you to come down from your own elevated platforms of god-hood, before God steps in and knocks you off of your high seat of pride.

There is a difference in a domestic kingdom and the

Kingdom of God; even though many leaders appear to believe that the sanctuary of their buildings has become their kingdoms! Many of today's leaders have body guards who carry weapons and personal servants who care for them almost around the clock. They have become kings in their own eyes, and in the eyes of their followers.

It is not against God for a leader to be successful in every since of the word, and neither is it against God for them to live like it. But it is against God for them to forget where the success came from, and who it is that prospered them. I can always remember being told to never forget where it was that I came from, citing the fact that I would not have always been successful.

It's ok that they felt it necessary to admonish me to never forget God. Only, many of the same pastors seem to have forgotten who God is themselves! They project themselves as being above the ordinance of the gospel, and the messages they preach over the pulpits to the people; AREN'T APPLICABLE TO THEM! People always seem to forget the fact that the law is for the lawless! Obey now, or pay later!

> And the Lord said to Samuel, behold, I will do a thing in Israel, at which both the ears of everyone that heareth it shall tingle. In that day I will perform against Eli all things which I have spoken concerning his house: when I begin, I will also make an end. For I have told him that I will judge his house forever for the iniquity which he knoweth; because his sons made themselves vile, and he restrained them not. And therefore I have sworn unto the house of Eli, that the iniquity of Eli's house shall not be purged with sacrifice nor offering forever.

> I Samuel 3: 11-14

If the word of God won't convince you that being out of

order with the Lord is not acceptable, then absolutely nothing will be able to reach you other than the hand of the Lord correcting you.

Eli was the High-priest; the pastor; or the shepherd of the house of God, for which he was responsible to admonish the behavior of anyone that may have gotten out of control, to administer correction whenever they failed to line up with the mandates and the laws of the house of God. But because they were his own sons who were causing the displeasure in the sight of God, he thought that a simple mentioning of the facts that they were causing a spirit of unrest among the people, would be enough to suffice their behavior.

Eli chose to judge the situations according to his own heart disregarding the mandated laws of God, concerning the behavior of the people in the congregation.

You might want to reconsider your position concerning the people in your own congregation who are freely living vile, outside of the will of God, who are involved and trusted as leaders in your church where you are the shepherd! God, can never ever close his eyes to your misbehavior or to turn away from the direction of your insubordinate demeanor and spirit as a leader, who claims to be God's leader!

…when I begin, I will also make an end!

This very powerful statement, in the scripture suggest that only God can stop whatever He starts; or finish whatever He initiates. I have always attributed the latter portion of that scripture to the relativity of time, which all mankind has been allotted, relative to our stay here on the earth. But God's revelation to me is that, God is saying, that it doesn't matter if every intercessor in the country goes on a fast and pray for you, God will not lift the hand of His wrath, until He's satisfied to do so!

It is no wonder that many of the preachers of the modern day Theological persuasions stray away from the old testament? Certain accounts like the scriptoral depiction of the king of Babylon, will cause us to look at ourselves in the mirror very closely. We need always to pay attention to ourselves, even while we are caring for the flock of the Lord Jesus Christ, so that there will be no judgment, or the wrath of God to come back to hit us hard, for being out of control.

On my way to worship the other Sunday morning, being tuned in to the radio broadcast, I listened to a particular minister admonishing the people that it is the will of God for us to partake of the bitter cup many times in our lives and to rest assured, that God would not take the bitter cups from us. Too many people are angry with God, so they take the positions, like the ministers, to suggest to the people that it is of no use for them to seek the Lord to help them in trying times.

He was very quick to conclude that God won't heal everyone, and that God won't bless everyone and remove their trials and situations. The gist of his message was that even as Jesus prayed til' sweat-like drops of blood fell from His brow, saying; "Father If It Be So, Let This Cup Pass From Me!", God did not let the cup pass from Jesus, even though He could have, it wasn't His will.

The people in the congregation were more-so given the option to look away from a prayer that would ask God to heal them or to remove the gut-wrenching pains that no other man (DOCTOR) could remove?

In his disconnected theology, he made a failed attempt to also connect the plight of the Apostle Paul, when he ask God to remove the thorn in his flesh, with his admonishment to the people. Suggesting that God is not likely to do all that He can do for you; God's reply to Paul was, "My Grace Is Sufficient!"

This is no indictment against God!

Look deeper in The spirit of God!

You can't beat God at being God!

For We Wrestle Not......Eph. 6:12

Three

WRESTLING.   *Catch as Catch Can Style.*

Thy Rod and Thy Staff!

And the Lord spake unto Moses and Aaron, saying,
when Pharaoh shall speak unto you, saying, shew a
miracle for you: then thou shalt say unto Aaron,
take thy rod, and cast it before Pharaoh, and it shall
become a serpent. And Moses and Aaron went in
unto Pharaoh, and did so as the Lord had commanded:
and Aaron cast down his rod before Pharaoh, and
before his servants, and it became a serpent. Then
Pharaoh also called the wise men and the sorcerers:
now the magicians of Egypt, they also did in like
manner with their enchantments. For they cast down
every man his rod, and they became serpents: but
Aaron's rod swallowed up their rods.

Exodus 7: 8-12

What Is It?

*T*imes change and people certainly don't remain the same with the passing of time. However, as the people go through changes, which usually only reflect the popular trends of society; as people experience multiples of variable changes, the leaders of the churches are constantly reminded to remember and to never forget, that God never changes!

The word of God, also never changes; though there have been new bible translations in the past few decades, let me suggest to anyone that might be concerned about which version of the bible we should actually read, to return to the original version of the King James Bible to review the originated translation. The original is always closest to the actual intended meaning of the originator.

We are living in the "somebody do it for me" era and syndrome, to the point, that people are no longer geared to search the scripture for themselves to know what the Lord is saying to those of us who believe and are determined to remain with the church.

Many of the new leaders of the churches, are also of the spoiled era of young people who were raised with the idea in their minds that someone else should do it for you, even though you were taught how to do it for yourself. They seem to have relied upon others who did not even have the right, nor the power to interpret the biblical meaning and the purpose, for the Shepherd's Rod and Staff, I'll explain;

To hear the terminological usage of the word *"ROD"*, sets

off an alarming slanted awareness, in the pit of the stomach of lots of people. Most people are taught to reference the meaning of a rod, to a stern rigid inflexible tool, that is used for administering correction; of which correction is also thought of as something that is often brutal and unforgiving, nothing favoring the love of God! For the better part, many people do not even have a true understanding of the definition of the rod and the staff.

It is not good, to look at a word in which you do not have the proper definition and decide that you disapprove of the usage of the word, or to choose a very negative position relative to acquiring an understanding of the word.

Just because a word sounds hard or sounds as if to be stern in its meaning, does not necessarily make it to be so?

Many people don't like the sound of anything that suggests that they are not going to be in control themselves. Their dispositions, relative to the definitive comprehension of certain positions of authority, is so vigorously stern, that they are often able to cause many of the leaders to back down from their own positions of authority, though they never physically remove themselves as leaders.

They allow themselves to remain leaders, like a puppet on a string at the mercy of the people. What the people will allow them to do, they do. Otherwise, they sit back and sulk over the fact that the people will not allow them to be the leader that they are suppose to be. They are okay with being the star of the show, like a monkey on a leash, as long as they have someone to turn the handle of the music box. The attitude is that of saying; "I'LL DANCE; JUST AS LONG AS YOU SUPPLY THE RIGHT MUSIC; OR MONEY; FOR ME TO DO SO!"

Can You Lead Without the Tools?

*W*ithout a rod; or a staff; as a leader you are to the likes of a police officer that has been armed with only a flashlight and a whistle, against criminals that are armed with high powered weapons. You may see a lot of things very clearly, but you are left to the disadvantage to only make noise concerning the matters; yet being impotent to take control of the situation. You are like a ball player without a ball or a goal for scoring the winning baskets.

Without the pointing rod; which is better referred to as the needle of the compass; there is no way for direction to be given to us, to help us find our way and to know of our geographical positions, when it is necessary to know where we are. We remain lost without hope and up the stream without a paddle to steer and to control our boats; our boats would be tossed and driven by the waves of the water.

Unlike the watch, the compass is at the mercy of the needle to exist as a productive instrument for the benefit of the user. The compass is made for giving direction, but without a rod or the needle, who would the compass be able to direct?

The watch; Many of today's leaders have become nothing more than watches! Especially in these latter times, have found ways to get along and to exist without the needles or the arms to point out the accurate times of the day and the night. [Second hand, Minute hand, Hour hand]

They have lost the ability to direct the people in the ways of the Lord, of which in my opinion; they are no longer to the likes of the compass. The compass is blessed with the realism of being the cause for mankind to find their way; while the watch in its greatest definitive detail, is only for the benefit of time.

No matter which way you turn the body of the compass, the rod or the needle always points you in the exact direction of the North. Looking at the compass you know that the East, West and the South directions are also there on the compass, but you also know exactly where you stand, as a result of the direction of the rod in the compass.

Whatever the test, or the rigorous challenge you put a compass through on any given day or night, the compass itself just keeps right on pointing to the north. I have never seen a compass lose its direction or its ability to give direction to anyone that uses it.

Many of the leaders, have begun their ministries as watches, without a rod or a staff, because someone told them that such mannerisms of leadership, such as directing the people to live godly, is outdated and no longer necessary. They were told that it doesn't take all of that to lead the people of the church. Alike the new technology of today, the needle-less, armless watches, are preferred because time is displayed by the digital picture of the numbers in the face of the crystal; LED.

I spent many years in the Boy Scouts of America; every summer it was part of our activities to go on an outdoor camping trip. In scouting, we learned that the compass was most important to us, we could easily get lost out in the woods. As long as we had our compasses, and paid attention to where we were when we got started, and watched the pathways as we traveled along down the trail, while we hiked through the woods, we could most likely always find our way back to where we started.

We were never taught to rely on a watch, not even to tell us what time a day it was, simply because our watches could lose the track of time, and give us a false sense of security, and leave us with the hope of having more time to find our way in the quickly fading daylight, than we actually had.

In the days of old, watches were powered by being wound up tightly, of which there was always the fear of winding the watch to tightly? As the watch would begin to wind down, whenever the wearer of the watch was not as watchful of the time piece, if the watch was allowed to almost completely unwind, the time keeping ability of the watch would begin to drag, slowing down behind the actuality of time.

Today, many of the wristwatches that are worn are battery operated. They are good time keepers, only for as long as the life of the battery. As the battery loses power, the watches simultaneously lose the power to accurately keep up with the time.

The watch only tells the time that it is projecting, whenever you look at it, whether it is right or wrong. The right time has to always be set into the watch, as the watch does not have the ability to know and to display the accurate time on its own.

An incorrect watch that is in working order and performing as designed, is never right, because it is always running against the movement of the exact motion of time. As long as it is determined to move at its own discression and its own choosing, the watch can never and it will never catch up to the speed of the actual motion of the minute or fall back and slow down to relax its time-keeping ability to land on the true position of the face of the watch at the right time.

A broken and disabled watch is at least right two times a

day; but, it is still an unacceptable mechanism for keeping the time; because, in such a case as this, time lands on the watch, when the design of the watch is that, the arms of the watch are supposed to land and remain on the exact time; at every mili-second of the day; and the night!

Usually my friend, you are the actual power of the watch, you have to keep up with the time-keeping ability of the time piece, if you are determined to rely upon its ability to keep time.

On the other hand; the power of the compass is unseen and totally unmanned! The life of the compass; is in the spirit of nature. There are no batteries or winds to keep a compass going, in other words the compass is never dependant upon people to assure that it does its job. I will go out on a limb and say to you that the actual power of the needle or the rod of the compass would have to be the Holy Spirit.

Direction is permanently set for ever; while time rolls on by the second, of which we had better be following time, as it moves on. It is one thing to lose the track of the time while knowing where it is that you are standing, you may only be at a lost for the period of time in which you had been standing there?

But, it is all together a totally different thing to realize that you have gotten lost; yourself! Whereas, time may yet be of the essence, but it is to no avail if you don't even know where you are in the first place. When you don't know where you are, you also don't know the way back to where it is that you are supposed to be!

Most of us are familiar with DAYLIGHTS SAVINGS TIME; at least by the time we reach the first grade in elementary school. But think with me for a moment: have you ever heard of DIRECTIONS FINDING TIME? Even in the dark times of the night or of the mid-night, the compass still points in the right direction;

to the north!

During daylights saving time; the actual time of the day is shifted either backwards or forwards, for the purpose of extending the actual daylight in a single day. But I know that you have never heard of directions being shifted from North to South, or from East to West, because the directions are set, just as the mandates for leading the people of the Lord are also set from the beginning of the time. As shepherds, we must follow the set patterns of leadership.

It is bewildering to me, that some people don't seem to mind being the leader, in title only. They don't seem to be bothered by the fact that they don't have any authority to perform their duties. They feel that people are best served if they are joined rather than led from the frontal position.

The bible likens such leaders to the worthlessness of old dogs that have lived out their time; whose strength is gone, whose ferocity has *waned*, and their ability to pose a threat has long since been challenged to the fullest extent of any dangerous potential, and proven to be impotent. The scripture goes on to say that they are even scared to bark. (Isaiah 56: 10)

They are referred to as dumb; meaning that they have either given up their rights to speak out and to speak forth, or they are speechless because they don't have anything to say. They don't know what to say!

My friends, these leaders are shepherd's without a *Rod; or a Staff!*

The Sun Dial*

While marching with the marching band in High School,

and marching with the Boy Scouts of America; there would be times when the forward progress of our movement had been stalled and we were not going anywhere, but we were not permitted to stop marching. We were told to *mock time;* which meant to keep the beat time that was set during the application of marching, in the rhythm of the time that had already been set.

At that time of marching or moving in place, we had actually become time keepers, which was not a chore for us after all, simply because the time to be kept had already been previously set, the work of setting the time had already been established by the drum-major and the drum line.

There is no real work involved in getting with an established movement of the church. Trendsetters are like compasses, they are responsible for the direction the ministry is supposed to take. Some who are at the helm of some of the ministries today, think themselves to be more successful than others, simply because they stepped into the work that someone else had already established and kept it going.

The Sun-Dial; which is noted as the first time keeping instrument to measure time, was styled after the design of the compass, which is the very reason that what we refer to as high-noon; and mid-night; are located in the very spot and the direction of the north point on the compass.

Time was established to determine the measured span allotted for traveling a certain distance, perhaps from one direction to the next, of which the directions were already set on the compass. The sundial; was said to have been used at least 2000 years before the coming of Christ?

Documentation, has it that the shadow of the *gnomon* , which is the center piece of the sundial, would change it's position with the changing of the seasons, and would render either favorable or unfavorable time changes for the persons that had to depend on the sundial for the time.

The sundial, was also dependant upon the daylight and the sunlight, in an effort to cast a shadow on the face of the sundial. The purpose of accurately showing the position of the sun, was to established the time of the day. Early developers of the clock determined that the face of the clock needed more than the *gnomon* of the sundial, in an effort to consistently give the accurate time of the day and the night.

On a cloudy day; and in the night; people were perhaps at a lost for the time, simply for the lack of sun light, unless they found ways to keep up with the time by way of the stars and the moon light.

It's Got To Be In Your Hand!

*M*ost people in the ministry are always looking to go up higher in the Lord. The problem is that they continue to show up before the Lord empty handed. Lots of people have got the mentality of saying to the Lord; "So I don't have what I am supposed to be working with in my hands; it doesn't really matter, you're God; give me the spiritual elevation anyway!"

Many of today's shepherds know that they are operating without the necessary tools for the trade, *(if you will allow me to say it like that)*. The equipment for leading the people of God has been left off of the desired list of things to ask the Lord for, concerning their leadership, and their shepherding tenure.

The perfect picture that comes to my mind, whenever I

begin to speak of the rod and the staff of the shepherd; is the picture of Moses wandering through the wilderness attending unto his father-in-law's sheep, with the rod in his hand. There has got to be multiples of uses for the rod of a shepherd, that perhaps could never be put into words for the purpose of giving a manual for the proper usage of the rod.

Alike many people of today, Moses had a desire to see God up close and personal; for himself. Moses, was not just entertaining empty hopes and dreams, for which he would have nothing to do with bringing the desires of his own heart to pass.

Many of the shepherds, that desire a closer walk with the Lord, first of all, they are standing idle and empty handed. Even though they know of certain issues that need to be brought to the forefront of their prioritized list of things to attend to, or when they see certain task to be performed in their own churches and communities, they will do absolutely nothing unless they are going to be publicly recognized.

The very same tool that Moses would need in order to lead the children of Israel through the wilderness, he had already; while tending to the sheep in the pasture. More than likely, you already have it, yourselves, but you may not even be aware of the fact that it has been given to you. It is possible!

I know a few very skillful and successful musicians, that put their talents down the moment they entered the ministry of pastoring. It could be, that they did not have a revelation of the true purpose for the talent that they had been given. Whenever Moses found the mountain of God; we know of the mountain as Mt. Sinai; Moses was well acquainted with the rod that he had in his hands to the best of his own knowledge.

Perhaps if more of the shepherds of today had a rod and a staff to lean on, they would never be caught leaning on the wrong thing or the wrong people, whenever the journey appeared to be getting a little long. The rod that Moses had was not for the purpose of holding him up because he had gotten old and stricken with age. Moses was a busy man, with a purpose.

I don't even want to imagine what things might have been like, had Moses decided to put the rod down, just because he heard the Lord calling him by his name. It's dangerous to have a revelation, before the Lord ever gives it to you. You don't know what the Lord wants with you before He tells you. Wait on the Lord; he's going to tell you what He wants with you, be patient.

Moses, recognized that the spirit of the Lord was moving in the midst of the fire, burning in the bush. There was no doubt that he was in the presence of the Lord. Being alone with God; proved to be the greater blessing for Moses, simply because he did not have anyone else present that didn't believe in the power of God; or perhaps they may not have even known the presence of the Lord; that could have led him astray, away from the very bizarre sight of a *bush burning, that never burned up!*

Whenever God called Moses by his name, He never suggested to Moses that he needed to get rid of the rod and the staff that was in his hand, already. God was more interested in letting Moses know, that He knew who he was. In my own opinion, it was more important for the relationship between Moses and the Lord to be established, to the point that they were on speaking terms.

Moses; was going to need the Lord to instruct him in the future concerning the use of the rod. For as long, as God; is in control of the usage of the rod, you never have to worry about the spirit surrounding your authority, being negative and out of order.

Now that Moses is on speaking terms with God, and not allowing fear to rule his ability to talk face to face with the God whom he had been seeking, God expresses to Moses; that He has an interest in the rod that is presently already in His hand, as he approached the mountain of the Lord.

And the Lord said unto him, what is that in thine hand? And he said; a rod.   **Exodus 4: 2**

God already knows what your task and your purpose is for being on the face of the earth, so stop trying to impress God; by throwing down your gifts and talents, unless the Lord says for you to do so. God never ask questions that He doesn't already have the answers to. He knew that Moses would need the same rod to fulfill his task, for which He would have to reveal to Moses; and the true purpose of the rod.

We Always Think That We Know!

*I*mmediately, God began to talk to Moses about the rod that he had in his hand. God has got a way of showing you whether He approves or disapproves of what you are working with. You have got to give God your undivided attention, so that you are sure to hear Him, and to understand what He is saying about the tools to which you are working with.

You should know, that God knows things about your gifts and your talents that you would never know, without Him revealing the hidden and undiscovered things to you. It's amazing to me; how that Moses had been carrying the rod around with him in the wilderness for a long time; only to approach God; face to face before the burning bush, where God begins to reveal to him the reality of what it was that he had actually been carrying around.

The more we as people, sharpen our intellectual skills, if we are allowed to become too confident with our own understanding, we begin to feel as if we are as sharp as we need to be on every platform! We will never even know all that God knows, about the knowledge that we have acquired.

Never allow yourself to forget about the infinite wisdom of God, which is immeasurable according to all human standards. I always say; that God knows more about forgetting than we as human beings, will ever know about acquiring information and retaining that to which we have learned. *HE'S GOD!*

> *And He said, cast it on the ground. And he cast it on the ground, and it became a serpent: and Moses fled from before it. And the Lord said unto Moses, put forth thine hand, and take it by the tail, and he put forth his hand and caught it, and it became a rod in his hand:*
>
> Exodus 4: 3-4

You would be astonished at the unknown hidden factors, that are relative to your gifts and talents? Just because they are yours, that doesn't mean that you have all of the information about the gifts that either you could have; or should have!

Remember, God took interest in the rod in Moses' hand. At this time He told Moses to cast the rod down on the ground. I could imagine God saying; *"Let me show you something about your rod that you didn't know."* We always lose ourselves, in the fact that the rod became a serpent, as if that is the only information possible to glean from this account?

Open your heart and your mind for a moment; listen to the reason in the revelation that came to me about the rod, or more affectionately stated as the *"tool of authority"* in the hand of Moses.

There is the possibility of a hidden sense of evil residing right in the midst of your gifts or talents, which you may not be aware of the fact that they are there. The evil that showed up in the rod of Moses was absolutely down right deadly, as well as evil.

The scripture gives us to know and to understand that Moses ran away from the ungodly discovery of the evil content in the rod, in astonishment and surprise. I don't believe that he would have fled otherwise, had it not been for a fact, that what was indeed revealed and showcased on the stage of truth right in the presence of God; was visibly manifested being both evil and deadly for humanity; and for the spiritual welfare of the church.

Most people would look at Moses, and suggest that the snake scared the living daylights out of him, so he ran. But you would have to be outside of your own mind to believe that you can handle the discovery of evil on your own, especially when you have been startled because it showed up where it should have never been found in the first place. Once the discovery is made, what is absolutely most important following your true findings, is the calculated response to your findings.

Fear; has the ability to abort any reasonable ability to react to the discovery of danger, and to put things back into the original perspective. Moses did not expect to find or to see such a thing as this deadly serpent manifesting from the changing shape of his rod, because he never had any idea that his rod could change shape or form from the beginning.

There are times when things will take a different shape and form right in the middle of your tenure as the leader, but be careful not to allow a hidden snake in your own rod to come forth? As a matter of the fact, lay your rod down in the presence of the Lord; before He has to ask you to put it there! Spare yourself the embarrassment of exposure!

Don't ever forget the fact that Moses was in the presence of God when the discovery was made. He may have fled the vicinity of the snake, but he only moved deeper into the presence of the Lord. Moses had the mind to realize that he was in the presence of the right person to solve the problem.

You need to understand, that God had a purpose for revealing to Moses, the hidden characteristics of the rod that was in his hand. Moses had already spent 40 years shepherding the sheep of Jethro, his father-in-law. So let's imagine that Moses had at least those 40 years of experience with the rod that was in his hand at the time of this meeting with God?

It really doesn't matter how long it's been since you've had the tools that you are working with, God; still knows more about what you are working with than you do.

A Chosen Rod!

*I*n resolve; the *rod* in operation, is a shadowed representation of the authoritative leadership of the shepherd, that has been called to lead and to instruct the sheepfold, while simultaneously being capable to administer reproof and correction when needed, for those persons of the congregation who willfully step out of line with the bylaws of the church and the word of God.

A true chosen shepherd, is often skillful at wielding the sword of the spirit, and handling the rod of correction, and the gentle staff of meekness necessary for shepherding the sheep. Regretfully, there are people who feel as if it is necessary to challenge the authority of the shepherd, and they will test the power of the shepherd's abilities to rule over the congregation.

I have been a witness to rebellious uprisings among the deacons and the board of trustees, in certain churches; as well as unconverted laymen in the congregation, who feel that they are more capable of handling the church than the shepherd. When at unappropriate times; because they did not like the way the church was being run, they would sound the very disruptive public alarm in the middle of a worship service, contentiously citing the fact that they felt the immediate compulsion to take the reigns of the ministry.

Most people that have been members in the church for longer than 2-5 years, have either witnessed this chaotic uprising of the members of the deacon; and the trustee boards for themselves, or they have been told of such disturbing uprisings in the church.

Though these types of things are frequent occurrences in the local churches. Such uprisings are not new to the body of believers for centuries and even for millenniums now. Moses also experienced the up-rise of disgruntled followers who wanted to take over the leadership of the congregation in the tabernacle.

Never worry about the opposition that arises against God fearing, chosen authority, which comes to overthrow the anointed leadership of the church, because they will never succeed.

Don't mistake the ability to disrupt the established flow of the ministry, for any successful defeat over the leadership of the church. Certain people of the ministry may split off from the congregation and start another group, but that doesn't mean that the shepherd has lost out as a shepherd of the Lord; and neither does it bespeak of an inability to lead the people of the Lord.

Any good shepherd, can lead the people of the congregation to stand still and to wait on the Lord; in the face of a crisis. There comes a time, when the shepherd has to follow his own advice and be still himself; when the same persons that have been followers of his leadership, rise up to oppose him. Wait on the Lord; you will win!

A wise shepherd will always fall back on the teaching that they have been delivering to the church. Any advise that is good enough to be delivered to the people of the Lord, has got to be good enough to be remembered in the times of a crisis, by the deliverer of the message.

A good shepherd, knows that the word of God works both ways, from the pulpit out to the pews, and back up to the pulpit. The word of the Lord is so powerful, that it always comes back full circle to speak to everyone that is a member of the body of Christ. No one is exempted from hearing the word of the Lord.

There are times when it might seem that no word will come back to the shepherd, advising them of how to handle certain situations in the church. At such a time, it is my advice to you; to just wait before the Lord because He will not leave you to yourself, to make the biggest mistake, possibly causing some to fall, or to turn away from the Lord to lose their soul.

Don't ever lose sight of the fact, that God cares very deeply about the choice that He has made to lead the people of the church. The only reason that Saul; was chosen in the first place, was that the people murmured and complained about following the anointed leadership of the high priest; Samuel.

They wanted to be like every one else, they wanted a king! People get tired of following anointed leadership for some reason or another, and they will jump ship and go after the flashier styles of leadership.

People choose leaders, who are stepping out of the pulpit and into politics. They like leading figures; who are always in the spotlight or the limelight; whichever you prefer?

Let me suggest to you, that all community service is not necessarily in conjunction with the mandated business of the church. So just because another leader other than the leader that God has assigned you to follow, is out in the community doing lots of stuff, his service to humanity does not negate another shepherd's service to the Lord.

Some are only after the quantity of people, because they have not been endowed with the excellence of God; that enables them to enhance the quality of the people in the congregation. I am always leery of those leaders that are very skilled at speaking, but not much bible is in their words, at all.

Thank God that I have come to understand, that it is not what I have to say that will bring deliverance and salvation to the people, rather it's what God has said already; that has brought salvation and deliverance to humanity all over the world. When people receive me, it's a good thing, but when people receive the word of the Lord; it's an eternal thing. My vote is for the eternal things, even though they have to receive me to get to the eternal things!

And the Lord spake unto Moses, saying, speak unto the children of Israel, and take of every one of them a rod according to the house of their fathers, of all their princes according to the house of their fathers twelve rods: write thou every man's name upon

85

his rod. And thou shalt write Aaron's name
upon the rod of Levi: for one rod shall be
for the head of the house of their fathers.
And thou shalt lay them up in the tabernacle
of the congregation before the testimony,
where I will meet with you. And it shall
come to pass that the man's rod, whom I
shall choose, shall blossom; and I will make
to cease from me the murmurings of the
children of Israel, whereby they murmur
against you. **Numbers 17:1-5**

God; always knows His own choice, and His purpose for choosing the leader that He has chosen.

God; gives Moses; distinct instructions for the rod of the house of Levi. *LEVI- IS A NAME THAT MEANS INSTRUMENTS OF WRATH.* God was not in the dark about the meaning of the name of the house of Levi; of which the bearers of the name, boar the exact characteristics of the name. They had no problem avenging the righteousness of God among the children of Israel.

Isn't it amazing, that God chose the rod of the house of "Levi" to reveal the fact that He had established His own choice in Israel? The tribe of "Levi" better known and affectionately referred to as the *"Levites";* is where the LEVITICAL LAWS, of the priesthood were established. The Levites were the priest of all of the houses of the children of Israel, and Judah.

When God give laws to us, He is intent on the people of the church, to keep the laws that have been given. While the shepherd's purpose is to lead the sheep of the Lord, their job is also to maintain the order of the sanctuary, and to keep the people in check with the established laws of God.

Lots of people say that they are looking for a church that doesn't have too many rules and regulations. They don't want anybody telling them what to do; not in the church anyway!

This is the reason that I know that every shepherd has got to abide in his own calling, with the rod and the staff in his hand ready for use at the proper times, and in the appropriate situations.

Only The Chosen Will Bloom!

God calls a leadership, that is ready to operate in the stead, as the shepherd. God knows that a leader cannot be inferior to the people, who are to follow their leadership. The leader must be strong and not passive, as some would have you to believe. People will run all over a leader that is weak, in their demeanor and in their positional authoritative stance.

And Moses spake unto the children of Israel, and every one of their princes gave him a rod apiece, for each prince one, according to their fathers' houses, even twelve rods: and the rod of Aaron was among their rods. And Moses laid up the rods before the Lord in the tabernacle of witness. And it came to pass, that on the morrow Moses went into the tabernacle of witness; and, behold, the rod of Aaron for the house of Levi was budded, and brought forth buds, and bloomed blossoms, and yielded almonds. And Moses brought out all the rods from before the Lord unto the children of Israel: and they looked, and took every man his rod.

Numbers 17:6-9

The word of God shows us, that the rods of the children of Israel were laid before the Lord to be established by the Lord, in which the rod would represent the truly chosen leadership of the Lord. Even God gets tired of disgruntled people, who only need to follow the leadership that He has already established to lead and would settle the gripes that they are having.

When leaders make up in their own minds, to lead the people in the ways of the Lord without wavering and crumbling under the weight of the opposition, they soon discover the willingness of the people to follow them. They Can Do It!

We have only been able to see that this dried out partially worn out stick of a rod, which had long since been severed from the tree it originally belong to, how in the presence of the Lord, the rod budded. I personally have never heard a successful pulpit explanation for the budding of Aaron's rod. But it is clearly written in the word of God for us to understand, why God chose this rod.

It was for a show of witness, to speak to the murmuring children of Israel who were opposing the leadership of Moses, and his brother the chosen high-priest of the people of God; "Aaron." They really didn't know just how close they came, within seeing the wrath of God unleashed upon them, for speaking out against the established leadership.

Rather, God; chose to give them a sign that the leader was indeed chosen by Him. The Israelites, had been captive to the Egyptians for more than four hundred years; for which they had adapted the ways of Egypt, after having been there for so long. The Egyptians; were sign seekers! They believed only after seeing signs, that would reveal answers, to questions they were asking.

The flip side to God revealing the snake to Moses; would be for the fact of God assuring Moses that he would also indeed have signs and wonders working, whenever he would go before Pharaoh and thé Egyptians. This is the reason that the magicians threw down their rods; they thought that Moses had only gone away from them to learn new magic. They didn't believe in the God of the Israelites!

Whenever Moses; made it back to Egypt, God struck the land and the sea and surrounding waters, with many plagues. These occurances were only signs to the Egyptians, that were indeed too powerful for any of their own magicians. Through Moses; God proved to the Egyptians, that He was truly more powerful than any of the magic they believed in.

In Israel; there were twelve tribes; TWELVE is the number of GOVERNMENT; or of the governmental grace given to the Israelites. Of the twelve tribes, there were twelve leaders to represent each tribe. But, God; in His infinite wisdom; He knows that only one leader is capable of being the head of all leaders.

It is no mistake, that God only chose one leader to be the head of the congregation, which in my own opinion, is not to be confused with a pastor and their spouse, as pastor and co-pastor of the church being more than one leader; because the two of them make only one true leader to begin with. It was the Lord's intentions from the beginning that the two of them *(husband & wife)* would work closely knit together to make up one complete head.

As we fight over who is going to be the leader; or not, many souls are being lost, and the ministry of the Lord is being left undone, simply because someone has got their lips stuck-out in rebellion to the leadership.

To avoid standing firm in the church as the leader, is not a presentation of godliness or meekness. Though you may not be a weak person, you may be operating as a weak leader, whenever you don't take the stand that pleases the Lord, even when the people don't seem to like it, or if they appear to be confused about your actions as the leader.

If you are not careful and stern, the people will lead you, and you will never be happy and satisfied that the work of the ministry is going forth in the way that God has given it to you as the leader.

Just because the people are murmuring and complaining, that does not mean that it is time for you to pack your bags and begin looking for another church to pastor.

God gave Moses a sign that would always be there for the people to witness and to respect; or die! Shepherd, where is your sign?

Perhaps it is about time that you went before the Lord to ask Him for the help that you have been seeking through the Bishop or the Moderator; with all do respect to these leaders. Their positions are for leading the leaders; your purpose is to lead the people of the local congregation, where you have been called upon to shepherd the flock of God.

The Lord will show up for you just like He did for Moses, but you must remember that He showed up through Moses' rod; by the way of Aaron; his brother and ministerial companion.

Where Is Your Rod?

For We Wrestle Not......Eph. 6:12

Four

WRESTLING.   Catch as Catch Can Style.

Sheep Led Shepherds

And Saul said unto Samuel, Yea, I have obeyed the voice of the Lord, and have gone the way which the Lord sent me, and have brought Agag the king of Amalek, and have utterly destroyed the Amalekites. But the people took of the spoil, sheep and oxen, the chief of the things which should have been utterly destroyed, to sacrifice unto the Lord thy God in Gilgal.

I Samuel 15:20-21

My sheep wandered through all the mountains, and upon every high hill: yea, my flock was scattered upon all the face of the earth, and none did search or seek after them. Therefore, O ye shepherds, hear the word of the Lord; Thus sayeth the Lord God; Behold, I am against the shepherds; and I will require my flock at their hands, and cause them to cease from feeding the flock; neither shall the shepherds feed themselves any more; for I will deliver my flock from their mouth, that they may not be meat for them.

Ezekiel 34:6, 9-10

But when he saw the multitudes, he was moved with compassion on them, because they fainted, and were scattered abroad, as sheep having no shepherd. St. Matthew 9:36
For ye were as sheep going astray; but are now returned unto the shepherd and bishop of your souls. I Peter 2:25

TELL THE LEADER TO GET INTO PLACE!

*Y*ou have got to be kidding or joking; somebody shake me! The sheep have taken over in many of the pastures! It's quite a scene to see the sheep pushing the shepherd around in the field, telling them which way to go.

GOING RIGHT TO THE HEART OF THE MATTER; I don't believe that God would have ever appointed leaders, had He intended for them to be led by the people they were supposed to be leading! Someone is seriously out of character, and out of their rightful place in this picture.

Either the sheep have taken on a new role in its nature, or the shepherd has somehow lost a backbone out in the pasture. Sheep were created to be led, and were never intended to take leadership roles, especially in the church. Someone forgot to either read the word of God, or to teach the uncompromised word of God to the people who were supposed to be led under their authority.

No matter where you feel your place is in the ministry, if you are not the shepherd, your assignment is not in the role of the *Pastoral* headship. You are not to be in control over the decisions of the leadership whether you like it or not.

The local churches are out of control mainly because the people don't have respect for the leadership anymore, regardless of the foul behavior that may have taken place in the clergy across the country, reported in the media; that has absolutely nothing to do with the biblical instructions that have already been given to the church.

Too often people are looking for reasons to disobey the word of God, or for excuses, for haven broken the laws of the scriptures, simply because they don't want to be held accountable for their actions according to the word of God.

The people have literally forced the shepherds of the flocks that should belong to God, into forms of religious practices that are so far to the left of true and pure righteousness, that the inner-church behavior is no different from secular humanistic societies.

Leadership that truly reflects the heart of God is often shunned and looked upon as outdated and unnecessary for these modern times we are now living in. Leaders, who still have a heart for the people, are often taken for granted and are usually mistreated by the very people to whom their heart has been given.

People don't attend the church to be taught and trained in the word of God anymore, rather they will attend to be religiously entertained, and to get a handout of some sort. They have no determination to please the Lord with their life styles, and they often dare certain leaders to say anything about the way they are living.

This group of people in the church are more like wild herds of untamed goats, or misfit beast that were mal-formed in the middle of the birthing process. Somehow they appear to be the products of rotten or otherwise badly decomposed seeds, which were incapable of producing humble godly sheep.

These spiritually disfigured specimens will tell a shepherd where to get off and where to step out of their business in a heart beat, without any fear at all. It is not really obvious as to whether or not the fear of God had left them, or if it had ever been there to begin with! These people are so callused around their hearts, that you wonder if God could even enter and bring about the change that they need, although they may feel that they are okay just as they are.

Shepherds are Nobody Special?**

*T*he average people of the church today are determined to believe that the shepherd, the pastor, the leader of the flock is no more special than anyone else. They believe that if they study enough to bring new information, which by the way, does not even have to be new bible revelation to enhance their biblical knowledge and spiritual growth, well they might say that they are worth listening to and possibly financially supporting.

Far too many shepherds are preaching from heavily restrictive sermonic manuals that have to be approved by the board of directors and the deacons. The shepherds are terrified of being terminated from their pastoral charge, so much to the point that they wouldn't dare offend any of these leaders or a sinner in the congregation for the sake of the gospel.

Nowadays the pastor is called on the carpet to answer for a sermon that came across the pulpit to the church. In my opinion, the people no longer believe that the shepherd has the ability to hear from the Lord, for a word and neither are they necessarily interested in hearing that the word came from the Lord. Believe me, they know how to find a church where the shepherd is definitely obedient to the board.

I was once approached by a young man who was about to start a bible study that eventually developed into a church, he invited me to attend his initial bible study with the stipulations of understanding that absolutely no one would be respected as having more knowledge than anyone else, regardless; because everyone has got something to say? He informed me that everyone was going to be sharing their opinions from the bible.

The look in my face answered for me that time, simply because this fellow had only been attending church for only a few years, and he was not biblically astute, even in the least. You see, this is what I mean; the sheep have the nerve to demand that the shepherd sit down and listen to them now, as if to suggest that the shepherds have had it all wrong in the past.

His demeanor, in my opinion, was as if to say to me that my prayer time, many years of studying the bible and following spiritual leadership meant absolutely nothing to him at all. People have been deceived into believing that they are just as anointed as the shepherd?

Angrily, they will tell you that as a leader or the shepherd of the congregation, you are not higher than anyone else, as related to spiritual authority. Literally speaking from a natural perspective, the shepherd stands taller and higher than the sheep out in the pasture, for the simple reason of the fact that the shepherd has to be able to watch out for the sheep. God made this fact to be so!

I never see people challenge the position of a court appointed judge, or a politician and even the president of the

United States of America. Any ranking official in any branch of the armed forces is usually agreeably respected for their ranking authority, without the common opinion attempting to demean their given positions of authority.

The police and the FBI are respected and feared for their positions of authority, while it doesn't stop criminals from committing offensive crimes and doing wrong, in retrospect, criminals do everything possible to avoid being caught in the wrong, and prosecuted by these law enforcement officials.

Only in and around the church, do we find so many people who are determined to pull down the persons of authority, from their authority in the anointing. People are now determined to do wrong in the presence of the leaders.

WHO'S LEVEL ARE YOU ON?

Sheep are naturally on all fours in a position of humbleness, whereas they are easily led and entreated. I don't know about you, but I have never seen a sheep stand up on its hind legs and walk around like a bear and assume a position on the offensive, or the defensive for that matter, ready to engage in a viscious assault against another, or even with another sheep.

Whenever a predator will approach the flock, the sheep will naturally retreat for a place of safety, leaving the shepherd behind to handle the element of danger. It's normal for the sheep to unintentionally set themselves up for an attack, and that's the reason they have the shepherd to watch over them and to fight for them.

And David said unto Saul, Thy servant
kept his fathers sheep, and there came a
lion, and a bear, and took a lamb out of
the flock: And I went after him, and
smote him, and delivered it out of his
mouth: and when he arose against me, I
caught him by his beard, and smote him,
and slew him. Thy servant slew both
the lion and the bear. I Samuel 17:34-36A

The shepherd is supposed to fight for you without having to fight with you, or even to be beaten up by you. Perhaps you can help me figure out who is to blame for the fact that a shepherd has been beaten and cowered by the sheep of his congregation?

Written biblical accounts of sheep and shepherds, never report that the sheep have demanded that the shepherd come down on their level. The shepherd does not need to be eye level with the sheep, because, the shepherds need always to see above and beyond the sheep through the eyes of God.

They don't need to be at ear level with the sheep either for the simple reason that they need to always hear from God. What difference does it make for the shepherd to listen to you grumble and gripe about all of your problems, when you know that the very moment the shepherd might begin telling you about their problems, you would have absolutely no ear for what they have to unload concerning their problems!

You are never the ones for the shepherd to talk to in the first place, and of course I'm very sorry that too many shepherds don't seem to be cognizant of this fact. The shepherd's problems are usually too much for the sheep to deal with, in that they are often overwhelmed to realize that the shepherd is living with problems that would take most others out of circulation. It is very easy for the shepherd to be misunderstood and misinterpreted relative to their ability to live on through life's most viscous oppositions.

The shepherds of today seem to agree with the people in that they say that the trials and the tribulations of the church are often too much for the shepherd to endure. Although shepherds still observe a sense of fellowshipping with other shepherds and their ministries; (or flocks), they themselves collectively, are so led and influenced by the sheep, that they possess no reflective repose to the good shepherd himself, being Jesus Christ.

I have never read any accounts of the shepherds being so preoccupied with what the sheep think of them. In the development of relationships among the shepherd and the sheep, it is the shepherd that has the ability to reasonably judge the relationship with the sheep, as a result of the spiritual authority to which they have been endowed.

I was minister of music for a particular ministry several years ago, where the pastor often made the statement that he wanted everybody to like him and to love him. I KNOW; DOESN'T THAT STATEMENT JUST STINK OF COMPROMISE?

There were several people in the ministry that kept major drama going all of the time, of whom were never chastised or put in their places. These people manipulated their way around the ministry doing everything they felt would please the pastor, and I mean to tell you that they never had any drive to please the Lord.

Some were ministers and evangelist, in title anyway, because they never had any time to seek the Lord, or to study the word of God in depth, for reason of their allegiance to the leader, who was also manipulatively led by them.

Spiritual Compromise!

$\mathcal{F}$or a while this pastor was praying for the sick and the people were being healed, miracles were manifested during the services, but all of a sudden things changed for the sake of the high dollar members of the congregation, who were not quite interested in witnessing the move of God.

Whenever the Lord would truly have his own way in the service, we would be in service a bit longer than when we were in control of the program. They did not want to have to wait in long lines at the restaurant for dinner after service had ended. The spiritual food was both ignored and compromised for natural food.

People know that they are hungry before they leave the house to attend the worship service. It's amazing to me how irritated people become whenever they come to the house of worship. They will sit through a 2-3 hour movie and almost never complain about the length of the movie. Some people would never even take a restroom break in the middle of the movie, because they are concerned with missing part of the movie.

On the other hand, whenever the sheep lead the shepherd, their spirituality is compromised, in that the message that the Lord has for them is often lost, because the Lord is not going to take the message from the shepherd and give the message to any of the sheep to deliver, simply because they feel that they are just as anointed as the shepherd.

Wayward sheep are in sure jeopardy for the reason of their own willingness to step out of line and to remain defiant to the linage of spiritual authority. People have all sorts of reasons in their own minds, which cause them to feel that they have the right to override the leadership of the church, and to be quite vocal about their attitudes.

Many new converts to Christianity allow others to fill their heads with all types of rebellion and stubbornness, they feel that they don't need a man to teach them in the word of God. They feel that they can teach themselves. Some of today's leaders have emerged from this very same ideology of having been self taught, and in my opinion, this is the reason for the many different sinful outbreaks of rebellion in the church. *IT'S IN THE HEAD!*

No Shepherd is called to please the sheep. These new fangled leaders feel that people should be made happy and comfortable around the church. They feel that everyone should have a pleasurable experience at the church, regardless of the spiritual conditions of the people, and regardless of the reality of their present sinful status.

The alternative lifestyles of homosexuality and lesbianism are comfortably fitting into too many of the local churches, daring anyone to ever say anything against their agenda, as if to suggest that they are the new church coming on the scene. Sheep Led Shepherds are afraid of lawsuits from the gay community, or either they are terrified of exposure because they are also a secret participator in such sexual perversion, and these other allowed persons are aware of the fact.

See then that ye walk circumspectly, not as fools, but as wise, Redeeming the time, because the days are evil. Ephesians 5:15-16

No shepherd could ever lead the people down a straight path, while walking crooked with the people, or while being led by them. The church is now filled with too many people who refuse to change, usually citing the fact that they know a leader who is not everything that they ought to be, so as a result they are not going to change their ways either, unless God comes down out the sky and tells them to change.

They Say That You Are Going To Hell! Too!

Sheep Led Shepherds are usually silenced from the discussions of hell from the pulpit. Let them tell it, God is pleased with everyone, simply for being on the face of the planet, so it's ok to just go ahead and live their lives to the fullest. They have also refrained from teaching the congregation to seek the infilling of the Holy Ghost, according to Acts 2:4.

There are more and more sermons being preached from compromised pulpits, on the subject of the fact that there is something wrong with everybody, and that nobody is perfect, so God understands.

It is very unwise to become what I will refer to as a *Pick-Nick-Pastor!* Ever so often, the church has a pick nick, where the pastor mingles with the people on very common grounds. Allowing people to become too common with you as a shepherd of the flock, is extremely unwise. Lots of people are button pushers, and for sure being used of the devil to do so. As the shepherd of the flock, they are after your buttons too; to keep you from hearing from God!

I have noticed that certain people will show up for a pick-nick sponsored by the church that will not even show up to the church for service even on a Sunday morning. People use to always show up for a church service on Christmas, Mothersday, and Easter, but not anymore, people have definitely changed!

The very people, that you thought understood the fact that you were pushed over the edge, which would be the only reason for any reaction that did not reflect God, are usually the same people who have sentenced you to hell for being a humanbeing also! Common people, who are allowed to get common with you, will expose your weaknesses to the people who might think of you as a strong leader otherwise.

While you are so determined to lower the standards of shepherding the flock of God, because the people don't appear to believe in you as the man of God, because you gave in to their control and to their antics, they have determined that since they are going to hell, that you are going also, for sure.

Let me ask you a question; are they right about you, Shepherd?

> Woe be unto the pastors that destroy and scatter the sheep of my pasture! Saith the Lord.
> **Jeremiah 23:1**
> Not everyone that saith unto me, Lord, Lord, shall enter into the kingdom of heaven; but he that doeth the will of my father which is in heaven. Many will say to me in that day, Lord, Lord, have we not prophesied in thy name? and in thy name have cast out devils? And in thy name done many wonderful works? And then will I profess unto them, I never knew you: depart from me, ye that work iniquity.
> **St. Matthew 7:21-23**

While it is very important to find working strategies to establish a sense of organization within the local body of the church, you had better know and understand the fact that if whatever you are working doesn't work eternal life with Christ

Jesus, you need to junk it, scrap it, burn it or whatever you have to do to get rid of it!

Shepherd; could you imagine being in **hell** with the people who rejected your leadership, and refused to turn to the Lord?

It will be a terrible day for those individuals who said that you were going to hell with them, to look at you and say; "I told you so!"

You won't have a thing to say in defense of yourself, because they will have been right, and of course you will be feeling their opinion of you; by then!

For We Wrestle Not......Eph. 6:12

Five

WRESTLING. Catch as Catch Can Style.

Now Who Will Care For The Sheep?

And the word of the Lord came unto me, saying, Son of man, prophecy against the shepherds of Israel, prophecy, and say unto them, thus saith the Lord God unto the shepherds; woe be to the shepherds of Israel that do feed themselves! Should not the shepherds feed the flocks? Ye eat the fat, and ye clothe you with wool, ye kill them that are fed: but ye feed not the flock. The diseased have ye not strengthened, neither have ye healed that which was sick, neither have ye bound that which was broken, neither have ye sought that which was lost; but with force and with cruelty have ye ruled them. And they were scattered, because there is no shepherd: and they became meat to all the beast of the field, when they were scattered. My sheep wandered through all the mountains, and upon every high hill: yea, my flock was scattered upon all the face of the earth, and none did search or seek after them.

Ezekiel 34: 1-6

*Counting Sheep!

*I*n this progressive era of the organized churches of our vastly growing modern communities, it's become more than obvious, that the main focus is the number of people in the sanctuary. Many of the leaders of today are in a competition for the number of people that they can get to fill the sanctuary of the churches on Sunday.

When the building itself is inadequate for the projected growth of the ministry, a building project for a much larger ediface is put into place to accommodate, whether the people will actually be attracted to change from a life of sin, or simply attracted to the new building.

The common perception is that a bigger crowd would bespeak of the blessing of the Lord over a church, even though many of the leaders are not righteous examples of the word of God. The leaders have become Secularly Iconic in their pastoral demeanor, and without a doubt they are not at all spiritual; their behavior suggests the fact that they are not personally acquainted with the spirit of the Lord.

Several years ago, I became rather disinterested with the idea of eating out after church. Many of the pastors are in the restaurants just shortly after Sunday morning services, dressed to perfection, shaking hands with other known pastors and bragging on the number of members that were taken in to their church that particular Sunday morning.

You could see the sunken facial expressions of the other pastors, who had not experienced what is being charted as a successful right for pastor's to brag? If you would listen closely, you would soon discover that the number of people, is all that many of the pastors present as a showing for the success of their ministry?

As many of the pastors are encountered in the post office, the grocery store or walking through the shopping malls, when asked about the status of their church they automatically rattle off the number of people they took in to their ministry as members. Someone has deceived these pastors into believing that successful pastoring, is being able to rapidly count the heads and bodies of the church's membership base, exclusively!

People need Jesus in their lives, not just an opportunity to adjoin themselves to a local church body to be numbered as a member of the church. I am of the opinion that the purpose of the church is to maintain the status of those who have truly been changed, and to equip them to further build the Kingdom of God.

The former generation, who were still quite familiar to the lifestyle of the farm life would say; that we were "pulling the cart before the horse!" It seems to be okay if things are out of sync to the actual establishment of the church, as prescribed by the Lord.

Whenever we'd see a cartoonist depiction; of an individual lying down in the bed underneath the sheets attempting to fall away to sleep, they would show the animated pictorialization of sheep leaping a fence over the bed to be counted peacefully, to cure the sleeplessness of those having difficulty with sleeping.

For as far back as I can remember, counting sheep has always been depicted for the purpose of lulling an individual to sleep! Very slowly, but quite cunningly; the enemy has lulled many of today's churches to sleep right from the pulpits. The detriment has been that the leaders themselves have also fallen off to sleep on their feet, and haven't realized that the gathered state of the local bodies, is stagnation and the purpetration of fraudulant, so-called Christian behavior.

Sleep; is a good thing for the physical body, and to be honest with you, I don't get enough of it! Sleepiness breeds laziness; laziness breeds poverty in every sense of the word, for which the problem with poverty is never relative to any number of people that are gathered in any one place; but, it is relative to the lack of substances, and even to the substandard and low quality of the substance that is available to any of the people in the number.

As a result of the subverted focus in leadership, the church has almost been rendered impotent to effect change in the society. While churches are more capable of handing out clothing and some small food items to the homeless, they are often powerless to reach the homeless by reason of their minds to encourage them to change their behavioral patterns and to become productive citizens of the society, as result of the church.

Some are successful at getting people off of the streets for a while, but without altering the thought process of those individuals, they find many of those same people right back on the streets where they came from.

We will not be successful at reaching 100% of the people that we are reaching out to, but to become settled on the fact of less than perfection by reaching even less than 50% of the people that we are capable of reaching, and pushing those individuals that are purported to have been reached, on through a religious ringer, only ensures that they will never be changed, as a direct result of an experience with the church.

What shall we say then? Shall we continue in sin, that grace may abound? God forbid. How shall we that are dead to sin, live any longer therein? Know ye not, that so many of us were baptized into Jesus Christ were baptized into his death? Therefore we are buried with him by baptism into death: that like as Christ was raised up from the dead by the glory of the Father, even so we also should walk in newness of life.

Romans 6:1-4

Guilt Under Grace?

I have heard so many people speak of a perfect church; probably meaning: looking for a church that is better at relating to the people that are regularly in attendance? People want to find a church that is everything it's supposed to be whenever they find it!

What they don't know, as a result of a lack of adequate teaching, is that perhaps they are the next piece to the puzzle that is supposed to make the church whole and complete?

Being left alone to become the more productive sinners in the community, as a result of the self serving Theology; that is delivered to the people over the pulpit, people by the scores are entering the entrance to hell right through the aisles of the church, and through the pathways of the grave.

Just because people's names are on the roster of any church, does not guarantee them a place in Heaven. As members of the church, we are always admonished to stand up to be counted! I have found myself asking the question; "Counted for what; Counted as what; Counted in relation to what; and on and on, relative to taking the stand to be counted?" People are already being counted as a group of willing people that will support the cause of a church; that may not even truly support the cause of Christ.

It is heart breaking, to see people that are so gullible, that they will hurry to get in line, and to stand in that same line until the cows come home, for a chance to give their last dime, for the sake of pleasing a leader that may not even be interested in pleasing the Lord.

Some people, will receive whatever they are given as the truth, especially, when that, that is given to them appeals to the softer side of their emotions, even though it allows them to resist the even flow of change that passes through their minds, as a result of the word of God. If it sounds good; most people want to hear it! Many people will drive for hours, just to hear what sounds like a new idea; or an easier way out of living according to the righteousness of Christ, through the living word.

So many people, have determined in their own hearts that living holy is totally impossible, or totally unnecessary in this late age of the Christian church. I hear people say all of the time; and so do you, if in fact you are not one of the persons saying these things; that God doesn't want us to live a life that is boring and dull! Living set apart for the glory of God, is what is said to be boring and dull.

Many of the churches have now come forward, to tell people that it is only necessary to properly conduct themselves at the party, rather than to refrain from the party crowd; disregarding the fact that the party crowds are usually people that are prone to live outlandishly sinful and disobedient to the word of God.

The message of the grace of God, is taken and turned inside

out, relative to the understanding of many of the leaders that deliver the message to the people, as if to turn it back on the giver of that same grace, to suggest to the people, that grace allows us to be forever forgiven, even in the future where we have not yet been privileged to live?   The lie that has been released on the people of many of the churches, is that we are forgiven even before we commit an act of sin, without asking for forgiveness!

People are even influenced to believe, that the grace of God blindfolds the eyes of God; whereas, when He looks upon the people of the church, they are seen as innocent even though presently they are gravely guilty of living ungodly, with no desire for repentance.

Let not sin therefore reign in your mortal body, that ye should obey it in the lust thereof. Neither yield ye your members as instruments of unrighteousness unto sin: but yield yourselves unto God, as those that are alive from the dead, and your members as instruments of righteousness unto God. For sin shall not have dominion over you: for ye are not under the law, but under grace. What then? Shall we sin, because we are not under the law, but under grace? God forbid. Know ye not, that to whom ye yield yourselves servant to obey, his servants ye are to whom ye obey; whether of sin unto death, or of obedience unto righteousness?

Romans 6:12-16

It is a pitiful shame, to continue to live consistently guilty under the grace of God; where God's grace has been freely given to us for the cleansing of our souls from the power of sin. Jesus Christ; is given to be the propitiation of sins, for the entire world, but, everyone individually, must receive him in the pardoning of their own individual sins.

There is a mental and spiritual malfunction within any leadership, that is determined to encourage people to remain as they are, with no desire to change the lifestyle that they are living. I'm not talking about encouraging people to come to the Lord Jesus; just as they are at the time and point of receiving Him as their Lord and Savior.

What is the reality of a change, for the person or persons who confess to being changed, if they never live according to the change that has supposedly taken place in their lives, through Jesus Christ?

Who is actually changed if no one lives like it; or who will ever be challenged to make a change in their life through Jesus Christ, if there are no living examples of the Christian kind of change?

I had a neighbor, whose pastor would come and eat bar-b-que outside in the front yard and play dominoes in the garage, while smoking cigars and drinking beer. They would curse and carry on for hours even up into the night, which usually took place on Saturday night prior to Sunday morning services.

People that I have shared these views with, who are members of the church at large, feel that I need to live a little, and lighten up on the people of the church, simply because, those other people confess to being committed members of a local church somewhere. Many feel that people should be left alone to live their lives, as they choose to do so.

As it is, the new breed of people in the church today, prefer the night-club-like atmosphere, and a comfortable climate within the church to create a sociable cushion against the impact of change. They don't even want the church to resemble the glorious atmosphere of God that convicts the souls of people everywhere, and cause them to come to Christ. It doesn't really matter to most people, if the persons leading the ministry have the power of God flowing in and through their lives, or not.

Many leaders are passionate with great zealous desires to lead the people; however, they are also equally as guilty of adamantly determining to continue behaving themselves in the old riotous ways of the flesh, relative to what should have been their past lives. They are ever ready to fight and to get their point over to everyone who opposes them. They will not back down for anyone, if a fight is what you want, a fight is what you will get.

You might be a bit surprised, at the number of shepherding leaders that are sitting on ready for a confrontation, void of civilized reasoning that would enable them to work through situations with other irrational people that are usually prone to take preachers for granted. I am not talking about those individuals that are masters at hiding behind a calm smile; I am speaking relative to those people that will curse you out, and whip you in the sanctuary, should they feel that they have been pushed to do so.

My point in purpose; is not to criticize the fact that shepherds are people too, but I am appalled at the shepherds that are always operating in the spirit of the flesh! There is no obvious control of the spirit of the Lord emanating from their demeanor, that would even suggest that they are truly people of the Lord.

We will never be successful at getting people filled with the spirit of the Lord, if we are always in the spirit of the flesh before them, having absolutely no restraint whenever it comes to showing high tempered emotions when we've been crossed in the wrong way.

There were things that I would not have experienced in

my church, that were beneficial for the spiritual welfare of the church, had I chosen to handle things according to the will of my flesh. I had a way of smoothing certain things out, that would have sent the wrong message to others, that may have had the same idea to cause trouble in the church. Besides, no one would have showed support for me publicly; had I been arrested for taking actions against the perpetrators of the offensive actions that were committed against my ministry.

Whenever we are found guilty of getting into the flesh with brawling people that have come into the church, we will soon discover that we will have also been found guilty of compromising our witness.

I ask the question; "Can you really be as effective as you need to be when you have been found guilty?"

Some people have determined in their own minds that all preachers are guilty anyway, simply because they are preachers? People talk all of the time, however, we are able to continue on, within the fact that whatever it might be that people are talking about, could never be substantiated.

Lots of people, have no prior experiences that allow them to stand on the fact that all preachers are scandalous individuals, that should never be given the benefit of the doubt, relative to their innocence. It's apparent that the understanding has to be renewed within the clergy, that the odds are against us, because, the world hates Jesus Christ; whom we represent.

Don't ever forget the fact, that we had already done things in our own past that wouldn't be profitable for any honorable mention of our reputation, as members of the cloth? However, those things from the past are not the things that represent who we are today, and of course there should be absolutely no association to those things.

If it weren't for the word and the blood of Jesus, many of the things that were done in the past would still have a tendency to bring agonizing shame and the re-emergence of the faded remorse from the past pains that we had unintentionally caused others, which had finally dissipated with the timely erosion of our past sinful behavior, through repentence.

As it is, there are always people from the past who are determined to keep us in remembrance of the past failures and the mistakes that were made, when we were not tamed ourselves and washed in the blood of Jesus. God; wooed us for years and months, pulling us towards the end of ourselves, showing us the right method in which to find the directions, to exit the low roads, leading us to our present life in Christ.

Whenever we realized, that we had truly been changed from the self serving lifestyles of our past, we had some problems ingesting and digesting the idea that God really wanted to use us to minister to other people!

Although I knew that I was called of God at 3 years of age, I still could not grasp the fact that God really had a very specific purpose for my life, that was far greater than my wildest imagination could have ever dreamed.

I was always in the church, where I also learned the skills of undercover sinning from other people, that often included the pastor's children; some of the pastors that I met along the way; deacons; choir members; musicians and lay-members as well. When we learn to sin, while being in the church consistently, often times we may have an even greater since of guilt and shame, simply because we are under the teachings of righteous and holiness, consistently. We should know better than to sin; one would think?

Staying in the church, even though we had been

disobedient to the word of God, is also what helped us to get over being guilty and shameful of the fact that we had committed sins. After all; I learned after a while, that as I matured in the word of God and in the spirit, that there would be things that once intrigued me, that would never have an effective grasp on me ever again. Learning to walk in the spirit would also serve the purpose of teaching me to forsake the drive to walk contrary to the word of God, and to live Holy.

There is therefore now no condemnation to them which are in Christ Jesus, who walk not after the flesh, but after the spirit. For the law of the spirit of life in Christ Jesus hath made me free from the law of sin and death. For what the law could not do, in that it was weak through the flesh, God sending his own son in the likeness of sinful flesh, and for sin, condemned sin in the flesh: that the righteous of the law might be fulfilled in us, who walk not after the flesh, but after the spirit. For they that are after the flesh do mind the things of the flesh, but they that are after the spirit, the things of the spirit. For to be carnally minded is death, but to be spiritually minded is life and peace. Because the carnal mind is enmity against God: for it is not subject to the law of God, neither indeed can be. So then they that are in the flesh cannot please God.

Romans 8:1-8

I have had the experience of ministering to many people who were so ashamed of their past lifestyles, that they would not even entertain the idea of being truly washed and forgiven, to the point that they could ever be of any effective service to the body of Christ.

I have also had the experience of ministering, (at least I thought that I was ministering) to so many people over the telephone and in person one on one, where the spirit and power of the Holy Ghost manifested in our presence, but the persons of which I had ministered to, were just like King Agrippa; *"almost I persuaded them"* to believe that God truly had a plan for their lives, and a design with them in mind!

I once had a conversation with a former friend of mine, that lasted for about two hours, exact. As the spirit of the Lord led me to speak to him, I would do so, and he would confirm that what I was saying was indeed from the Lord! To me, he sounded as if he was about to leap through the telephone at one point during the conversation.

When we arrived to a certain place in the conversation, after haven spoken for quite a while, he said to me; "I WISHED THAT I COULD BELIEVE WHAT YOU ARE SAYING TO ME LIKE YOU DO! IT SOUNDS SO GREAT, BUT I HAVE JUST GONE TOO FAR AWAY FROM THE LORD FOR ANY OF THAT TO BE TRUE! GOD; DON'T WANT ANYTHING TO DO WITH ME!" With that statement, I was left to do or to say nothing else; but to end the conversation and to hang up the telephone receiver.

Back several years ago, I received a telephone call from a young woman who was in distress, and thought to be somewhat suicidal? From the very beginning of the phone conversation, she spewed anger and disgust over the past failures and the mistakes of her life which she felt were the direct result of being the victim of incest and outright sexual abuse.

She explained to me that her abuse started maybe as early as 5-7 years of age. She was very angry that so many of her male family members had taken advantage of her sexually. She had even been the victim of some female sexual abuse. She said to me that many of the abusers blamed her for their actions against her. She was a very confused little girl and she is still confused as an adult.

I listened and did everything that I could do to keep from being religiously motivated to rebuke her, as she spewed profanity into the phone receiver and raved over her past treatment from the people of the churches who had misunderstood her, as well as those who had also misguided her. Some of the things that she had been taught by members of the church who were indeed indoctrinalized by way of their denomination, was so far to the left, that even when I heard of the teachings in my own ears, I knew that the teachings were erroneous and self motivated.

While ministering to hurting people in the past, it has been a sense of self healing to allow most people to talk out the feelings of their past pains, and to tell me why it is that they feel that they are still hurting.

On this particular occasion, I was dumped on like a garbage landfill. When I was as full as I was going to allow myself to be, I stopped the young woman from speaking, and made a failed attempt to minister to her.

I tried to pray as she talked, and mind you, she was vulgar enough without going into the sexual details of every attack, that's not what I'm talking about! This woman was definitely demon possessed! She had a spirit of unforgiveness like no one else that I had ever encountered. What she wanted, was an opportunity to tell somebody her story, in her own way. She had no desire to respect anyone, especially a minister or a pastor from the church.

Thinking to myself; that there is more than one way to skin a cat, or to even get the attention of a person that may need to be reached, I allowed my wife to speak to her, but to no avail. By now at that particular time of her life, she had given herself to a multiplicity of sinful behavioral patterns, and had also thrown away the fact that she had known since she was a little girl that God had a special calling for her life.

She said to me; "BROTHER BILL, YOU ARE NAÏVE AND CRAZY, OR STUPID IF YOU THINK THAT GOD IS GOING TO USE SOMEBODY LIKE ME FOR ANY REASON!" She had chosen to condemn herself, and to judge herself to be good for nothing more that to live and to die, expecting the damnation of hell fire and brimstone, for eternity!

Once a year, at the Spoken Word Center, we would have what we dubbed as our Jubilee revival, where we would see the power of God eminately flowing through the atmosphere of our sanctuary. In the late spring of the year 2003, we were in revival again experiencing the power of God, when I invited a very frail homeless gentleman to enter the sanctuary.

He had been sitting on the curb, out in the parking lot of the church, because the service sounded so inviting to him. He didn't come inside because he was too ashamed. By now I should not have to give the description of a homeless man that was hooked on drugs and alcohol, a person who never bathed and rarely ate food. He drank alcohol instead.

I happened to notice him sitting outside, and I invited him to come on the inside of the church where the spirit of the Lord was indeed moving. He very graciously accepted my invitation and came inside. As the guest evangelist finished the message for the evening and began to minister to the people in attendance, he came up to the alter to receive ministry.

He asked if he could tell his testimony, which we allowed him to speak for a few moments. During his testimony, he informed the church of how sick he was in his body. He told the church, that even as he spoke that he was in serious pain.

The evangelist laid hands on him, anointed him with oil, and prayed the prayer of faith; that the Lord would touch his body.

The power of the Holy Ghost; touched him and he was slain in the spirit, for real! It was not a courtesy fall, to make the preacher feel as if he was really powerful? Whenever he got up from the floor praising God; and shouting I'm healed and showing the church that he could do things that he could not do when he first entered the church; he began telling the church how he had always believed that being slain in the spirit was a hoax.

That night, he had to acknowledge that the power of God is real. He praised God with us for a while. He told us about his friend who needed a healing in her body, and he vowed to bring her back to church with him the next time that he came. He came back to the church and she came with him the next time. She was homeless also, and her body was in very bad condition. I will always remember these people in my heart and I will refer to them only as "Merritt & Beverly."

I Cared To No Avail!

We, at the Spoken Word Center, ministered to these people for a little more than about $1^{1/2}$ years. I personally poured my heart into these people day by day. I spent hours talking and listening to them as they sketched their life stories.

Some days they shared for hours, while other days they only spent 30-45 minutes with me at the church. I really believe that they both learned to love and to respect me, as a man of God, and they discovered that I would take time to make them to feel human and significant again.

Mind you, these people were yet homeless, most of the time they couldn't bathe themselves. They smelled, acted and lived the part of truly being homeless individuals. I could not help but realize that these people had not always been in the shape that they were in. During our conversations, they each confirmed my suspicions.

I won't go into the details of our conversations, but I will tell you that they both had it all at one time of their lives, and they also lost it all. Bad memories; from their youth up unto their adulthood, plagued their lives, playing to the tune of devastating sharp cuts, rips and tears in their souls, that never cease to throb at the beat of recounting recollections of their failures.

These two individuals, hurt so badly, that their stories were painful for me to even listen to. I hurt for them for a number of reasons. Firstly, I hurt because there was absolutely nothing that I could to improve the quality of life for them, naturally. The ministry of the Spoken Word Center; was gravely under attack from surrounding church organizations, who felt that SWC should have come under their headship.

I would love to have been able, to house these people in living quarters where they could have lived in a different atmospheric surrounding that would have been comparable to the change that had happened in their lives, but we did not have the available finances to serve their total needs, and to also handle the needs of the ministry.

I would almost cry each time I would see them leave the church, knowing that they were going back out on the streets for the night, or to the home of a friend of theirs, where the drug conditions were definitely unfavorable for them. According to their testimonies, they would lose what few items they were either given from other ministries, or the Government; to the people in the home where they would sleep. Their things would be taken and sold for the purchase of crack-cocaine.

The very best that we could do for them was to feed them, and each time we did, they would sit down and eat and sometimes cry for one another, for the joy of having a good meal to eat. I realize that I am not special, in that I share the like passion with many in the ministry, and likewise we all have seen some very shocking and heartbreaking behavior from the people, who live on the streets as they struggle for survival.

Merrit's story; was that as a toddler his mother would put beer and alcohol in his bottle to shut him up and to get him to go to sleep. As a result he died an alcoholic. While being with the Spoken Word Center; though he never totally broke the habit of drinking, his alcohol consumption diminished from 8-10, 40 oz. bottles of beer per day, within a 24 hour period; down to 2, 40 ounce bottles of beer; by his own confession.

Knock Blockers!

*B*everly, confessed to the most extreme low level of what I will call *"Junkyard Prostitution"*, and the fact that she did it to get drugs. She was an intravenous drug user, who looked as if she had acquired the HIV/AIDS virus, with no bath for a while, but her soul was important to me.

Beverly & Merrit, would come to our services and sit attentively and even ask questions relative to the word of God and holy living. They even requested to sing their favorite spiritual songs and would come up for prayer at the alter. So even though they continued to come to the worship services as they were; we accepted them and provided for them in the very best ways that we could.

They seemed to grasp the idea that God had more for them, which I gathered from the slight but noticeable changes in their behavior. For a while I thought that they had begun to dig in to the knowledge of God; just a little deeper. The smile on their faces were priceless, as they began to appear to feel loved and accepted at SWC. They began to confide in me more and more about their past life, and the mistakes that they each had made.

To listen to them talk, you would soon discover that they were not hopelessly illiterate people at all; they had actually done well previously in life. They spoke very intelligently, and they articulated well. They had no problem getting their point across when given a chance to talk. They wanted to be loved once again in life, by someone of meaning and substance. Most of the people of the church would show them love, and respect them as people.

Unfortunately; everybody in the ministry did not share our like passion for the lost and the downtrodden. Some people who were not even a quarter-of-a-mile away from the life of sin they lived, whenever they first came to SWC, had the nerve to judge these people, and to make negative remarks about their condition. They embarrassed them and hurt their feelings very badly, which in my own opinion, set them back further than they were before they ever came to the church.

People that are living on the bottom of life, don't need anyone to define their status for them; they know exactly where they are! The very snotty hypocritcal reaction of a few people toward them, sent them reeling backwards away from God. Beverly cried and sobbed very intensely, and she said to me that the people in the streets treated them better than the people at the church.

As I watched them, I was convinced that they had begun to hear the Lord knocking at the door of their hearts! They informed me that they had begun to feel confident to pray again, citing the fact that they did not feel as if their prayers were being unanswered any more. Believe me; I was working them towards answering the call of the Lord! God has a plan for everyone!

The enemy used these mean and nasty persons in the church, to silence the knocking that they had begun to hear in their hearts. It was reported to me that they had resumed the previous behavior, but even at a much greater measure than even before.

You should know that they disappeared for quite a while and did not come to the church any more during the week days to share with me.

> When the unclean spirit is gone out of a man, he walketh through dry places, seeking rest; and finding none, he saith, I will return unto my house whence I came out. And when he cometh, he findeth it swept and garnished. Then goeth he, and taketh to him seven other spirits more wicked than himself; and they enter in, and dwell there: and the last state of that man is worse than the first.
>
> St. Luke 11: 24-26

As the time passed on we were back to the point of revival again, of which was the same point and time they were intrigued to come and see what was going on in the storefront church.

Like usual; we had a guest minister speaking, and in the middle of his message, Beverly walked through the door and sat down in the service as she had in past times.

She had an eerie spirit about herself that even the least spiritual person in the church could discern? The pleasantry, that had once draped her countenance seemed to had been stripped away. She did not want to be bothered by anyone. She wanted to be left alone to herself. It was as if she had known that death was on her and she had decided to give in to the will of death?

The evangelist called her out for prayer, which she reluctantly accepted. As she came forward, she set herself to reject the ministry that would later come forth. As the shepherd of the house, I make it my business to be watchful and to pay attention to everything, as much as possible. She fell in the floor as if to be slain in the spirit; I could see that it was only a COURTESY FALL! Absolutely nothing was going on with her and the spirit of God.

I asked her to get up off of the floor and she complied to my request. I asked her why she would not receive; she replied that she couldn't and that she did not have a desire to receive from the Lord anymore. The evangelist began to speak prophetically to her saying that he could sense the spirit of death all over her and that her time was indeed very short and that she needed to make a decision to come back to Jesus now!

She refused and she openly said no! I stepped in to attempt to minister to her being that I had spent just better than a year ministering to her previously, but to no avail. This service was on Sunday night; late Monday; the very next day, Beverly laid down to sleep for the last time; she never woke up again! She died in her sleep before daybreak, Tuesday morning.

You might think to yourself, being as spiritual as you are, that no one could have stopped her from answering the Lord; if she really wanted to answer? But, I want you to consider the fact that some people have got to be taught how to answer the Lord. The High Priest; Eli, in the 3rd chapter of I Samuel had to teach the little boy Samuel how to answer the voice of the Lord, that was calling him in the night.

These individuals were naturally adults, but they were little children spiritually, relative to their understanding about the things of God. I'm sure that they did not know what most well-churched individuals and spiritually matured individuals would know about hearing the voice of the Lord calling them, and responding accordingly, even though most people who say that they know what to do, still don't answer!

The final incident; whereas, Beverly & Merrit were offended during the service, was brought to my attention only after the perpetrators had been long gone from the church that evening, and they never returned to face me as the pastor of the church. You get the feeling that they knew they were out of order and that they had succeeded to block any further progress in the lives of those people? They did damage to the purpose of these people and they didn't even care that they hurt them, or that they will have to answer in the judgment before the Lord.

I would always spend time in the office at the church during the day on a weekly basis. On a couple of occasions, Merritt would come by the church seeking money. I reached out to them and sent word to Beverly to try and get her to come back.

I did not hesitate to admonish the congregation, that we are to be very careful about how we handle the people that come into the church. Though I spent weeks on the subject, the damage had already been done and we would not be given another chance to repair the breech.

I take full responsibility for what happened in the church, after all I'm the leader. I can say that I learned a very painful lesson through this situation that I will never have to be taught again. I have learned to keep the sheep, as well as to care for them, while they are under my leadership.

It is devastating to realize that the greater fight against the flow of the ministry is actually levied from the people docked in the pews of the church. Many who refuse to assist the ministry with building up the ministry of the church, have no problem at all, tearing away at the success of the same ministry.

Shepherds, wake up and come out of those pastor's studies, drinking coffee, with your legs crossed, and pay attention to the people in the sanctuary of the congregation of your church. Don't give them the benefit of the doubt, see them for who they really are and deal with them accordingly. God will hold you accountable for them in the judgment!

Do You Care?????????????????

For We Wrestle Not......Eph. 6:12

Six

WRESTLING.   Catch as Catch Can Style.

Doubters & Haters!

X'S & O'S AND X'S & O'S

Then the eleven disciples went away into Galilee, into a mountain where Jesus had appointed them. And when they saw him, they worshipped him, but some doubted.

St. Matthew 28:16-17

For verily I say unto you, that whosoever shall say unto this mounntain, Be thou removed, and be thou cast into the sea; and shall not doubt in his heart, but shall believe that those things which he saith shall come to pass; he shall have whatsoever he saith.

St. Mark 11:23

I will therefore that men pray every where, lifting up Holy hands, without wrath and doubting.

I Timothy 2:8

They Really Do Exist In The Church!

*I*n the Christian church, there are people who doubt the reality of the Lord, that have actually brought themselves to hate others for truly believing.

To properly begin the chosen dialogue of this chapter, I will honestly admit to you, that over the years past, I have met some of the most loving and lovable people in the church. People, that make living holy for God and being a member of the church, a reality most realized. I am talking about people who made you want to come to church, they kept you looking forward to the very next time that we were to gather together for worship.

I have met people that I felt that I could at least go out on a limb and say that they were truly living for the Lord all of the way, with every fiber of their being. These were people that I could say the types of things about them that could not be said about most people found around that church. They sort of stood out from the norm, and made it easier to love them.

I thank God for allowing me to meet people who cared if I loved them. You only knew this because they were so aggressive in their efforts to love you, at all cost. No matter what you needed they would see to your need and never expect recognition for it, nor would they place stipulations on you as a result of their care for you. They were determined for you to see Jesus in them, and for you to know the Lord for yourself.

The more it appeared that you had begun to grow and to

mature in the Lord, the more excited they became, as a result of you. They could rejoice in the Lord with you, about you; *AND TO BE HONEST*, they would actually go off and leave you in praise, while praising the Lord, for you! They would be just that excited about your spiritual development in the Lord.

Whenever those people checked on you and questioned you about the way that you were living from day to day, you knew that they were genuinely concerned about whether or not you lived a lifestyle that was indeed pleasing to the Lord. Their purpose was never to get you planted in the Lord, so that they could see if they would be able to pluck you out of the will of the Lord later, for any agenda of their own.

They were never concerned if you knew the latest gossip of the church, they wanted you to know the word of God for yourself. They were in a hurry to get you filled with the spirit of God, which would enable you to get a grip on the reality of living saved, quickly! Many people come forward nowadays to be saved, who just as quickly as they came, also return to their original wayward lifestyles, because they lack the necessary infilling of the spirit of God. They need the Holy Ghost!

When I speak of the Christian church, I am speaking of the <u>Christianity</u> umbrella at large; world wide, relative to the supposedly, "Bible Believing Churches" that teach the gospel of Christ Jesus.

Many members of so called, Christian churches, have chosen to take neutral positions, as it relates to the Holy Bible; the King James Version of the scriptures. It has been suggested that perhaps the bible that we adhere to, may not be the word of God after all. So as a result, fewer people have chosen to embrace to an offensive positions of the Bible, which is to agressively believe it!

We are not likely to find as many people of such a genuine passion for loving and caring for the Saints in righteousness in the church, for the fact that the world has indeed made its influential landing in the local church.

The aisles of the churches have become a runway for the ungodly spirits that have been flying through the air needing a place to land for centuries? As a result of the attitudes of the people of the church, who scour the sanctuary of the churches to find the people that are noted for keeping it real; quote-un-quote; those certain people have actually become doorways and gates of entry for the worlds influence and ultimately, the devil.

Alike yourself and others; whenever I came into the church to be saved, I never expected to encounter the devil with a tambourine, or with the microphone at the front of the church, in charge, leading the service.

At the age of 14; coming to the Pentecostal church, from the Baptist church; I realized that there was something more spiritual going on among the Pentecostals that just simply was not happening among the Baptist. The people were spirit filled in their expression of worship. The actual power of God flowed throughout the atmosphere, among the people, whereas, it was a common practice to experience the working of miracles, and to witness the operation of spiritual gifts during the worship services.

Being overwhelmed with the magnitude of the spirit of God in the services, immediately, I associated the people in the Pentecostal church with being true and righteous, even more-so than any other people that I had ever encountered. If you told me that you were saved, I believed you without a doubt! I didn't believe that you could hang around such a spirit filled atmosphere and be anything less than saved!

On the other hand, I have encountered some of the meaner, hateful, unforgiving and just down-right nasty people, in the same churches. I'm talking about people that were mean without a purpose! They were evil and stubborn without a cause! I'm talking about people that would not hesitate to inform you that they hated you just because they could, or just because they wanted to!

Before you get too spiritual on me and begin to judge me for my true observation, I need to inform you of the fact that I am not just talking about people who were supposedly just sinners that hung around the church, my reference is to the people who claimed to be truly saved in Jesus Christ! Don't rebuke me; because it was their claim to being saved!

Many of the people that I encountered were pastors and deacons. They were the leaders of the churches who should have been teaching others how to behave themselves as a child of the Father.

I am well aware of the fact that Jesus taught us that we would be hated without a cause; I'm not lost concerning that fact. He did not hesitate to tell us that the world would hate us for the cause of Christ! You would have to show me in the scripture where Jesus made a reference to the people of the body of Christ; that part of their character would be to hate you without a cause. Just because it happens to take place in the church, doesn't mean that it was the intended behavior for the people of the church! *Where are the True Lovers?!?!!!*

Need I tell you that I soon realized that people are people everywhere you go, and that I was made aware that every one in that powerful atmosphere were not all partakers in the teaching and the convictions of the church? Some of the people that I encountered, I wondered how they even made it past the front door without passing out, or being scrutinized by the elders of the church. Such encounters made me to know that the Grace and the Mercy of God were indeed for real and truly at work in the church!

Just because we allow hateful people to continue to hang around the church causing trouble among the believers, that does not constitute that God is at ease with the behavior of ungodly people around the church as many people of today are indeed pleased to have them hanging around the church. I once heard a pastor say from the pulpit, that he needed a person that was indeed acquainted with the devil, to deal with the devils that might come into the church for a confrontation.

I could care less if you agree with that particular pastor; no demon on the earth, in the sky, or in hell; should ever have the people of the church so scared that they are looking to other demon spirits to handle the problems that arise as a result of an evil presence, or any evil influence in the local church!

It has now come so far past the time of need, for angry people to come to the altar of God, to have the *"demon of anger and hatred"* cast out of their spirit. The only problem is the fact that there is too many angry people standing in the stead of the shepherds, to do anything about the other angry people in the congregation. Angry shepherds, produce mad, raging GOATS, who cannot follow God; or leadership.

The consensual attitudes of the people around the churches nowadays, is "Mad is; Mad allowed!" In other words; since I'm angry, I might as well allow the others to be angry as well, and leave them alone just as they are! It never makes any sense to people who are yet in need of deliverance, to seek after other people in the congregation of the church to get them delivered from whatever has angered them. Angry people, usually only become more enraged when others are set free from their bondage, they are not often encouraged to seek deliverance for themselves.

While the church should be spilling over in command, to influence the world, the influence of the world is in many of the churches now. We all have to admit that the church is filled with hypocrites, who falsely confess to being truly changed. But, however; we also shop at the same grocery stores as they do, we frequent the same restaurants that they do, we even shop for clothes at the same clothing stores that they do, as well as attend the very same churches that they do.

I know that what I have just stated, about being the hypocrite in the church is true, because it just might be you! Just as sure as you are alive and breathing, the reality of hypocrites are just as true and real in the church. As a matter of the fact, if it were not for the reality of the church, there could never be any hypocrites. That which is true, has to always preceed that which will later be determined to be false!

The hypocrites are the ones that are most angry at the fact that there are other hypocrites hanging around the church. They are territorial predators alike the wolf, and other wild predators. Much of the hatefulness that I have mentioned, is spawned by way of the like spirits that are in each others way. They are consistently stumbling and colliding into each other!

You're Outdated; Doubter!

A vast majority of those who attend church have always chosen to be analytical, rather than receiving relative to bible teachings, they are repulsive to the idea of faith; believing beyond the shadow of a doubt. The greater exemplary intent to openly scrutinize the scripture, is on steroids to the 5th power!

The observed demeanor of many people who are hanging around the church, is the excessive posture to openly choose which part of the scriptures that they are going to accept. It doesn't really matter whose preaching or teaching the word of God, most people are not choosing to believe anymore.

Teachings; that are relative to the lifestyles that people are living today, just might be drowned out with the *very high volumes of extreme silence!* Picky people, who choose to ignore the truth of God's word, bring their nerves and disrespect with them to church, and when the messenger is too persistent during their delivery, to suggest that people live by the principles of the word of God, they show a sense of protest to the message by walking out of the service!

Plain and simply, there are some people who cannot bring themselves to totally settle their belief in God, who are angered and enraged once they discover that others do believe, totally!

I am talking about people who attend church regularly without missing, and are dedicated workers in their local ministry! People are dangerously taking on a very secular humanistic approach to believing in God relative to the scripture.

Because their hearts are filled with doubting, relative to the word of God in the first place, they have allowed themselves to believe that the preacher or the church has got no business at all, telling them how to live their lives? However, the very same picky people who choose to disbelieve the word of God; somehow find it possible to start believing whenever they find themselves facing a life-threatening crisis.

It has now become very difficult to minister the word to this educated generation of people, who understand the English language a little better than the average people of the church. The smarter people become, the more they appear to project an attitude towards the church, as if to suggest that the church is filled with a bunch of simple minded dummies, which is a very unintelligent assumption. They enthrone themselves as being the only smart people in the church, now that they have a college degree.

People choose to psychologically silence teaching or preaching that condemns their personal behavioral patterns, now that they claim to be a believer in Christ Jesus. They are more determined to pick through a message from the scripture, than they are at picking through a very bony piece of fish! People know how to eat fish and throw out the bones, figuratively speaking?

> *Brethren, if a man be overtaken in a fault, ye which are spiritual, restore such an one in the spirit of meekness; considering thyself, lest thou also be tempted.*
>
> Galatians 6:1

Haters Expose One Another; Not the Enemy!

*M*ost people don't seem to know the danger in exposing another individual in the church, without any attempt to restore the person to their rightful place in the Lord through repentence. In the past decades, we have seen churchmen fall themselves, who had indeed exposed other churchmen, spotlighting their weaknesses and their frailties and their propensities to sin.

Solomon said; that all flesh is as grass! We are temporal and fragile to the natural process of life, to the point that there will be times when an individual will not be as strong in the Lord as they ought to be always.

Some people are so holy, *(at least they have convinced themselves to believe anyway)*; they feel that they have the right to sit around watching the lives of other people of the church, keeping them in a binocular-like judgmental focus for the purpose of being able to document the patterns of behavior of the other people. They doubt that anyone could be living more holy than they may be living themselves.

Sometimes they might watch another individual for months or for years before ever seeing anything that they think in their own eyes; truly warrants even an honorable mention of anything worthy of being cited as acceptable behavior. To be accountable is one thing, however, to be spotlighted, as if an individual is on stage performing a play or participating in some type of a competitive sport, is altogether a totally different thing, which by the way, does not even belong in the church.

Some people in the church, choose certain persons to pick on, never giving them any rest at all. They make it known to others that they are keeping their eyes on that other individual, as if they have been hired to privately-investigate that person. My; the nerve of some people who have knighted themselves little gods in the local church; it's nerve racking and shattering to the faith of other individuals?

See if you can wrap you mind around this? I have been hated by two of the same people in the church, who by the way, they hated each other! Often! You be advised, that I am not at all crying the victim here, while I am crying, foul!

They could not even come together to serve the same

hateful cause against me, they were so hateful towards each other. You'd be knocked out to realize, that the very same people who hated me and felt no shame while showing it, were the same people who often determined that they would require me to show LOVE to others! That's Crazy!

While the term "Haters" is used as a slang among people, it does also bear the ring of truth in every since of the word. If you go around hating people, determined to knock down and to tear down everything that other people build up, seeking to destroy their influence with other people ultimately, then you are a hater! It is not at all possible to hate people on a consistent basis, and love God. It is not even wise to hate other people even for a day!

I know that it's difficult to wrap your mind around the fact that some people around the church are still as hateful as they were before they ever came to the church, but they are in the church right in the mix of things, up front and quite visible. Don't act as if you are not aware of the fact that there are hateful people in your church, truth is that you really don't even have to look hard for them at all, they avail themselves to be known!

Be advised; God doesn't hate people and neither do I! I hate everything that people do against God, things that God hates about people according to the truth of the word, and so should you! If people are going to change who they are, they have to change the things that they do that make them who they are.

To give others the benefit of the doubt, does not necessarily bespeak of your ability to love beyond the finding of fault in another individual, it does most often show that you are capable of denying the actual purported behavior of another individual.

When you purposefully fail to acknowledge what you see in the spirit and behavior of those that you may endear, because you actually despise having to face the truth about someone that you love, that does not suggest that you are actually spiritually blind or even incapable of seeing what is actually true about another person? Perhaps your own apathetic spirit have caused you to become vile in your affections, relative to seeing the need for a change in the lives of others.

I am not suggesting that we can change anyone, but I am suggesting that we can point them in the direction of the one who changes all people; which is God in Christ Jesus. Love covers a multitude of faults; but, how do you cover any fault that you may be unwilling to even see? We have to see it to cover it!

What we do will have the power to exact the probable cause in allowing others to define who we may be, though they often get it wrong when pointing us out to others, holding what they feel that they have come to know about us, against us! They often think themselves to be the most loving around the church, while being the same individuals who will hold others hostage for any wrong doings. Learn to forgive people quickly, and release them from the judgemental grip of your own unforgiving spirit! You're not God!

Where Is Pointer?

Figuratively speaking, the average finger Pointers in the church, do not often reveal themselves to the general membership body, because they would not dare have anyone mark them as a busybody. They want everyone to receive them as true and honest, blood washed children of God? Pointers are more dangerous among the people of the church, than the silent slithering attack of the Giant Anaconda in the African Nile River. Anacondas are quite sizable in length, and very bulky in weight; they are masters at swiftly surprising prey, when launching striking, lightening flash, quick; attacks!

Anacondas are silent killers; by crushing and squeezing the bodies of their prey until all breath and blood pulse algorhythms are ceased, they then swallow their prey whole. It's been reported and documented, that even full-grown adult men have been swallowed whole!

Finger pointers around the church, are often like Anacondas, they are usually very sneaky, while they generally ask the persons of which they are revealing their findings to, to keep confidential, the information which had been divulged.

In elementary school, we used to sing a little song because we were learning to recognize all of our little body parts, we would sing;

"Where is Pointer, Where is Pointer,
Here I am, Here I am,
How Are You Today Sir,
Very Well I Thank You,
Run Away, Run Away!"

Here's how I interpreted this little song; "Pointer", would always identify himself so that we could recognize him, and distinctly know him from now on. I have always known Mr. Pointer, ever since Kindergarten and Pre-School. Everyone in the class would be looking for Pointer, and we would soon discover on the playground, that the rest of the school had also been looking, and had found him!

I don't know about you, but I have met a lot of pointers in the church over the past forty years. I am always appalled at how well received these persons are by the leadership of the ministry. They are often rewarded gracefully for the private investigation of others around the church, as if the church could not have proceeded without their hunting skills.

Leaders often overlook the damage that may have been caused in the lives of the other persons, and some have even suggested that they could care less about the spiritual welfare of the other persons. No leader should allow another person to be fingered without bringing them together with the investigating pointer, who has brought accusations against them.

In our little song, Pointer was told to run away, and we would put pointer behind our backs. Whenever one of the other students would point their finger at another student, they would immediately be reminded to put Mr. Pointer away, and also given the instruction that it wasn't very polite to point at other people. As a matter of the fact, we were taught that it was down right rude and disrespectful to point the finger at another person even when we knew what we were talking about.

Also in our little song we were encouraged to enquire of the welfare of Mr. Pointer, saying; "How Are You Today Sir?" We were taught to seek after diffusing any unfavorable situation in the life of Mr. Pointer, once we recognized him for who he is.

The leaders of people who point the finger at other people around the church, should be encouraged to recognize the inner outcries and the serious need in the life of that person, who couldn't possibly have a life of their own, that they are happy with? You would have to be miserable to always desire to see another person's happiness destroyed, or to see the possibility for deliverance in the life of another person totally wiped out. Misery still loves company; it has not changed over the years.

Many leaders, seem to have forgotten this fact about misery, as a matter of the fact, they themselves are not passing out as much Holy Communion; as they are passing out little cups and sometimes big cups of *HATER-AID!* People may be going through the motions serving communion, but it is not God to whom they are communing with!

Picky Choosers!

$\mathcal{Y}$ou would be shocked to realize, how it is that some people are just now coming to the knowledge of the truth, after being in the church for most, if not for all of their lives. I mean that they have been in the church anywhere between 20-50 years as a doubting, hateful member of the church, and they are finally deciding on truth. I cannot help but wonder what it is that they have believed, or what has been the driving force that kept them going all of this time?

Late comers always think that they are doing something unique, whenever they rebel against the teaching of the church. They are fooled into thinking that they have started a new revolution.

People who have never surrendered to the Lord in the first place, are the very same people who always think that the church needs to change, for the sake of people like themselves.

The problem is that, they are so doubtful, that they almost

never embrace the fact that they are completely faithless? Faithlessness; breeds hatefulness, when others who are in fact just hanging around for religious purposes, when they witness the hand of the Lord moving in the lives of others.

In many colleges, and Learning institutions, several of the instructors and professors are Atheistic in their beliefs. They don't keep their beliefs to themselves, and neither do they hesitate to dissuade others from believing. They are real haters!

America, has definitely become quite scientific in the belief systems, for which the average American is encouraged to think objectively, outside of the Christian box, beyond the scriptures of the Holy bible; rather embracing the experimental findings of Science, over and above that of any faith in God.

Science does not purport within it's practices to prove the reality or the truth of any findings; rather science and scientist seek to disprove a thing, and to establish any sustainable finding as a fact, if possible. Faith yields the truth, that God really does exist and that He lives! However, the doubtfulness of Science seeks through scientific evaluation, to dissuade the possibility of believing in God's existence.

Haven't you noticed, the basic level of college degrees are referred to as, "The Bachelors of Science?" The emerging professionals are trained in the expanded knowledgeably impacted usage of the mind. The cunning craftiness of college professors is often subtle, but damaging to the knowledgeable acquisition of faith in God.

Sadly, but most truly educated persons, often seem to lose their faithful adherence to the word of God, as they begin to doubt, having had their minds infiltrated with information that is not necessarily new information, but it challenges the necessity to believe God. Yes, people are smart now, but they are also spiritually disfigured, and disconnected from the truthful reality of God, because they were never really faithful to begin with.

If you really knew the word of God, you would know that doubters were prevalent during the life and times of Christ, and even before He came to earth to save us. Many of the Roman cultures have always embraced what we know of today as *"GREEK MYTHOLOGY." MADE UP, PHILOSOPHICAL, IMAGINARY LIES!*

Other civilizations of people during the Old Testament bible times, also embraced other idle gods; in which, there were many. People prefer believing that God, is only an inflated figment of the imagination. Whereas, the individual mind is actually in control, therefore *god* to them, is whatever they choose for him, or it, to be. People, have always preferred a god, for whom they could be in control of, never ever having to be concerned with obeying and reverencing any deity.

Is It Really Reasonable To Doubt?

*Y*ou may in fact be very smart, but allowing yourself to doubt God is not very intelligent, so just how smart are you? People have become so big headed and brainy, that in spite of the fact that people continue to die one after the other, another individual still emerges to proclaim the title of being the one to rule the world. How smart is that; if you cannot bring yourself to acknowledge that God is in control?

In the courtroom, all a jury has to do to convict an

individual of a crime, is to believe the preponderances of the evidence beyond any reasonable doubt. Often times, the purpose of the defense attorney is to prove reasonable doubt in the prosecutor's case, or rather to scientifically disprove the prosecutorial theory which will in turn win an acquittal for the defendant. The prosecutor, and the defense attorney, are usually smart individuals who can interpret the letter of the law with accuracy, for the common individual, and even for those persons who are judicially astute.

They verbally spar over issues in the court room, often making moves with the lives of people who are on trial, being charged with a crime, like pieces on a Chess board. As result of these intellectual mind games, some people walk free, who are in fact guilty and others are incarcerated, who are in fact many times innocent, simply because one of these major players could not prove their case against the other.

Before you ever take God into the courtrooms of your minds, for a trial relative to your own reasonable doubt against Him, I'll save you the expense of your reasonable time with a very important news report:

GOD *Is;* GUILTY AS CHARGED!!!!!!!!!!!!!!!!!!!!!!!!!

> *But without faith it is impossible to please him: for he that cometh to God must believe that he is, and that he is a rewarder of them that diligently seek him.* Hebrews 11: 6

He is neither remorseful, nor apologetic for being God. He won't be changing His requirements for us in the earth, according to His written word, believe it or not! God, was already sentenced to Eternal Life, long before any man was formed on the face of the earth.

If there was a case, of *"GOD VS EVOLUTION"*, to determine the responsibility for the actual behavior of man since being on the earth, upon the preponderance of all of the evidence of this sometimes "monster of a creation," the truth is that evolution would definitely still be innocent of all charges. You might be surprised to know that God would not even attempt to dodge or to shun the responsibility for being your creator. He's Guilty!

YOU THAT ARE READING THIS BOOK RIGHT NOW:

How have you turned out in your own life? What have you done to make people wonder why God made you? Did you know that God is not shocked at your behavior? God is not sitting on the throne in Heaven popping Rolaids, and drinking Maalox, because of an upset stomach, because you have disturbed Him so badly?!

Mankind has turned out to be destructive, deadly, scheming, conniving, drunkards, whoremongers, perverted, liars, thieves, predators of sexual crimes against other people, and on, and on, all over the earth! But, you will never be able to find that God tried to change His identity! He is forever God!

All doubters will eventually hate the fact that they doubted! Your own doubt, will eventually turn on you. Some of the ideas that people have developed, who profess to be born again believers, are sickening at best. Any ideas that you have developed about God, are irrelevant, if they did not come from the written word of God. No matter how accurate you might feel that you are in your own personal findings, you don't have the power to defy the truth of the word of God, therefore, you are wrong!

My friend you do not really have the time to read everything that I could say about God, I am only one person, and there are many people who can tell you about God and what He has done for them.

Since you are such a deep thinker, why don't you rethink your doubting and hateful positions in depth!

For We Wrestle Not......Eph. 6:12

WRESTLING.   Catch as Catch Can Style.

Seven

Sheep Gone Wild!

Then King Agrippa said unto Paul, Almost thou persuadest me to be a Christian.

The Acts 26: 28

But fornication and all uncleanness, or covetousness, let it not be once named among you, as becometh saints; Neither filthiness, nor foolish talking, nor jesting, which are not convenient: but rather giving of thanks. For this ye know, that no whoremonger, nor unclean person, nor covetous man, who is an idolater, hath any inheritance in the kingdom of Christ and of God. Let no man deceive you with vain words: for because of these things cometh the wrath of God upon the children of disobedience. Be not ye therefore partakers with them. For ye were sometimes darkness, but now are ye light in the Lord: walk as children of the light:

Ephesians 5: 3-8

If ye be reproached for the name of Christ, happy are you; for the spirit of glory and of God resteth upon you: on their part he is evil spoken of, but on your part he is glorified. But let none of you suffer as a murderer, or as a thief, or as an evildoer, or as a busybody in other men's matters. Yet if any man suffer as a Christian, let him not be ashamed; but let him glorify God on this behalf. For the time is come that judgment must begin at the house of God: and if it first begin at us, what shall the end be of them that obey not the gospel of God? And if the righteous scarcely be saved, where shall the ungodly and the sinner appear? Wherefore let them that suffer according to the will of God commit to the keeping of their souls to him in well doing, as unto a faithful creator.

I Peter 4: 14-19

Biblically N-Correct!

Shepherds need to stop the local churches in its tracks, and tell them that they are out of control! Has anyone ever told you, that you were out of control and out of the will of God? Perhaps someone should?

Just because you say; that you have confessed Christ; as your Lord and savior, doesn't give you the authority to do whatever you choose to do in the name of Christianity, under the protection of grace. LORD; HAVE MERCY ON OUR PITIFUL SOULS!

Whenever I was saved, at the age of fourteen, we were constantly reminded that somebody is always watching you, no matter where you are and no matter what you are doing, there will always be somebody looking at you, so live like the child of God; that you profess to be.

Sometimes I felt that a reminder to be on my best behavior, was unwarranted, because it came at a time when I was doing my very best and I felt that I was pleasing the Lord; daily? But, to the persons who encouraged me to behave myself, it was a sense of duty for them to keep me in mind to be accountable for myself at all times. The older saints used to wear us out at the very sight of what looked like a slip or chance to get out of the will of God.

They adamantly refused to stand aside and see us falling or slipping and say absolutely nothing to correct us. It didn't matter to them, who your parents were or were not, when you got in the wrong in their presence they would let you know, and without asking your permission for fear of hurting your feelings or embarrassing you, they would lay hands on you on the spot and begin to pray for you in the name of Jesus.

We were conditioned, to take the criticism and stern correction. They did not sugarcoat the truth for us, and pet us on the back to excuse us, when we were indeed found in the wrong, boy; they hit us very hard. They often had us wondering if we even belonged to God! They knew how to keep us in check with our confessions and the word of God.

Our feelings were the last thing to be considered, when it came to telling us the truth about Holiness and Righteousness, as it related to daily living among our peers and our fellow churchmen.

There was a common practice of teaching us to care for one another, and to share with one another, and never to allow anyone to lose their souls if there was anything that we could do to help. Simply, they taught us to know God; by his spirit, and to respect the working of the spiritual gifts in the local church.

We learned the importance of knowing how to come before the Lord; and how to behave in his presence, understanding that there are many things that are unacceptable to God; regardless of our feelings about those things.

They taught us that it was nothing short of being suicidal to come before the presence of the Lord sinful and wickedly pressing forward to attempt to force the Lord to accept worship from us.

They taught us that our only purpose for coming to the Lord, knowing that we were indeed sinful and unsaved, was to be cleansed from our sins. Don't Play With God!

There were many things that certain people made an attempt to introduce to the worship service of the local churches, that the scriptures clearly disapproves of; if in fact the presence of the Lord was expected to be in the midst of people; however, those persons were met with a swift rebuke and stern admonishment to change their behavior, from the anointed leadership of the church. Those leaders were no cowards, and neither were they weak and fearful of the people that they were to lead?

I can recall the love and the respect that we poured on the leaders of our churches, and the relentless determination that the average member of the church exemplified in obedience, despite the dashing assaults that were coming at us from friends and many family members and secular leaders of the community, suggesting that we as members of the church, do as we please!

Of course, I will also be one of the first to admit that those leaders were concerned that we would not enter into lifestyles that could cause us to lose our eternal rewards.

We have way too much flesh on parade, and instead of

people being sensitive to the spirit of God, people are just simply too sensitive; period! People become members of local churches, brandishing the attitudes that they remember where the door is, the same way that they came in, they can leave out, and they do walk out of the local churches with the quickness to find another church to join; and to leave! And the cycle still goes on, and on, and on…

More of the leaders of today's churches are fearful of putting people in their respectful places, as it relates to being out of order behaviorally and spiritually. Seems as if, when people are at their worst, they are preferred to do things around the local church above those persons who are indeed living clean before the Lord?

In light of some leaders, and other members of some local congregations, it appears that clean living is too clean for their taste, so they spend most of their time looking for the dirt! People have lost the sensibility of knowing the difference between being a pig that live with it's head down in the dirt, and a sheep whose head is often down submissively feeding on the provided nourishment. I've heard sermons on the discussion that "sheep are dirty animals?" What the messengers are conveying, I'm not really sure, all I know is that the message is vague and left wide open for any stretch of imagination?

People like to think of themselves as broad-minded nowadays, but what they think of as being open to objectionably thinking, is actually deceptive apprehensiveness, leaving them outrageously mad in their thinking; as it relates to holiness and clean living.

For this reason alone, many of the churches resemble a mad house of people who confess Christianity; of a different brand? The atmosphere around some churches is no different from being at the park or on the beach in bathing suits, lying in the sand. Show time at the Apollo; does not even have as much dancing energy and finger popping as some of the churches now days.

The new breed of churchmen can definitely dance, *NOTE: (WITHOUT THE SPIRIT)*; while they are truly biblically illiterate and incapable of impacting the lives of people who are ready to change. People are not seeking to find just another nightclub or a different gang, and call it a *CHURCH* without the life impacting power of Christ. They want Jesus to come into their heart, but they are consistently being told by people of the church that they are alright just like they are.

Didn't you know when you needed to change? Not only did we know that it was time to change, but we also knew that there was no one on the face of the earth that could change us. I knew that anyone who was as subject to sin as I was, or worse, that they did not have anything to offer me, relative to changing my life from the inside. It doesn't make sense to listen to people as they influence you to stay in their company, still in need of being changed, when you can rest in the presence of God and be changed all in the same process.

Everywhere we looked, there were people who had major problems; some seeking changes, others were seeking to keep going just as they were, while believe it or not, some people were actually working on making their lives worse than they were already!

And if it is not bad enough that the church at large is in disarray, once on the inside of the church, little groups have been spawned and nourished to segregate one group from the other in the congregation, these groups for decades now have been referred to as *"cliques."*

The prosperous; are often separated from those persons who may not appear to be so prosperous. People have gained knowledge of another individual's job and financial status, or they have been secretly made aware of the amount of tithes that a person may be giving, or watching the offerings and the donations that are made by an individual.

You would even be shocked to realize that certain people walk the parking lot just to see what type of an automobile a person may be driving. They watch for name brand clothes and shoes and purses, which they feel might tell the story of an individual's financial status, though they are often grossly mis-led.

Certain families automatically establish a sense of eligibility to be inducted into the hottest clique in the church. Some churches allow certain families that have seniority in the ministry, to have precedence over others in the church that may not have been in the ministry as long.

An all out war will ensue, should a new family to the ministry be allowed to be involved in certain activities that the clique might disapprove of. Cliques; usually run the church from the pulpit to the front porch on the outside of the church.

People, who allow themselves' to be involved in the clique, are totally deceived and unwise. In my own opinion, these people have gone stark-raving-mad in the brain! You have never really had a problem with anyone in the church until you run into a person that has been allowed to feel as if the church could not exist if they were not in it!

Christian?; Or Christi-aint?

I have witnessed members of the cliques in certain churches bully their way through a testimony service, whenever they took more time to tell their testimony than what was originated allotted to them. They made you feel as if no one else's testimony was of any essence but their own. As others would share their testimonies, you could hear the counter-comments to the details that were being stated by the other people, as if to suggest that they were telling their own story wrong, or as if to imply that they were lying?

I like to refer to these persons of the sheep patrol, as the "Modern Day Pharisees!" The most that they have to offer to the church, is a great big show. When the time comes for the church to be cleaned, they don't have time or the dedication, to put their hands to the wheel, a broom, a mop, a dust rag or anything else that cleans.

You will not be getting much volunteer services from these people, because generally they feel that they are too important to be asked to perform tasks that may be demeaning to their reputation. *THEY STINK OF THE DEVIL'S PRIDE;* and you can tell them that I said it! They can't see the needs of others for looking at themselves in the mirror, AND I DON'T MEAN THIS IN A POSITIVE WAY. They are pathetic and selfish in that they think of themselves only.

I know that these people are gone wild because they think that they are pleasing the Lord; and they often feel that they are projecting a Christian demeanor in their daily walk.

Somehow it has slipped from their understanding, that everything about God stems from His love; and the fact that He always gives to us; even when He takes from us!

What it is that exudes from the personalities of these nasty persons of the church's *[gang]* (clique), is the very same attitude perception that emanates from the crips and the bloods out on the street! They are protective of their territory in the church, just like the gangs are territorial out on the street corners, for which they become deadly at the signs of their territory being invaded.

It is not a common practice for these persons to use firearms, or knives, or other physical weapons to handle their disputes in the church, but don't exclude the possibilities; carnally thinking people do come to church bearing firearms and other weapons. They are not nearly as godly and spiritual, as they might have been led to believe. Holiness and righteousness is not what you make it, it is what the bible says that it is, and that's settled.

For Instance : the clique may feel that it is right to shut a person out from being nurtured by the pastor, because they don't want another person to be as close to the pastor as they are, as if that's what really matters to God, relative to making it into Heaven.

If you look through the eyes of the spirit, you will see the spiritual blood shed of many Christians; who have been stabbed in the back and the others who have had their spiritual throats lacerated from ear to ear. Members of the clique are murderers just like those persons that carry semi-automatic weapons, and knives.

Listen : Who are you and what happened to the heart that God gave you, that you could knowingly, totally destroy another fellow member of the church and continue to carry on as if you've never done anything wrong?

The older saints would tell us that; "GOD IS LOOKING AT YOU", that would cause a sense of control to come over us, for fear of being caught by God; in the wrong. Whatever we were doing came to a halt especially in the presence of the saints! We left their presence watching ourselves!

There used to be a time when the sinners would cross over to the other side of the street to walk down the sidewalk, simply for the respect to the Christians; that were walking towards them, as they were approaching. They didn't have the nerve to come face to face with the people of the Lord; they had respect. Although those were respectful times, the sinners of those earlier times were respectful of the people of God; because of God.

Now, we have people who carry themselves as if God; had better move across the street and stay out of their way, before He gets dealt with. More and more, people of this free country that we are living in, are beginning to have the nerve to curse the name of God; and to make light of the reality of the local church without showing any fear.

Don't be fooled, God; is not even backed into a corner! Because of the grace of God, we of these latter generations are given more chances than we obviously deserve. This is the only reason that people appear to be getting away with saying things that are against God; and living on to talk about it. God; has told us not to fret over evildoers; don't you think that there would be something gravely twisted, if God were to fret Himself, over these people who are out of control?

The love of God; is stronger than death, and He is longsuffering to the point that He is not in a hurry to strike any one dead as a result of saying or for doing the wrong thing. God always search the motives and the intents of the heart before judgement occurs. Don't ever forget the fact that God is all too wise to ever move ahead of His own manner of dealings with the people of the earth.

The Christian church; has become a place where we seem to believe in burying and finishing off the weaker persons of the faith, that fail to get a grip on the reality of being saved. Some people who were truly wild whenever they came to the Lord, might somehow continue to struggle with the reality of their nature being changed, whereas their behavior would no longer be acceptable. So because they don't appear to be transformed from bad to good in a hurry, we may tend to believe that they are indeed defected and worthy of being religiously euthenized?

When it comes to supporting one another in the body of Christ, we tend to believe very strongly in the buddy system. When a person is not very well acquainted with others in the congregation they just might be left to figure out the strategy of staying among the people of the church all by themselves, learning to abandon the ideas of going back into the previous life.

The Devil Got HYPE from the Church!

*T*he church has always been significant in the community for an opportunity to change the lives of people from the inside; out! Whereas, changing is visibly noticed by those who know an individual best, is it also eventually noticed to all that come into contact with any changed individual.

Whenever people come into the church, they are required to change their associations with the people of their past, and their negative dealings that are not conducive for altering their lifestyles, and their personal decision making that will keep them above the lows that they came to the Lord bearing.

Love covers a multitude of fault and changes the way that we view one another. True Christians, will do everything possible to avoid believing and thinking the very worse about an individual, often mentioning the other persons in their prayers, asking the Lord to help them. As long as the others desire help, those who are truly capable and destined for helping them, will come to the aid of those persons, and they will see them change.

However, many people have been allowed to come into the church just as they are, but, with no determination to change. They have come to the church with a mind to do what everybody else does and to know what everyone else knows, while they are yet determined to remain worldly and carnal in their thinking relative to what makes the church; the church.

Many believe, that it is acceptable to God, to still be everything that they were when they came to Christ, and they feel that they should not be hypocritical about who they are, so they show whatever side of themselves that they want others to experience, and could care less about what they think, even though they came to the Lord asking for Him to change them.

What they showed is that the change they asked to receive, is really not what they wanted? They wanted relief from the pains of the trouble that their own ungodly behavior brought upon themselves, but it is for certain that they did not want to change!

Many mature Christians of the church have been viciously

attacked, as a result of taking it upon themselves to encourage the new comers to conform to the teachings of the bible that are relative to living the Christian lifestyle. People need desperately to understand that the spirit of the Lord must fill their souls in effort to begin the total process of controlling and guiding the lives of those persons who have indeed confessed Christ; as Lord and Savior!

New converts, who come to the church for the first time, seldom understand that it doesn't signify a change whenever they come to the gathering of the church under the influence of controlled substances. They may not have learned as of yet, that the nightclub is not the atmosphere conducive for remaining under the shadow of change.

They simply do not have a complete understanding of the true atmosphere of freedom that is in the church, which is a sphere of spiritual release, whereas, the unseen binds and guilty, shameful bands attached to the sinful soul of an individual, are totally severed.

They come into the church, not being spiritually minded enough to know that freedom is spiritual first. They might believe that the church is the place where they can do whatever they choose to do, because it is a place of freedom?

People that are unchanged, but have developed a strong desire to get involved in the activities of the church, don't always ask for permission or seek the consent of the leadership or the more mature persons in the congregation, they move forward on the impulse of their own feelings to satisfy their own desires.

Waiting on the Lord or even waiting before the Lord is often not a very desireable thing, so they do as Saul did in I Samuel chapter 13:

It seemed that Samuel would not make it to Gilgal in time

to offer sacrifices to the Lord for Israel and Judah to worship the Lord; Saul leaped out in front of the necessary spiritual order of worship among the congregants, offering the sacrifices himself and later found himself in trouble with the Lord.

If God says not to touch a certain thing, it drives most people so intensely wild that they are driven to touch it anyway. More now than ever, we see a highly diminished respect for the things of God. People prefer the absence of the spirit of the Lord in the services, which allows them to operate as they choose.

Most times, people respect the physical things in the sanctuary of the church, in that they will usually avoid touching them, but they do not respect the things that are truly attributed to the spirit in the church. People always have a desire to lay hold on the anointing of God; seeking a sense of control over the anointed people of the Lord. They believe that the preacher is fair game to them in every since of the definition.

People don't always keep their feelings under the cover of discipline and respect these days; they are controlled by their feelings. Christianity; is not about a feeling, it's all about faith and trust in the Lord Jesus Christ!

People don't hide undercover when launching an attack against the pastor or the church. Openly, they bear the crux of their attitude to everyone that will give attention to the situation. You ever hear of the term: *"The more the merry?"* They do whatever it takes to involve other people in the malee.

People feel that damage has not been done until the destructive information is made public knowledge, both on the inside and on the outside of the church. People used to be ashamed to mess with the children of the Lord for any reason, but the shame of coming against the people of God is no more the same, they don't even care.

I've seen adults literally engage in a fist fight in the church during what should have been a worship service. They began to use profanity and to swear to the tops of their voices over matters that would never have an impact on their spiritual growth. They turned the sanctuary of the church into a boxing arena and began to showcase their fighting skills.

There is way too much drama that is being allowed on the inside of the church. Used to be that whatever happened in the church stayed in the church, for reason of the wisdom that the leaders of the past, seemed to observe. They knew that people would disrespect the church even more if they knew that there were people who hung around the church consistently causing problems.

Bearing It All!

*T*he church should have never come into this type of sinful agreement with the ways of the world, because, Satan is the ruler of this world. He has always desired the fall of the church, for which other demon spirits would have to be loosed in an effort to secure the fallen state of members of the church, in desperate situations. Jesus said to Peter;

> *Upon this rock I will build my church, and the gates of hell shall not prevail against it.*

St. Matthew 16: 18B

Many people have gone wild in the church, acting like a bunch of barbarians and heathens who have never met the Lord? But, whenever they are exposed for their outlandish behavior, all of a sudden it's the devil's entire fault; the devil made them do it!

People don't spend enough time in bible instruction to know that the devil has to get his permission from the church, to wreak havoc in the world because the power of total control, is in the church. The shepherds; have got to make up their minds whether or not they are going to be a *shepherd* or a *pimp!*

The persona of the pimp's total concern, is to make sure that the money is coming in by proportions that are enough to support whatever their desired lifestyle is? The attitude is; *"by any means necessary bring me the money; and I don't want any excuses!"* *"That SHEEP better have my money!"* So because people feel that they are being pimped from the pulpit, they have chosen to take the advantage of the people who are ignorant to what's really happening. They allow those individuals to get caught up in the hype, and all of the hoop-la of the shallow excitement, that many people call; really having church.

Jesus said ; "the gates of hell shall not prevail against the church!" In other words, the power of the evil spirits of hell would never be in control of the church, and neither should the people of the church be controlled by such evil spirits of hell.

Some people do feel as if the spirit of hell is the controlling power of the church, simply because there are way too many people in the local church memberships, who have never been converted. They have refused to change, based on what they witnessed in the lives of the people, who were already confessing to be Christians.

It is time for the church to come to the understanding that the people of the world feel that if the people of the church endorse certain behavior patterns of the people, to allow them to be active in the church, that it must be alright to project such unrestrained living, as a lifestyle that is pleasing to God? The

Apostle Paul said; "that all we like sheep have gone astray"; but that's not exactly what I'm talking about.

Just because we are confessing Christians at the time of a particular committal of a sin, that doesn't mean that whatever we have done wrong is no longer a sin, since we have already confessed to being changed! Sinners are changed; while sin in and of itself will always remain the same! Sin Will Always Be Sin!

Being a Christian, means that we should not be found in the midst of sinning, especially in the presence of sinners who have not yet confessed Christ; as their Lord and savior.

Misconduct, as children of the Lord, in the presence of the devil and his followers, gives a misrepresentation of our position as the church, relative to which side we are on, as it is obvious that we have compromised our authority and the power to be witnesses, which is invested in us as believers.

What a sinner sees from sinning Christians, lends a misdiagnosis for their own sinfulness, which is to go ahead as they are and not to worry about how they are living, because evidently the church doesn't seem to be too concerned with how they are living either. Of the more highly debated issues of the church, are the indulgence of alcoholic beverages, drugs and elicit sex.

How do we reach a world, where the sale of alcohol increases, even with the number of drunken-driver fatalities; when we cannot even keep the shepherds of some churches sober, of alcohol; and drug free?

I often come across certain pastors, at restaurants which serve alcoholic spirits and wine on the menus, sitting at the bar or in a booth sipping on martinis and mixed drinks, as if it is nobodies business? Just how a preacher of the gospel of God, could be caught up in alcohol and control substance abuse, is far beyond my understanding. Even though there is undo pressure in the clergy; That's the reason that we have to always pray!

I have ministered to young people who have confessed to me that they bought their very first drug purchase, from their pastor! *Isn't that wild?*

Of course we often wonder why it is that the church is losing so many people, both male and female, to the influence of the party animals? What should we expect when the pastor can't lead the people to the present power of God, but certain people of the congregation wait on them when the service has ended, so that they will lead them to the present party.

The world can't believe that there is no party like a Holy Ghost party, because the people of the church keep on coming to their partys! That's not the kind of party that they have been introduced to from the average people of the church. Many have been invited to attend better partys among the people from the church, than they did while hitting the popular nightclubs every night!

The world is saying to the church; you all need to get real and stop dashing salt and hater-aid on our parties. Seems like too many people of the church have aspired to the message of Pop-Eye; he said; *"IF YOU CANZSK BEAT-EMZSK, THEN JOIN-EMZSK! EK-KE-KE-KE-KE..........."*

The World is hyped because they feel they have won the argument against the church. The world knows that a great percentage of the support they get comes from the people of the church! The people of the church are the ones buying over half of the tickets to the secular concerts, and supporting pornographic videos and magazines, and gambling. The music that is recommended for sensorship, is both bought and sold by the members of the churches.

The people of the church have not all as of yet come in to Christ, which makes it quite difficult to enforce the installed biblical mandates for the church at large, to separate the style of living as a member of the church, from the people that are still in the world, which have no desire to know Christ.

There are as many people on a single Sunday morning, sitting in a football stadium for a professional football game, as there is that will show up for a special crusade or revival meeting at one of the sporting arenas. They get hyped whenever they discover that the leadership of the church is in agreement with ending the services a bit earlier so that the people won't miss the game! What are they supposed to think?

They're hyped because the sheep are gone wild over the things outside of the grazing pasture, over the fence in the world, while they reject the things of the church of God; in Christ Jesus! The people of the world are not clueless fools, they know when the so-called Christians of the church, who attend every time the church doors are open, when they don't even want anything to do with Christ!

Because you are a member of the church who confess to being finished with sinning, it is really outrageously wild to think that you can offer to sinners who are genuine in their sin; that that you do not even have a desire for, that would free them from the bondage of sin; which is Christ!

No matter how deeply entrenched we are affixed into Christianity, how deeply we explore into the spirit realm, or how knowledgeable we become as a result of studying the bible, it is not possible to discover that we can get beyond Jesus Christ, as the center of the church!

It's amazing to me, how so many people have gotten board with the idea of Jesus in the church, as if there is an alternative to Christianity, other than Christ. I have worshipped with people that totally reject the more spiritual people of the church, calling them spooky? Yet, they embrace S̲KUUR-R̲E̲E̲ Halloween?!?!...........

Too Willing to Deal!

*E*very other chosen practice of religion; places an individual on the outside of true Christianity; the only real church! Jesus; is the reason; period! The religious communities often interject that saying, which during holiday festivities they often leave Christ out of the picture during celebratory occasions. Many organizations of the church, have chosen the much lighter sides of celebrations, as it relates to recognizing and including the name of Christ; for the sake of creating comfortable atmospheres and cushions, for the unsaved and the unbelieving to attend celebratory functions.

We have become too willing to tolerate the demon spirits that surface in the lives of the people that attend the church, and the demonically influenced society that has come about to breed such reclusive renegades against the agenda of the church, that should have been cast out and cast away from us, where no physical, emotional, or sociable harm could be possible ever again, among the people of the church.

So as a result, instead of being able to sense the spirit of Christ, intentionally, during the holiday seasons, we rather wildly expect for people to over indulge in alcohol consumption, over partying, over spending and using drugs. We expect more tragedy and death, as a result of people being truly out of control, lacking the spirit of Christ.

We are really not surprised when people go into a fit of rage and begin to fight and make an attempt on the life of another individual, citing the fact that they have celebrated a bit too hard, further resolving, that they will return to their normal selves, a soon as the substance induced high wears off?

Baa Baa Bad' Sheep**

*I*t has become normal behavior for the wrong people to come together sexually, misbehaving themselves relative to the word of God, because, the people of the church have gone wild! From as far back as many can remember, those people seem to have the approval for their wayward behavior, from the leadership.

The children of the saints, their wrong doing is often covered up, whereas, excuses are made for them, and provisions of restoration are set in place to restore them back to their rightful place as one of the children of the church. They are given chance after chance, although they have proven over and over again, that they are not going to do what is rightfully required of them.

> Brethren, if a man be overtaken in a fault, ye which are spiritual, restore such an one in the spirit of meekness; considering thyself, lest thou also be tempted.
> Galatians 6: 1

When another person of the congregation, who is not the relative of the saints, commit a sin or make a mistake, there is not often the same level of compassion or determination to restore those persons.

There is an all out persecution and open sacrifice of that fallen individual. They are put on the altars of the church, both naturally and figuratively speaking, for the crucifixion of public opinions of the much lesser persons of faith in the congregation, to decide what the fate of these individuals should be, sort of like Jesus; and Barrabus; in the presence of Pontius Pilate, the Jews, and the Romans.

Jesus caught trouble from the religious communities and from the political agendas of His times. The religious conformants, and the un-churched people sought to damage the reputation of Jesus; or in other words they desired to destroy the name of Christ; which was, and is, and will always be impossible, because God had already exalted Him, and given Him a name, higher than any other name; a name too high to be touch by corruptible hands, words, spirits or even the association of other corrupted names.

My friends, we have gone wild for sure when we forget the fact that we had also made mistakes and even outright sinned since we confessed Christ, whether we would want to admit it to anyone or not. The only real proof that we have, that there is absolutely no perfect people on the face of the earth, is the hard facts, that the written word of God states the fact to be so. (Romans 3:23)

Whenever we desire to penalize other people for the very same things that we ourselves have been guilty of, we, my friend, have gone wild!

Whenever we become too deeply engrossed into getting the scoop of the circumstances about another individual's problems, or the sins that they have committed, to ensure that we have the right ammunition to bring that other individual down to the ground, perhaps we have gone more wildly than anyone could have ever imagined!

I know of some pastors, who thank God for certain people who are members in the congregation of the church where they are the overseer, but the only problem is that the persons of which they seem to be so thankful for, are nothing more than religious busy bodies, who nose around in the affairs of people in the church for the purpose of reporting the behavioral activities of the people when they are away from the church, to the pastor.

What some people don't know, is that the pastor never transforms into God, and they never become the judge and jury for the behavior of the people. As pastor of the church, our purpose is to point the people in the direction of the Lord Jesus Christ, who is the only righteous judge.

Some people wouldn't dare remove themselves from judging other people to allow the Lord to be God to that individual. Lots of people feel as if God moves too slow to render judgment in the lives of certain people that they themselves, all alone, have found to be guilty as charged, even when there has been none or very little evidence to corroborate the perported guilt.

Even wilder, is the fact that the other persons have absolutely no shame for vigorously attempting to expose the hidden things in the life of someone else, knowing that they have issues that would bring down equal, or sometimes even greater judgment on themselves, should their skeletons be disclosed to those persons who matter the most.

Many times, the person at the center of the open discussion are only the people who might have gotten caught in the wrong, but to those who are yet under the cover of their wrong doings, it would be very wise to start right now repenting for those things, presenting them to the Lord for the purpose of dismemberment, so that absolutely no one could ever remember them!

You might want to consider the fact, that if for sure you were really living clean prior to dealing with the unclean things in the lives of the other people, that as a result of touching those things, you are no longer as clean as you were before you started tampering with the matters of the other person.

You know how clean an individual might be before they begin to wash a filthy dog, as soon as they begin to handle the filthy animal, the dirt, the unclean smell, and the even the water which will eventually become dirty as they begin to bathe the animal, will often get all over the person cleaning the animal.

Touch not; taste not; handle not;
Colossians 2: 21

You've Got Other Sheep's Wool All Over You

People have died for touching the wrong things to which they were never ordained to touch. I believe that people would keep their hands to themselves, if they understood that whenever we touch another individual, or certain other forbidden objects, (alike the Tree of Knowledge of good and evil; in the garden of Eden), people's reputations, their character, their ministries etc., inadvertently, with little, to almost no effort on their own, they touch us back, having never stretched fourth their available extremeties to voluntarily do so. It's ordained of God for the laws of reciprocity to be activated upon these circumstances; just keep living!

When was the last time that anybody told you to keep your hands off of the things that did not belong to you? Many people have their hands all over everything and everybody that they can get their hands on. They never realized or either they hadn't actually considered that the people that they were touching, often secretely from behing their backs, those same people are touching them in retrospect, even when they are never even in their presence physically.

Lot's of people would definitely be happy if I were to air all of the dirty laundry of the people of the sanctuary, in many of the local churches. I mean that if I were to get down right dirty and nasty with it! People love to read novels, and books that are entertaining. But, I would be no different than the deranged sheep that have gone wild, *now would I?*

Who's sleeping with whom', and who's in an adulterous affair, or even who's child is either pregnant or who's son is responsible for the impregnation of the young lady, are all realities in many of the churches? But, my purpose for disclosure of any of the information that I might have written in this particular chapter, or even this book, is in no way at all for the purpose of gossip!

However I am honest, as you should know this by now! We all know that the people of the churches have lost their sense of direction, and their sober minds. Everything that there is to get into, even since they have been saved, at the church, they have gotten into it! We could spend the next several months naming the different things that the people of the church have gotten themselves into, but it would only be a waist of time; it wouldn't change the facts!

Wild people, need wild things to capture their wild attention spans, or else they lose interest very quickly. Just as those persons who are truly sexually addicted, seek out and find pornography, to entertain their thought process. In effort to remain a slave to any sin, your mind has to be conditioned to follow that particular pattern of thought on a consistent basis.

More people than we know of, have knowledge of the fact that the sheep have gone wild. Truthfully, most of them who have the knowledge of the rambunctious renegades around the church, are also likewise one and the same, as well as, partners to those that have been cited as the worst of the worst, and the busy bodies hanging around the fellowship of the saints.

The church is the only place to find real hypocrites! They are not faking it, they are truly living the part that they have been accused of portraying daily among their peers, and to the other people of the church who are truly living holy and sanctified. As a matter of the fact, I have never ever seen any one fake being a hypocrite! The people that I have seen over the years have all been for real.

Let it be known of you, that there could never be the reality of hypocrites in the church if it were not for the sake of the true saints of God.

So many people have gotten mish-meshed all in the midst of the outlandish people of the church to the point that they are no longer capable of knowing a true saint of God, even when they are in their presence. Jumping into fellowship with the wrong people around the church will cause you to conform and to even transform into the image of the disfigured "AINTZ!" You will never become a Saint of God, staying in the company of the wrong people. You will become a bleep, but you will never be a Sheep!

As intelligent as many people are nowadays, whenever they come into the church, they don't always make smart decisions, choosing to distance themselves from those persons that are truly dangerous to the body of Christ. Somehow they always seem to enter into friendship with the wrong people, who are not even seeking the Lord to know His will for their lives.

You've got to know when to separate yourself from certain people, and not be ashamed for having to do so. You need to be aware at all times; just know whatever it is that you desire from the Lord, and be willing to recognize when you're in the company of people that will hinder the blessing from the Lord that you seek.

Sometimes it's easy to misinterpret the behavior and the activity of loose wild sheep, as being mature in the Lord, because they always portray a sense of strength, which is often headstrong rebellion leading them as they go out on their own, never seeking the counsel of the more mature saints. These people are truly out of control!

In Closing : So many of the shepherds have knighted themselves Kings, or Magistrates; they have taken the power to themselves to declare war on other ministries and even several other members of the body of Christ. In many instances they have demanded that the sheep go wild, disregarding the word of God, and any good judgment, to choose behavior that would reflect, not only our salvation, but the God who saved us.

By no means am I interested in shifting the blame to the leaders for the behavior of the followers, but I am suggesting to you that perhaps another look into the rambunctious renegade behavioral patterns of the people in the church who are trully out of control, is at least necessary.

Followers are always prone to do as they are told, even when they have found themselve to be regretful of the denegrading orders to which they have carried out. People often find themselves basking in the shame and the embarrassment for haven levied an attack on another member of the body of Christ, only to find that they have been deceptively coerced into making a judgment call to deliver punishment, though they know no true facts!

One of the most dangerous statements ever made in the church from the leading shepherds was; "DON'T DO AS I DO, DO AS I SAY DO!" Those people who aspired to following such leadership, were of course, very easily led astray? The overall problem is that people don't usually feel that they need to repent for doing wrong when thay had been giving an order or a request from the leadership of the church to do whatevet it is that they might have done. So they never repent or even ask the person or persons, that they have wronged for forgiveness.

It is true that those that are responsible for leading the flock astray, that they will answer in the judgment before the Lord. But in the mean time, the mess that they create does not help the body of Christ to live in the peace of God, and to go forth in the power of the Lord, to love the hell out of the sinners and the ungodly.

Sinners know they're wrong and they are well aware of their error, relative to the word of God; they just choose to do it anyway, even though the word of God speaks clearly against it. By their own choice, they make decisions to disobey the written laws of God.

The ungodly, on the other hand, they live totally outside of the knowledge of the truth in the word of God. Not necessarily on the outside of God's grace?

Too often, we in the church are the reasons that the sinner and the ungodly never come in to the fellowship of the saints of

God to be saved, to have their lives changed. Haven't you noticed that they already know how to Gang-War outside of the church before they ever come to the church?

They don't want to leave a life of fighting and war out in the streets, while bar hopping and club hopping, thinking that they have escaped a life of fighting and crime through repentence and the shed blood of Jesus, only to come into the church and have to learn the strategy of fighting and war all over again in order to exist with the people of the church!

As the sheep of His pastures, we are all on the move in the ministry, but, I guarantee you that we are not supposed to be going wild!

That's the wrong direction!

For We Wrestle Not......Eph. 6:12

Eight

WRESTLING.   Catch as Catch Can Style.

Sheep Bites

But if ye bite and devour one another, take heed that ye be not consumed one of another.   GALATIANS 5:15

As we have therefore opportunity, let us do good unto all men, especially unto them who are of the household of faith.   EPHESIANS 6:10

From whence come wars and fighting among you? Come they not hence, even of your lust that war in your members? Ye lust, and have not: ye kill, and desire to have, and cannot obtain: ye fight and war, yet ye have not, because ye ask not. Ye ask, and receive not, because ye ask amiss, that ye may consume it upon your lust.   JAMES 4:1-3

A Disfigured Image!

*O*prah Winfrey", "Montel Williams", "Morey Pulvich", and many televangelist, psychologist, psychiatrist, physicians and an innumerable host of others who have the power of influence, often talk of "Dysfunctional Families, and of Individuals;" which does have substantiated relevance to the behavioral patterns of many people; even to those who make up the body of Christ.

People, and their family units, are considered dysfunctional, because of the clear sense of failure to function as originally designed. Let's face it; the family unit is not often functionally operating the way that it is supposed to, someone has got to acknowledge the fact of truth. If we are going to find remedies for the dysfunction of the local church family; in that we are failing to reproduce the image of Christ, we are going to have to step forward to acknowledge that the controls in the leadership are out of whack!

The intense levels of dysfunction, in that it has been ignored for so long, have allowed many local church bodies to produce what I will refer to as the "Disfigured Images" of Christianity!

The local church has been disfigured for so long, that the new members of this generation's churches, are determined to recreate their own ideas of the church, which is even further to the left of the presently disfigured image of the denominational churches, totally slanted away from the commanded biblical image required.

Even the unchecked sinners, on the inside of the local churches, have decided to force the church to accept their idea of what they think the church ought to be to them, and/or even for them, whether they believe the bible agrees with them or not.

We can never fix the problems of the local church, adding more destructive behavioral patterns to the originally damaged image of the church, of which is the only thing that people who have not surrendered themselves to the Lord, could possibly ever do!

Neither should you attempt to fix the problems of the church when you do not even possess the necessary skills to reorganize the fragmented puzzle-like conditions of the church and the knowledge of what caused the broken-ness or the damage in the first place.

Further damaging the originated image of the historical church, destroying any possibility of putting the broken pieces of the church back together through prayer, as was established by the Apostles of Christ, will be a disaster, eventually most regretted.

Because sheep are always so unsuspecting of attacking one another, is the reason that I refer to the attacks of the people of the church, who evidently have not realized the we are the Sheep of His Pastures, as; *"SHEEP BITES."*

What's Under Your Skin?

*I*n past times, many acronyms have been used to identify the diverse types of enemy behavior of the people around the church and the religious communities. For an instance: it is common to speak of a "wolf in sheep's clothing," relative to scriptoral dialogue.

I bet you've never heard of a "SNAKE IN SHEEP'S CLOTHING?"

Sounds as if to be dangerously deceiving and deadly, doesn't it? The very thought of one form fitting into another that is totally out fitted and mal-figured to its natural shape and structure, is far to the left of anything we have ever heard of.

Just as the wolf could never change the God-given clothes of its natural fur, and body structure: simply because it has hair all over its body and walks on all fours like the sheep, we tend to accept the metaphor of the deceptive trait within people.

However, an even more sinister and shocking reality of an even deadlier enemy, has long since emerged to shake up the peaceful fellowship of the church, to bring utter chaos and destruction to the body of Christ. Here's a grim fact for you to face; there are definitely more snakes around the church, big snakes, and even more than there has ever been the presence of wolves wrapped in sheep's clothing.

Try for a few moments to wrap your mind around this sinister concept and the very analytical description of some would be sheep? I'm talking about sheep whose tales are dragging the ground, because they have taken on such low down under ground behavior, like smiling in the face of others with the intentions of deadly betrayal.

No wonder we always seem so baffled and bewildered to face certain members of the church who appear to have no shame at all for having caused tragic uproars and mad rages around the church. These people; haply they walk about their lives as if they have been called by the Lord to create the disturbances that also lend substance to the evaluation of skeptics and critics of Christianity.

We use the term often; "getting under my skin", to signify the fact that an individual has gotten on the inside of us, in ways that anger us to the maximum, taking away our focus to succeed at any level in life, and on any platform.

In order to keep others out from underneath your skin, you are going to have to identify who or what it is that is underneath the skin of the opposing attacker, whomever it may be!

I have come in contact with many people in my own life who confess that it is really not that difficult to get to people where it hurts them, or to disturb them mentally to the point that they are now in control of the other person.

Some people enjoy playing mind games and the tactical execution of undercutting one another for a position of authority in the church. They don't even mind backbiting and lying on another person to make themselves look good.

This behavior is often sickening and depressing; to think of people who confess to being born again of the shed blood of Jesus Christ; on the cross of Calvary, to see them operate as if there had never been a change in their lives. The very same people, who are smiling in your face, shaking your hand, complimenting your ministry, and even kissing you on your face like Judas Iscariot; are actually trying to set you up for a disaster to bring you down from that place of recognition.

You Would Never Believe It!

ctually, sheep only have bottom front row teeth in their lower jaws, and no upper front teeth to aid in cutting or biting off tough meaty substances, of which they are incapable of launching vicious brutally mauling attacks that are designed to down prey. It's not common to even hear of sheep latching on to another sheep in the pasture for the sake of hurting the other sheep for no apparent reason.

Scientist, have documented the animal behavior of almost every un-humane life form on the face of the earth, and in the sea. I don't believe that it is some form of an oversight, or a mishap that the documentation of SHEEP have omitted to reveal that sheep are as deadly to one another as their predators are to them, in that we as people should be aware of their unsuspected behavior.

The fact is that God made the sheep very humble creatures which are tamable, though they are wild instinctively. They are not given the predatory killing behavior of many other animals in the wild.

The natural nature of the sheep would never bring the sheep to rise up on its hind legs and roar like a lion, to excite fear into prey. As a matter of the fact, sheep do not even have claws, which are used to snag a fleeing prey and to hold on to its prey assuring the catch and the kill. Maybe you didn't know, but sheep are herbivars, they eat grass, which is naturally sheep food.

Sheep don't have to kill in order to eat, so they have no need for deadly teeth and claws. Sheep are often attacked, so as a sheep or a child of God, we are never to retaliate and go on the defensive to launch deadly counter-attacks; we ought to always pray, as the good shepherd will always provide for the sheep. In His provisions, the protection that we might need whenever an attach has been launched against us; can also be found.

For this reason alone, the shepherd is given to watch over the sheep in the pasture, and to lead them to the best feeding pastures where there is rich green grass. Because sheep are prone to follow the leadership of the shepherd, there is no need to worry themselves, of the whereabouts of good nutritious feeding grounds.

Spooked From Within!

Sometimes, circumstances arise that alarm the sheep to shake up the entire herd. For an instance; the very sight of a wolf in close proximity of the sheep is alarming, because sheep know that the presence of the enemy also means the presence of the spirit of death.

Just because the sheep are humbly submitted to the leadership of the shepherd, it doesn't mean that they are clueless and stupid to the intentions of the wolf. Sheep may miss the signs of their shepherd leading them to the slaughter to be killed, but they almost never miss the danger signs of the wolf lurking about the pasture.

Any individual that may not be skilled at using firearms would still know the imminent danger that they may be in at the sight of the weapon being pointed in their direction, right at them.

So just because the wolf may not be momentarily charging in the direction of the sheep, is no reason to be at ease having a wolf in the midst of the camp. The nature of the wolf is to kill and to devour after chasing down its prey. The wolf is a stealth hunter in that it is relentless to capture the prey of its choice.

We use the terminology in the church whenever we refer to gossips talking other people's business, we say that; *"THEY ARE RUNNING DOWN ONE ANOTHER!"* See the connection between the stealth of the wolf that chases its prey and runs it down until there is nowhere to run, and gossips that chase after information that is capable of destroying the character of another individual in the body of Christ, successfully exploiting the information until the damage has been done.

Just as the wolf does not stop until it has successfully captured and killed its prey, gossips don't quit until they have gotten the attention of enough people that will listen to their negative report, so that the credibility of the persons that they are talking about is brought into question under a cloud of suspicion.

The wolf bites with several pounds of pressure of which at times may only leave its prey severely wounded and incapacitated, but not dead. There are times that the attack of the wolf is only for the sake of its territory, and the fact that the wolf feels that it's territory has been invaded. Naturally the wolf will launch a good fight for its position and it's authority in dominance to teach the intruder a valuable lesson.

This is the only reason that many people of the church are fighting so hard against others, it is for the simple fact that they want to be in control and others who are truly deserving of the positions of control are blocking any present possibilities for the position because it is their time and their season.

They desire to be the more popular known persons of

their surroundings, so if it means that another individual will have to be destroyed in the eyes of the people, their character assassinated, and for the power of their influence to be disintegrated, well so be it!

A wolf will bite even in its own pack, whenever it feels threatened, to reestablish its supreme dominance over the rest of the pack. Sometimes I believe that they rather bite to stay in practice of their ability to do so. In other words, I don't believe that the intention of the bite is always meant to be deadly or even offensive. Sometimes they just want to establish which one has the biggest teeth, the baddest bite, and the fiercest attack.

All bullies like to keep others in mind of the fact that they are the baddest, the biggest, and the toughest around. Bullies are often seen shadow boxing to brandish their skill, or sparring often to show what trouble another individual would be in should they choose to engage themselves in a fight with them.

Another characteristic of the wolf, is that they often howl in the darkness. They don't mind revealing their presence to all under the sound of their voices within a certain radius. Howling is also for the purpose of locating others to stand with them in the attack. Hardly ever will you see a wolf fight alone, they fight in packs, together! Remember this fact!

So sometimes the lone wolf's howl; is nothing more than blowing in the wind, huffing and puffing to get attention, but be advised that even a lone wolf is yet deadly. They will come out of a corner when pushed and backed into a corner or a tight spot. The more evil it gets, the better they are at operating and working their way out of the situation. When caught in a trap, a wolf will bite through its own leg to free itself from the power of the trap, to escape dying.

Whenever a *"WOLF IN SHEEP'S CLOTHING"* has been spotted

in the congregation of the righteous, the wolf must be swiftly exposed and bound up to be put out of the company of the Lord's sheep. You must understand that there is absolutely no surrender in the wolf! So, cornering such an individual who has the wolf-like spirit operating on the inside of them, once they have been discovered, only citing them for the purpose to excite them or to scare them, won't work!

What I refer to as wolves; are those persons around the church who were never converted, though they have confessed Jesus Christ as their Lord and savior. They are not necessarily in search of the truth of the word of God in the church. They have never invited the Holy Ghost to fill their heart, and to live there. Often they will not hesitate to tell you that they are not ready to receive the Holy Ghost, even though they have recognized the need for a spirit filled life.

They are not going to leave the church because they say that when the time comes to make that decision, they want to be close to the church already.

Often very religiously dedicated to the local church, they wouldn't dream of being absent from the presence of the gatherers who come out to partake of the weekly services, because they don't want to miss a thing! They always make sure that their voices are heard in the congregation in one form or another. The deception of wolves in sheep's clothing is that they are always present in the midst of the crowd. They know how to fit in to the mix with everyone else.

They are hand clappers, and foot stumpers; they sing in the choir when allowed to do so, they pray out loud, and some even preach sermons; as long as they are able to keep other members of the congregation at a distance from their own personal flaws, and the fact that they are not true believers.

They can be quite adaptable to the church environment, whereas, they know how to conduct themselves, and they do a very good job, all the way to the point of launching their surprise attack! You should be familiar with those persons around the church who frequent the popular night-clubs and all secular affairs, such as, secular concerts, and bloc-parties where drugs and alcohol is being consumed.

The wolves are supportive of secret criminal behavior and usually sexual deviance and misconduct, whereas they feel that everyone should be allowed to express themselves in the way that they think is best for them, whether the behavior is offensive to the word of God; or to the righteous posture of the church.

Real SHEEP, will not be given to such behavior of ungodliness and down right spiritual degradation. Of course, that is if they are truly filled with the spirit of God, and are living by the word of God; which teaches us to do the opposite of what has been previously mentioned relative to the behavior of the wolves in the church.

The Borrowed Bite!

*E*arlier, I spoke of the actual inability of sheep to launch biting attacks, relative to the lack of teeth to do so. They don't use their bottom row teeth for any other purpose other than eating grass. This information is relative to the natural animal characteristical make-up of the sheep.

On the spiritual side; the people of God, who are styled as sheep; have become quite prone to bite one another with deadly vicious bites that are tailor made to destroy and to permanently kill other sheep of the fold of grace, often away from the presence of the shepherd. Though sometimes it is with the shepherd's consent, in some certain churches?

In my own biblical observation; the snake never gave up on the ability to be used of the devil since the Garden of Eden, in the beginning of time. The deadly snake-like characteristics of some people in the church is shocking and often unsuspecting in that they usually present themselves so harmless; and as if to genuinely care for others.

The silent slithering of the snake on the ground, is so subtle that the snake could actually be right upon you before you ever knew it! Biting, spiritual sheep; are also usually upon you so fast that you never knew that they were targeting you. You remember that person who left you with your mouth hanging wide opened, because you discovered that they were the individual that was responsible for causing the unrest that involved you around the church?

The contrasting differences between the bite of the wolf; and the snake; the snake bite is deadly because of the venom that has already poisoned the bite before it ever takes place. The wolf uses powerful jaws and very large teeth and muscles to accomplish the purpose of the bite.

The snake's needle-like fangs, pierce; injecting its venom into the veins and the flesh of the victim so quickly and precisely that an individual may not even realize the fact they had been bitten for a moment or two, and until the venom will have begun to do damage to the victim from the inside first.

The wolf's bite; on the other hand, does damage beginning with the external frame of its victim, working its way to the internal organs of the victim. However the snake's bite starts killing its victim from the inside damaging the internal organs first, working its way to the external frame. By the time the evidence of the snake bite has been revealed. For many; it is already too late! Get it; Too Late!

The very bite that has indeed downed many persons of the body of Christ; had been borrowed from the characteristical nature of the snake! The subtle movements of the people of the church that are undetected, and the bites that are unsuspected have often done the intended damage long before any telling evidence had come to the forefront to be noticed. I have encountered many snake-bitten persons around the church who are dying spiritually on the inside, but often they don't even know it!

Try to understand me whenever I suggest to you that the very "BITE" of the sheep, does not even belong to the sheep in the first place. Therefore, sheep have to borrow such a biting temperament, and the fang piercing ability to penetrate the skin of another sheep.

By the way; *"HOW TOUGH IS YOUR SKIN?"*

It is dangerous to allow the devil to place you in a position of attacking another member of the body of Christ, because your spiritual nature does not call for deadly venomous bites. So, there is no way that you could possibly know the extent of the damage that was caused! It is ignorant, and quite a negligible spirit of portrayal, to willingly attack one another.

You may be subtle, but you are not innocent in no uncertain terms, whenever you allow yourselves to launch such deadly attacks in the body of Christ. You have no excuse for your behavior, and of course you will never be excused, so if I were you I would not allow death or judgment to slip upon me in an hour that I am unaware of.

REPENT! Because, the damage to which you have caused others in the body of Christ, is probably irreversibly permanent, leaving you in need of an eternal fix for your own declining profile, as a deadly predator hanging around the fellowship of the sheep. Although you may feel sorrowful in your own heart, you really can't take back the damage once it has been done.

It's Not Right to Bite!

By now I know that you have gotten the message loud and clear, relative to how uncharacteristic and unnecessary it is to launch after one another in the body of Christ, as children of the Lord, more affectionately endeared and referred to as; "His Sheep."

You need to be sure that you make it easy for others who are standing on the outside of the relationship that we have with the Lord, to definitively comprehend the true hand of our shepherd on our lives, causing them to desire His touch.

Put away that vicious bite, and forsake the attitude that keeps you charging in the direction of others for the purpose of attacking them. Stop using the bible to justify the fact that you are entangled with the evil ability to fight like no other in the body of Christ. The book of Hebrews: tell us to live peaceably with all men, as much as is possible. Disruptive behavior, chases away the holiness that is required of us as children of the Lord.

You do not need to prove any points to anyone! The Apostle Paul suggested that we should greet one another with a holy kiss, and James also admonished us to refrain from biting and devouring one another.

It is not possible to kiss and to bite simultaneously, and neither does the two scenarios represent the very same meaning, no matter who it is that will place a kiss or launch a vicious bite. In this perspective instance; it is not at all about who you are that makes the difference, it's all about what you did!

You may be able to explain why you did what you did to others that will ask, but be advised of the fact that they will hold it against you for a long time to come, even if they themselves truly understand your reasoning, they may know why, but they may never let it die!

The fact may be that, many of the people of the church may not pack a pistol or carry a knife on their person, but, don't ever overlook the fact that many of the same people pack a mean and very nasty bite!

As sheep; we are all vulnerable in a sense to the attack of the enemy, so by all means we need to support one another, and believe in one another to the point that we would even go to bat for one another, and even fight together when necessary, to ward off the fending attack of any evil predator.

Don't be fooled, we need each other in an effort to stand in the power of the almighty God as the church. I hear people all of the time say; *"I don't need them"*, or they might say; *"we can make it without them!"* The truth is that we can make it without others, but the journey will definitely be longer and much harder than it would have been had we chosen to join forces with those who are of the body of Christ.

The world always used a term which stated; *"The More The Merry"*, if the world can do it, then so can we in the church! The Church is in Charge! Let's take the world together for Jesus Christ.

For We Wrestle Not......Eph. 6:12

Nine

WRESTLING.   Catch as Catch Can Style.

Leg Of Lamb

Wherefore kick ye at my sacrifices and at mine offerings, which I have commanded in my habitation; and honourest thy sons above me, to make yourselves fat with the chiefest of all the offerings of Israel my people?

I Samuel 2:29

And he fell to the earth, and heard a voice saying unto him, Saul, Saul, why persecutest thou me? And he said, who art thou Lord? And the Lord said, I am Jesus whom thou persecutest: it is hard for thee to kick against the pricks.

The Acts 9: 4-5

We'll Have it Our Way!

*M*y sister Jane (1959-1990); was very friendly. She always mixed well with the others in the neighborhood that would play with us. At that time, we were all school aged children living at home with our parents, without a care in the world.

The boys would separate ourselves to play touch football in the street, or we would play some other game that wouldn't involve the girls. The girls joined their arms together, swinging their legs, chanting a popular cheer that our school cheerleaders would shout on the field during a football game. I can remember that, just like it happened yesterday. They would say; "IF YOU DON'T GET OUT THE WAY, WE'RE GOING TO KICK YOU OUT THE WAY!"

They were not going to be denied the opportunities for having the same fun that the boys were having, so they would sort of attempt to force their way into the excitement without our permission.

We never really minded letting the girls in for a while, being that they were our sisters and our friends, who lived only a few houses away from us; we were sort of a big family in our neighborhood. However, the boys noticed that whenever we would let the girls in to participate, they would attempt to take over and turn the tide of events that were taking place.

They would suggest that we play one of the girl games that they liked to play, that may have included all of the children who were outside playing at the time, and sometimes they might even knock on the door of another individual to have them to come outside and join in the fun with the rest of us.

Of course, you should know that we would have to abandon our football game for that time and come back at another time to finish the game, or just start all over on another day. Those were indeed a few of the fun times that I have truly missed as an adult, having to mind the more serious things that are certainly attributed to the more mature individual.

But, now, we are not playing anymore, at least we are not supposed to be playing! It's been discovered that quite a vast number of the people in the church are playing a make believe game with their salvation.

People still like to play the game of "TAKE-OVER" that allows them to be in control, and they usually don't mind that their tenior as the leader would definitely be short lived. They prefer to disregard the biblical rules and mandates that have already been pre-set for the church. What they really want, is to have things go their own way, whether there be consequence for any one else or not.

This brings me to the place that enables me to disclose the meaning of the title. While the topic is rather animated in its metaphorical state, it is by far a very serious topic of concern, which is the reason that I chose it as a topic of discussion relative to the sheep attacks in this book.

LEG- was regarded as one of the choicest parts of a sacrifice reserved for the priest. (Lev. 7: 32-34)
HOLMAN BIBLE DICTIONARY

1.one of the limbs on which men and animals support themselves and walk.
THE WORLD BOOK DICTIONARY

KICK-3.*informal* to complain; object; grumble; find fault.

2.verb text to strike with a strong impact:
3.part B   to force or make (one's way) by kicking.

THE WORLD BOOK DICTIONARY

If you just look out over the vast population of the world, you would be able to recognize the magnitude of people, who don't approve of the mandates of the church, that are relative to lifestyles, according to the bible. We really do not have as much stress over the people who stay away from the church, because they have already determined that they are not going to respect the rules of the church and follow them.

Rather, the confrontational issues about rules and the regulations; are usually internal problems from the people who are supposed to be sold-out to following the biblical mandates of the church, whether others understand them or not.

Everywhere you go in life, there will be rules or regulations that are to be followed. Just imagine what the church would really be, if there were no rules or regulations, to establish the boundaries for living within the Christians confines in this present world with the present mindset of the people today.

*Recreational Thinking?

*O*utsiders, as it relates to Christianity, most of them usually don't have a problem letting the people of the church know that they are not governed by the teachings that are relative to the bible. Most outsiders don't believe the bible to begin with.

I can't speak for others, but, I can respect those persons that are truly real; relative to their own choice of living. I know just as you know also, that their choices will not be the best decisions they could have made should they be found standing before the Lord in judgment, in a state of adherence to their own system of living outside of the word of God.

The sooner we as people of the Lord; learn to see people as they are, whether we like it or not, we will discover the more successful methods of reaching the people that are in need of Christ, to change.

Usually, what we are taught to do from within the church, is to shun those individuals who have not as of yet chosen to come in to the salvation of our Lord Jesus Christ. While we do need to shun the things that the sinner does, and refrain from going to the places they go to establish their active status as a sinner, we need very desperately to embrace the sinners with the love of God.

HERE IS THE PROBLEM: too many people around the church will not attend the training sessions of the ministry, for the purpose of learning why the church does, and why the church doesn't do certain things, as the church. So as a result, they often meander in and throughout the church with a chip on the shoulders, about the treatment or the non-treatment of the people who are not church attendees.

You may not have thought of what I am about to say, in the manner of which I will say it; we have what I will refer to as, *"CHURCH VIGILANTES!"* They take the matters of the church into their own hands to work them out and to get to the bottom of the things, whether they know the circumstances or not. Most of them are not even called to this particular facet of the ministry. They have no authority at all!

They know the regulatory stipulations of the bible, but they would rather disregard those rules and mandates, to recreate their own set of rules to follow, citing a sense of anger or dislike for the leaders of the church, who have been ordained of God to handle the people of the congregation.

God thought; He created things; but whenever man thinks now since he has been created by God, he has the nerve to think that things would be better served if he re-create his own positioning around the things! Why don't we understand that God don't need for us to change His methods of dealing with mankind? What He needs, is for us to adhere to the word of God, and to work the word, while the word of God works in us, for us, and through us!

How simple minded we are to think that we actually have the power to change the things of God, for the sake of a few sinners that don't even have a mind to follow the Lord in the first place.

America, is definitely a country that truly believes in taking a vacation as often as we may be allowed to do so. Even while we are going about our daily affairs and routines, we are often confronted with the options of our choosing for recreation. In other words; we are found speaking of getting away from the necessary, to quote-un-quote; "relax in the unimportance of what is regarded as the insignificance of playing on the beach!" Most people need to unwind, only the mindsets of the people suggest that most refuse to seriously wind themselves up; or to be wound, for any serious reason!

How is it, that we are so stressed out with all of the alternative choices for relaxation and recreation?

We are conditioned daily to think recreationally in our thought processes, by way of magazines, television commercials, telemarketing, the internet ads, and spam-mail? Everybody has a solution for getting away from the needed, the necessary, and the normal.

Many people dread their regular daily routined schedule, seriously anticipating the opportunity for another vacation. Although this is the land of the free and of the brave, we are often probed to visit a foreign country that is not as free or brave, as it relates to the welfare of the people who live in those countries?

The way we think on a daily basis, is the determinate facter that establishes what we stand for and how we stand on it. As we opened this chapter we began talking about playful matters, only to disclose the fact that there are yet too many people in the churches who are still playing and are very playful in such serious times.

The church; for certain, is definitely not a playground or a playhouse, where play dolls and toys are to be placed for the purpose of having make believe fun. Many people, from the shepherds to the sheep, have turned the church into a fun-house and an amusement park.

Without a Ferris wheel, it may be impossible to please yourselves; in light of the fact that so many people demand recreation in their lives, but, the bible clearly states that without Faith it is impossible to please the Lord!

Now that most Americans are overweight; everywhere we turn, there is some sort of lite-food or diet drink to be consumed for the purpose of losing weight. Why weren't these weight loss schemes offered from the beginning, as preventions to weight gain?

I'M GLAD YOU ASKED!

Weight gain is definitely the result of recreational thinking, and /or the lack of serious consideration, as it relates to being careful about the food intake, and the count of calories and saturated fat, that come with our own desired consumption of foods. As we have settled down in the church as a participating member, we have also relaxed in our need to control our desired intake, of food and recreation. Most people eat more heartily while vacationing, disregarding the need to inspect the dietary intake of the food stuffs consumed.

Wherefore seeing we also are compassed about with so great a cloud of witnesses, let us lay aside every weight, and the sin which doth so easily beset us, and let us run with patience the race that is set before us, For consider him that endured such contradiction of sinners against himself, lest ye be wearied and faint in your minds. Ye have not yet resisted unto blood, striving against sin.

Hebrews 12: 1, 3-4

LEG- was regarded as one of the choicest parts of a sacrifice reserved for the priest. (Lev. 7: 32-34)

HOLMAN BIBLE DICTIONARY

2. one of the limbs on which men and animals support themselves and walk.

THE WORLD BOOK DICTIONARY

Over Weighted Leg!

I can imagine the very succulent, well prepared, roasted "LEG OF LAMB", seasoned with Basil; Garlic; Black Pepper; and other spices to bring out the hearty flavor of the meat? This very meaty part of the lamb was regarded and chosen as the prime choice, over all other portions of the meat, and it was preserved primarily for the PRIEST; or in layman's terms for today, they saved the best for the PASTOR.

Let's take a very respectful look at the Leg of Lamb: As a metaphor; relative to a certain branch of the ministry, that is set aside for the pastor; to aid him in his needs.

In this chapter, we will discuss the fact that sheep don't only attack each other but they also turn on the shepherd!

Just when the shepherd feel that they've got certain persons in their own corner in the ministry to assist them with the other sheep, and with the needs of the pastor, there are times when that entire leg of the ministry may turn and begin to kick against the pastor.

Symbolically speaking; shepherds are caught off guard in such a case as this, whenever their own support team will develop insecurities or jealousy, desiring to receive everything that the shepherd receives for no other reason than for the fact that they want it too? In some way or another, the idea of those persons being in total support of the shepherd seems to have gotten misconstrued.

Meat is protein, which is a source of strength and nourishment for the body to keep it strong. Body builders and major sports athletes are required to have very healthy portions of meat in their diet on a daily basis to maintain their own muscle mass.

The leg of the local church, of which we will refer to as the PASTOR'S AID; should strengthen and nourish the pastor in ways that are only unique to their own tailor made purpose and capabilities. There is usually a sense of understanding that is not necessarily made privy to the general population of the local congregation. Remember, these persons are set aside for the specific purpose of the pastor.

As long as the meat is indeed lean, it will do what it has

been deemed to do, but if for an instance, there becomes an over accumulation of fat, the meat is no longer fit for the shepherds use. (*Refer to Leviticus*)

The priest; and any other persons assigned to prepare the meat for the High-priest, were required to allow every trace of the fat to be consumed in the fire of the alter. Priests were not usually permitted to partake of the fat of the lambs, or the fat of any other meat sacrificial substances.

Perhaps, because certain pastors allow the overbearing, fatty, over weighted control, of the pastor's aid, for the sake of peace; the pastor's are forced, under these circumstances anyway, to settle for less than the required service protein of excellence from these persons, who have allowed their minds to be infiltrated by the counsel of the ungodly.

I have heard pastors say that it is better to just sit back and give the situation time to work itself out! There has got to be a lack of understanding relative to the actual purpose and the reasons that these non-conformative persons are allowed to remain in the leadership aid of the ministry?

> *Blessed is the man that walketh not in the counsel of the ungodly;*   Psalms I: I a

3. One of the limbs on which men and animals support themselves and walk.   THE WORLD BOOK DICTIONARY

There are other wayward thinking sheep in the same pasture as you, that will mess your mind up and corrupt your service to the leader where God has placed you to serve. Don't look so far away from the inner-sanctuary of the church seeking to find the ungodly; you just might be surprised to realize that they have been going to church with you for quite some time now.

You might ask the question; "HOW COULD THE SHEEP OF

HIS PASTURES EVER BE UNGODLY?" Jesus; is quoted in the word of God as saying; *"My sheep"*, not just the sheep, or sheep. All sheep don't belong to the Lord Jesus Christ; and don't ever forget this fact! Everybody at the church have not all been saved, as of yet!

Well, before you become too engrossed with the fact that the sheep are out in the pastures; Jesus said; *"My sheep hear my voice and I know them."* Who said that the ungodly were any of the Lord's sheep?

And by the way; how long does it take for an individual to become ungodly? The very problem with many of the branches of the Christian teaching environments, is that people are being allowed to believe that they are yet godly and living righteous; while they are living as ungodly as they could possibly ever live.

It's time that we stop believing that just because people show up at the church whenever the doors are open, especially on Sunday morning; that they must be the Lord's own sheep?

Just because these people will come to church, knowing that they are acting outrageously sinful on a daily basis, the ungodly people who will never attend a service of the believers for any purpose, lay the blame on the Lord that these people are out of control and that they misbehave, having stolen the Lord's name and placed it on their own backs.

If you tell a person that you belong to that church, the people that you are speaking to, will most likely believe it. Many churches have taken a bad rap for people who have claimed to be participating members of the church, whose names were never even on the churches records.

Some people had been arrested and put in jail and have demanded that a certain pastor be called to come to the jail, for which that pastor had never even known of that person, ever, even though they claimed to have been an active member of that pastor's church!/?

So come down off the idea that just because people attend the church that they are indeed sheep of the Lord. Don't ever forget about wolves in sheep's clothing, who show up for the raw delight of the *"LEG OF LAMB;"* as bloody and as messy as they can get it! They purpose to kill, to devour, and to destroy the fellowship of the believers, who have indeed humbled themselves to be the sheep of the Lord.

Aint That a Kick in the Head!

*O*ur jobs as believers; is to expose the devils business when it has infiltrated the fellowship of the church. But nowadays, the enemy is a friend; or a family member; and sometimes even a lover to one or more of the members of the church! So as a result, whenever they know for a fact that there is an enemy in the camp, they don't reveal it on purpose!

Whenever the leader has discerned those individuals to be an enemy to the purpose of the ministry, and calls them as such; those members who are close to those individuals are enraged and sometimes outraged that the pastor would openly voice such a fact, about someone that they love.

If the pastor is a genuine shepherd at heart, and holds fast to the position of authority, relative to the true endowment of the spirit indeed, having a validated revelation relative to that infectious person, the persons of the ministry who are supposed to be sheep in the pasture, will turn from that leadership and go seeking other pastures to settle on, as result of their anger.

Or, rather they take their devilish friends to find a church where they can all be comfortable fitting in, to destroy as many others as possible before being cited. What is amazing to me, is how they don't take their friends to the altar of God; before the church to receive Christ so that they can be saved; and so that their nature can be changed from those old evil ways?

Not many seem to care that the shepherd has a genuine sense of concern for the soul of that individual? They only feel that the pastor should not have had anything to say about the lifestyle and the possible damage to the church, and the inevitable destruction to any number of the souls of the people that attend the church, should that individual be allowed to roam free among the sheep. Aint that a kick in the head!

There is a story of a pastor, who was called to pastor of a particularly established congregation. The story is that he accepted the position and the opportunity to serve these people of the Lord as their new pastor. Of course the people were likewise excited, but, they were also loaded with the traditions of the past.

Upon taking on the ministry as the pastor, there would be a certain order of business to be attended unto. The minister of music; who had been with that ministry for quite a number of years, had a very degrading problem and a very sinful presence right up in the front, before all of the people. He was a practicing homosexual, who had no desire for a change, which was evident in the lifestyle that he portrayed.

The report is that the pastor met with the board and instructed them that either the homosexual would have to leave the post as the minister of music, or he, himself would have to resign as their pastor. In this particular instance; this person had far too much influence over the affairs of that ministry, for which he had been exercising for many years. In past times he had a say in how the former pastors ran the church.

The members of the board told the pastor that he would have to turn in his resignation immediately, because not only was the minister of music a relative of many of the people there, but that he had been there way too long to allow someone to come in and to ask him to leave. The people were really attached to this person and without them even knowing, they were emotionally attached to his sins as well; they did not want that to change!

The pastor left and went back to his home without even missing a beat. AINT THAT A KICK IN THE HEAD!

THIS IS A TRUE STORY!

Many other pastors said that they would have never made such a bold stance like that from the beginning as the pastor, they would have just dealt with the situation for a while until they had won the people over to them.

Reading this chapter right now, you might even be enrage at what I have written here, because you would have never ever asked a homosexual to leave your church for any reason? NOT A HOMOSEXUAL!

Maybe if it had been a man who liked women, or a woman who might make a pass at the men in the ministry for money, many leaders seem to have absolutely no problem asking these people to reframe from their attendance to the ministry, but never a homosexual or a lesbian, because they are too valuable to the music department? They draw too many other people to the ministry; even though the people that are drawn to the ministry, are often as demon possess as the persons that drew them!

Whenever I was coming up as a musician in the church; while I was actually learning to play the instruments in the church, I can remember that there would be musicians all over the place just waiting on an opportunity to grace the instruments. Musicians were a dime a dozen back then; they were everywhere, even the gay musicians.

My father was in total rejection to the idea of myself being a musician for the church, simply because of the high volume of homosexual activity that was already in the churches at the helm of the music departments.

The Baptist church that we had attended, were very adamant about hiring homosexuals to the office of minister of music. It seemed that the people of the ministry were never really satisfied with the music department if there were no gays participating or in control of the music department. My father was Vice-Chairperson to the Chairman of deacons, and a trustee to the ministry. He was always very strongly opposed to the homosexuals in the music department! But, his voice was only one among only a few. AINT THAT A KICK IN THE HEAD!

I assured my father; that God; *and the devil:* with absolutely no grief on my part; that we all knew that there would be none of that foolishness in my life because, God made me all man and I totally agree! I have absolutely no problem being the man that God made me! God made the woman for the man, and definitely, He made the man for the woman; only!

We really need to stop this artificially fake; conveniently posing of the question; *"what would Jesus do;"* whenever it come to hiring homosexuals and lesbians to the key positions in the ministry, before ever even requiring them to be changed from their alternative ways. Rather, we need to be gravely concerned with; "WHAT DOES JESUS THINK ABOUT WHAT WE'VE

DONE?" You might want to refer to I Samuel chapters 1-5, to see how God responded to the High-Priest; Eli, for allowing his sons to desecrate the temple of God.

Whatever the spirit that is in the singer; or the musician; the shepherd; or any leader in the ministry; whatever it is that they present during the worship service, the very same spirit that embodies them filters through their music, song, service, sermon etc., And you don't have to be prophetic to sense the spirit that is emanating from an individual.

Certain sexual spirits, relative to those of perversion and the alternative lifestyles of homosexuality and lesbianism, being that they are unatural and ungodly; are very dangerous to the spiritual atmosphere of the sanctuary where the worshipers are gathered together to enter into the presence of the Lord. In worship, we get deeply intimate with the Lord. I mean that true worshippers; go all the way into the presence of God with no reservations or fear, while allowing the spirit of the Lord to have total access into our spirits as well. It's a love affair; we actually get deeply intimate with the Father! WRAP YOUR MIND AROUND THAT!

As we come before the Lord to worship, our spirits are open before him. Satan, is intrusive to our atmosphere of worship; he seeks to distract and to hinder us from worshipping in the first place, because he already knows the power of intimacy with our God. The key word of which must be carefully considered, is the word *open*; loose unrestrained demonic spirits in the atmosphere of the church, are the fuel of the inner wars of the church.

Whenever the wrong people, who are playing church to begin with, are allowed to begin spewing out spirits that are not of God during worship; those spirits are seeking a place of entrance into the lives of others present. This is the reason that most people around the churches are so incapable of entering into true worship of the Lord, in the sanctuary of the church. They are truly hindered, and distracted as a result of those people who are playing church!

Should the enemy cause an individual to become distracted for even a few moments, and catch them looking away from the presence of God during worship, if for certain they are more vulnerable than others and not yet as strong in the spirit of the Lord, their spirits can be intrusively suppressed.

Some people emerged from certain services, where they might have felt that the movement of God rested upon the service, but, when they left that particular church service they noticed that they had begun to think ungodly thoughts, and sometimes to even have sinful desires that they had never experienced before?

A spirit of some sort seemed to have folllowed them away from that service? This is because the musicians, the singers or even the individual ministering on the floor; someone among them, were of the wrong spirit and no one took authority to bind any spirit that was not like God in the atmosphere.

Others began to have very demonically influenced dreams of devient errotic behavior, where things were chasing them through very dark places; and it appeared that they would never escape, all because of the wrong persons being up front, were out of control spiritually and out of place in the ministry.

Many pastors down through the ages before I was thought of, and since I came to know Christ and what it means to be in the church following pastors, and as a pastor myself; we have spent multiples, upon multiples of hours pouring ourselves into people, who eventually turned from our leadership without an explanation, and have very easily gone to other churches and pastors as if to suggest that the time and patience that had been invested into them, was of no importance at all. I believe that the pastors need to begin sending people back to the pastors where they left, to mend the fences. Pastors use to require a letter of transformation from the previous pastors, before allowing the people to adjoin themselves to their ministry.

There is no time for shepherds to compete for the attention of people, feeling as if they are more qualified or even more special than other pastors. Whatever people will do to one shepherd, they will do to another should the opportunity arrive for them to do so. You are only a good shepherd in the eyes of the people, for as long as they think that you are!

The members of the clergy, who have been investigated through the media, suspected of committing some sort of a wrong act of crime, are the very same individuals who were also respected as being among the most well beloved local pastors, simply because they finagled their way into the hearts of the people, although they were as sinfully wicked and dishonest, as the average street thug.

Sometimes drug dealers, hustlers and pimps, are better regarded as more genuine in terms of their character, than the preacher!

Certain people are able to bend the ears of the people of the church, influencing them to do wrong and to commit crimes and to sin against the church and the teachings of the bible. These persons aren't the ones that are really concerned as to where your behavior is going to land you after the fact!

There are some people, who really won't mind coming to get another individual out of the jail. But, usually, it's the preachers that are interested in keeping you from ever going to jail in the first place. The wayward sheep of the pastures, are the same people who walk around within the church disregarding the shepherd as being anyone special, allowing them to be attacked by those on the outside of the ministry. AINT THAT A KICK IN THE HEAD!

Faulty Legs Make Unstable Ministries!

*T*he ministry itself, as a whole, must be watchful of the persons that are elected and erected to aid the shepherd, for the simple fact that the stability of the ministry is often riding on the legs, on which the pastor is supposed to stand. That is unless you have been taught to believe that the pastor is but a servant on a string, who really don't have much to do with the stability of the ministry?

Many ministries are fallen simply because the legs are either broken or they are other-wise pulled out from underneath the place of support for the heads. We don't stand on broken, fractured, sprained or otherwise hurting legs, because the power of support is gone. If, when we find a way to stand, it is for certain that we are not yet able to move about on these legs.

The media, certain friends and family members can remove a very well beloved pastor, right from the heart of the people in the church where they are the leaders. Then all of a sudden you are nothing more than a rejected blurr. AINT THAT A KICK IN THE HEAD!

I know some people who have had nerve damage in their legs, which causes their legs to give out, lose strength and go out from underneath them with no prior warning. In such a case, the only direction that the head of that body is able to go is downward towards the ground, and the rest of the body following the way downward in the fall.

The church is dependent upon the support team in the ministry for much more than the teams member might have imagined. Mostly being ignorantly uninformed of this fact, they should never set themselves in agreement with an agenda, which purposes to starve the pastor of the support that is normally awarded to them for their services.

What the people may not have realized, was the fact that the starvation was actually turned back onto themselves, because God will not allow the man or the woman of God to suffer for too long, and to go under. What you do for God's man and woman, God will do for you! What you do against them, is coming back to you!

As these selected groups of people begin to fall, as a result of mishandling the shepherd, other members of the body also begin to fall, all on the premises of following the reports of those people, who are supposed to be closest to the pastor.

Whenever a pastor fall and suffer public humiliation, as a result of their fall, not many people seem to understand how it is that a pastorial committee seems to adhere to the exact support that they always offered to the pastor. Some are even strongly committed to the point that even after the shepherd has been proven guilty as charged, they still choose to stand firm accepting the ridicule for doing so.

Kick'-em Where it Hurts!

I can't, and of course I will not even try to defend all of the rumors and the accusations that are levied against the shepherds of many churches. We have to admit that we weren't there to witness any of the things that usually capture our affectionate concern for a brother or a sister of the cloth, that may have had accusations hurled against them.

I would never say; that a person who is doing wrong from the platform of the shepherd, should never be exposed, but to whom should we expose them? Before we decide to pull the cover from the people of God, perhaps we had better consider the motives in our own heart, and we need to be mindful of the imminent danger to the body of Christ, at large! Stop and examine the person's surrounding the exposure, to determine whether or not it is really worth it to take the lid off of the can!

God; is a God of mercy and restoration. Other members of the clergy and the media will usually suggest that we kick a foul shepherd while they are down, to ensure they never get up again, and because we have become so humanized in our process of thinking, we learn to ignore the bible, and the leading of the spirit of the Lord, in dealing with matters that would have been best served had it been left up to the biblically connected prayerful individuals of the church.

As true, as it is sad, we have allowed the business of the church to drift like a ship without a sale, so far out into the middle of the corrupt waves of the societal seas of the world, that we have lost any biblical sense of handling the affairs of the church.

The prison system and rehabilitation facilities are very necessary for the people of the society, and our churches who are out of control, but, we are of the church! If the church would refrain from allowing criminals to be in control of the ministry, the church would not have to find itself returning to the courts to have the judicial system to revisit one of it's own, of whom should have been finished with criminal activities.

> My brethren, have not the faith of our Lord Jesus Christ, the Lord of glory, with respect of persons. For if there come unto your assembly a man with a gold ring, in goodly apparel, and there come in also a poor man in vile raiment, and ye have respect to him that weareth the gay clothing, and say unto him, sit thou here in a good place; and say to the poor man, stand thou there, or sit here under my footstool: But ye have despised the poor. Do not rich men oppress you, and draw you before the judgment seats? But if ye have respect to persons, ye commit sin, and are convinced of the law as transgressors.
>
> James 2: 1-4, 6, 9

In my own opinion, white collar crimes are often undetected, as the same with those crooks in the church; because criminals in a suit are not easily spotted. Our society believes that the better a person dress themselves on a daily basis, gives the indication that an individual's patterns of behavior are acceptable to the society as well.

Many of the churches nowadays, are transforming to the less-dress; or to the dressed down church attire, as a result of creating an atmosphere that make's it much more easily to see people for who they really are. However, dressing down does not completely solve the problem either, as the real problem is not a clothes problem, it's a sin problem!

As long as the church is willing to look on the outer appearance to determine whether or not a person is worthy of conducting church affairs, there is going to be consistent indescressions.

God never intended that the church would be in the *read-*

only status; as it relates to being selective of the persons to be followed as a shepherd, and the persons to be allowed to forefront the business matters of the church and the kingdom of God.

"Read-Only" allows us only to look only at whatever it is that we have focused our sights upon. In this particular mode, all of the usability and the benefits are totally blocked! As it relates to software on a computer, should a problem arise with the software itself, being in the read-only mode status, the problems cannot even be eletronically addressed, nor explored for the purpose of citing the initial cause of the error.

Nowadays; the church is only reading the bible and looking at people if they look church-worthy, to be accepted by the people in the congregation, without any inner-personal evaluation, or background checks. Too often the church is left asking the question within the counsel of the board members chamber; "What Went Wrong!" and "What Would Jesus Do!"

It's time to tap into the church's spiritual properties through prayer to change the *read-only* status so that the shake up in the ministries can become settled among the people of the church, starting with the shepherd.

The time has come, long since before now, for decisions to be made, relative to the importance of moving the hand of God through faith to please the Lord, or whether we are going to remain stuck in the playful atmospheric mindsets of moving the line at the Ferris wheel; for the enjoyment of the people?

As real as God is; and all of the things of God that are real; it is amazing to me, how people seem to ignore the seriousness that is associated to the realness of God, never to even flinch at the sight of losing the potential to win the battle over sin, to which the church is vigorously engaged to fight.

I, have been told too often, by other Senior Ministers, many of them pastors to be exact, that I needed to relax and just take it easy, because "Rome wasn't built in a day!" It has often been stated to me, that I was taking the ministry and preaching the gospel way too seriously, and even advised that my ministry would last a lot longer if I would calm down? Jesus *AINT* Calm!

My concern in the first place is not Rome! The things that we need to put our shoulders to, are so serious, that if we don't get about the Lord's business, by the time we'd make-up our minds to get busy handling the matters that are challenging the existing freedom of the church, as we know of the church today, the local church may not be left standing free for much longer?

Leaders, that are not serious about the house of God, or the parishioners that attend and financially support the ministry, will also breed other upcoming leaders that won't be serious about caring whenever their opportunity has come to forefront the ministry, either. They won't care enough about the souls of the people to correct them whenever they are in the wrong, and they will most-likely neglect the seriousness of preaching the uncompromised truth of the word of God.

It's not always the shepherd that should have the covers pulled, there are some people that are absolutely no good for the business of the inner workings of the church. They're still worldly and very much involved with corrupt, illegal business dealings.

Many preach, that people should not be kept from the participatory operations in the church, because they need to start somewhere? This particular philosophy, gives people the wrong indications about pursuing the things of God, causing them to feel that they are fine just as they are, needing absolutely, no changes.

Others who have been required to meet certain criteria before being permitted to participate in church affairs, are usually infuriated over the fact that these persons are allowed to go free, without adhering to the mandated requirements of the ministry. The legs kick up against an agenda that allows for differences to be made for some that are respected as special, or otherwise exempt individuals.

They should kick!

Under these circumstances?

For We Wrestle Not......Eph. 6:12

Ten

WRESTLING. *Catch as Catch Can Style.*

Undressed & Unprotected

Put on the whole armour of God, that ye may be able to stand against the wiles of the devil. For we wrestle not against flesh and blood, but against principalities, against powers, against the rulers of the darkness of this world, against spiritual wickedness in high places. Wherefore take unto you the whole armour of God, that ye may be able to withstand in the evil day, and having done all, to stand. Stand therefore, having your loins girt about with truth and having on the breastplate of righteousness; And your feet shod with the preparation of the gospel of peace; Above all; taking the shield of faith, wherewith ye shall be able to quench all the fiery darts of the wicked. And take the helmet of salvation, and the sword of the spirit, which is the word of God: Praying always with all prayer and supplication in the spirit, and watching thereunto with all perseverance and supplication for all saints;

Galatians 6: 11-18

Dressed For Less!

While of these latter times, teachings that address the ehtical codes of appropiate attire in the body if Christ is definitely necessary, I am not about to deal with that subject from a carnal perspective, but rather from the spiritual aspect of dress. I have seen people of the church often dress more revealing than what is actually desired for the church, but, they projected more self discipline in their personal demeanor, than some whose clothing were always dragging the ground and buttoned to the neck!

So, I do believe that the dress codes should be taught as part of the healthier spiritual diet, whenever the sheep are fed. An attempt to dive into the subject of the dress codes, from such an outwardly influencing perspective, would only breed an even greater sense of fiery indignation in the spirits of the leaders who are in the stead of shepherding the flock of God.

They actually deserve the courtesy of being allowed to teach their congregations, as they are led of the Lord. They may be reserving lessons on dress codes for a later time which has its purpose in that particular ministry?

However I will deal with a form of dress that is relative to every church and for every ministry no matter where they are located.

Many so called born again believers are walking around naked on a daily basis, as a result of a lack of teaching or simply because they choose to ignore certain teachings that don't appeal to their interest. Everywhere you turn nowadays, people are beginning more and more to reject the word of God as a mandate for daily living. I don't believe that there is as much pride, relative to the moral standards of living as there used to be, just a short while ago.

Many members of the church, are extremely fearful of no longer fitting into their own secular realities of living away from the four walls of the sanctuary of the church, should they begin to dress in the clothes of righteousness. The much less spiritual dress, is often excused for the need to be more seeker sensitive in the local churches, citing the fact that the new comers to the church might feel left out and unaccepted being that their spiritual dress is yet unaccomplished.

The church has taken on the position of passionately reaching out to take more people into the sheepfold of the church at all cost, but they are often making the mistake of lowering the landmarked standards in the word of God. It's actually not even Christ that is really being presented in totality, to those who are indeed lost and in need of the savior.

It almost seems as if some of the churches have gone on strike against the bible, in that there is too much secular influence allowed in the midst of the sheep, that is not even in agreement with the bible itself. Too much interpretation; and not enough revelation; have infiltrated the teaching circles of the churches. Whereas, the teachers are better educated and more reading comprehensive and vocabulary literate.

Whenever we get to the place of comprehending what we have read in the bible, and begin taking the interpretive skills of our minds to be the defining factor for receiving the word of God, our own intelligence will blind us to the reality that we have only approached the doorway to the entrance of receiving the true revelation to what God is actually saying to His church.

Trust in the Lord with all thine heart; and lean not to thine own understanding. In all thy ways acknowledge him, and he shall direct thy paths.

Proverbs 3: 5-6

Wouldn't you conduct yourselves differently, if you understood that while interpreting the bible with your own mind on a consistent basis, that you are undressing your self spiritually, each time you place your mind and your own ways of thinking in front of the spirit of God speaking, to reveal the only living way to please the Lord, through the living word of the bible?

For every season of time, we have to change clothes to prevent ourselves from being ill, as a result of wearing clothing that do not match the present seasonal temperatures of the weather, leaving our bodies unprotected against the unfavorable elements.

Some people dress wrong in the natural on purpose, simply because the clothes that are designed for the seasonal weather change, may not be as eye appealing to the onlookers.

The lack of proper dress on a consistent basis, bespeaks of the lack of faith in God, and it signifies that an individual's disrespect for the seasons of their life to which they are presently living. Most people don't associate the season changes of their lives with the will of God for their lives.

Disassociated change; is the real breeding ground for the pains of separation, on every platform of our lives. When we seek the Lord through the word of God, we soon discover that there is nothing taking place in our lives, that hasn't been ordained.

Let's Go Shopping For Clothes; In the Bible!

*T*here is far too many people in the church that are only window shopping in the word of God, who never intend to purchase or to take anything from the SCRIPTORAL SHELVES in the bible. Most people, are spoiled anyway when it comes to shopping in the first place, as a result of the many different options, relative to the clothing styles of hundreds of different clothing designers.

I once heard Morris Cerrulo say that all truth is parallel. The way we practice living in the natural will often become applicable to our spiritual lives.

The shopping behavior of those who frequent shopping malls, and major department stores, is so out of control and often taken out of context, that it would be quite difficult for them to understand that there is only one maker and creator of the spiritual clothing that we are to partake of without choosing; but accepting all of the required coverings in the bible.

Many feel that they are capable of living holy without the Holy Ghost living through them, on the inside of them. People have convinced themselves, that the teachings and the requirements of the church from the past are now obsolete and unnecessary, for these present times. They have taken on more loosely fitting clothing in the natural that protects them from revealing the shapes of their bodies.

Guess what? Loose Fitting Spiritual Clothing; also prevents anyone from seeing your spiritual figure and shape. It's no wonder that people don't know who you are? We live in a cross dressing society that have developed cross-gender and Unisex styles, that may be styled to mask true genders, for the purpose of alternative styles of living.

People are trying to create uni-spirituality, and one world churches; whereas it is to be understood that everybody is the very same, and that there are no such things, as spiritual levels. They want you to believe that everybody has the very same spirituality, as long as their minds can comprehend the concept of teaching and achieve it.

People are no longer interested in reaching up higher to achieve spiritual oneness with God. They are deceived into believing that they can reach inside of themselves to find God and total spirituality.

WHAT A TOTAL DECEPTION!!!!!!!!!!!!!!!!!!!!!!!

Whenever this teaching is compared to the word of God, it is soon discovered that people who aspire to such teachings are spiritually undressed and unprotected. Isn't that ashamed!

There is absolutely positively no way to get around looking into the bible, to acquire the necessary spiritual clothing for the purpose of truly covering the soul. Earlier, I mentioned the fact that there is only one clothing designer for the spiritual clothes that we are mandated to wear, so be advised that there is only one selection to make. EVERYTHING!!!

There will be no picking and choosing for purchasing a garment to wear, and afterwards taking it back to the store. Or, in this instance, back to God's store house. One style fits all, tailor made for every individual, and the garments are made of pure authentic eternal materials that are warranted to last forever.

And one of the elders answered, saying unto me, what are these which are arrayed in white robes? And whence

226

came they? And I said unto him, sir, thou knowest.
And he said to me, These are they which came out of
great tribulation, and have washed their robes, and made
them white in the blood of the lamb. Therefore are they
before throne of God, and serve him day and night in
his temple: And he that sitteth on the throne shall
dwell among them. They shall hunger no more,
neither thirst any more; neither shall the sun
light on them, nor any heat. For the lamb which
is in the midst of the throne shall feed them, and
shall lead them to living fountains of waters:
and God shall wipe all tears from their eyes.

Revelation 7: 13-17

We must always be mindful of the fact that it is our purpose and our place to come before the Lord to worship Him. It is therefore imperative that we are prepared to appear before Him desiring His approval and His acknowledgement of us as His own children and the sheep of His pastures.

Serve the Lord with gladness: come before his
presence with singing. Know ye that the Lord he
is God: it is he that hath made us, and not we
ourselves; we are his people and the sheep of his
pasture.

Psalms 100: 2-3

I purpose to come before the Lord and to stay, not ever being cast away from His presence, because I might have showed up improperly dressed! Don't expect for God to treat you like many of the babysitters, who call themselves shepherds and pastors?

They allow you to continue showing up any way that you choose naturally and spiritually, intentionally giving you as much time as you think you need to understand biblical requirements, while you slow around, excusing your ownself from making the necessary preparations to meet the Lord, on a consistent basis.

Now that you have reached this portion in this chapter, you might need to consider the fact that you are probably at a crucial point of your spiritual growth. You've had enough time to get dressed but your focus has been on lesser things. You are determined to make sure that everyone understands that you are only human? You may not have been told as of yet, but God is not soft hearted, and neither has He been put into an awkward position, because you're only human.

Should you end up being cast away from the presence of the Lord, God will not be depressed over His judgment of you, because He is God and He already know the excuses that you have made always concerning being prepared to meet Him. Jesus wept over the people in St. John 11: 35; but get this and don't ever forget it, *God Won't Cry Anymore!*

Jesus; is the only human side of God; that there will ever be. God is A SPIRIT; and we that worship Him must do so in the spirit of the Lord and in the truth of the word of God. The truth is that you need to put on some clothes and get dressed properly before the Lord.

> *Create in me a clean heart, O God; and renew a right spirit within me. Cast me not away from thy presence; and take not thy holy spirit from me.*
>
> Psalms 51: 10-11

Has anyone ever showed up at your home to pick you up for a ride to school, to work, or to church, or to go anywhere else, and because you were not fully dressed when they arrived, you got left behind and had to find another way, or rather you missed out completely, and you had to stay home as a result?

News Flash! If you miss God; there is no other way; period! You may be a little twisted and confused relative to the Lord Jesus Christ being the only way, as is the truth in the

Holy Bible; but, that is the truth and you might as well receive it! Christ; is the only way, so go ahead and get dressed and prepare to meet Him!

Then Jesus said unto them again, verily, verily, I say unto you, I am the door of the sheep. All that ever came before me are thieves and robbers: but the sheep did not hear them. I am the door: by me if any man enter in, he shall be saved, and shall go in and out, and find pasture.

St. John 10: 7-9

Jesus saith unto him, I am the way, the truth, and the life: no man cometh unto the Father, but by me.

St. John 14: 6

Too late; always comes at the darnedest times in our lives, it never shows up at a time that would ever be sufficient to proper timing, and it is eternally incapable of showing up early! I've never met anyone that was in love with this misplaced, outdated, period of reality called "TOO LATE."

Being creatures of time, there is absolutely nothing that we can do with the expiration of time, when it has truly made its arrival into our existence. Everything that can be done to counter act what would be disastrous for us, has to be done afore time, and way too soon to be late!

Time; is like the air that fills a giant balloon called life to its capacity, from the start. But, the balloon of life, also has a consistent leak in it, whereas, we are to be assured that sooner or later one day time will run out for every individual on the face of the earth, leaving our life sized balloons deflated, empty and flattened. That's everyone, except for those that will see the rapture!

You must understand that this balloon of life that everyone is given, is only the necessary dressing room for us to prepare for the great coronation, one glorious day with the Lord. I know that you want to be there, so I am going to give you a few clothing racks from the word of God; where you can at least begin dressing.

God; wants us to come and be saved just as we are, but it has never been his intentions for us to remain as we are, after we have come to Him! He will redress you from your head to your toe.

Job 27: 17, 29: 14, Romans 13: 12, 14, Galatians 3: 27, Ephesians 4: 24, Colossians 3: 10, 12, 14

You Still Need The Armour!

The scripture teaches us extensively of the need for the armour of God, for every Christian. God never intended for us to be exposed to the onslaught of the enemy's attack against us. Everything that we need to successfully live godly; in this godless and perverse generation, has already been provided, before we ever arrived to take our rightful places, as the sheep in God's pasture.

Perhaps you're thinking that there is a lot of things to put on in Christianity; well you're right! For many of you, I offer the most sincere apology from my heart to you. I'm apologetic that you were never taught proper spiritual dress, and that dressing up spiritually, is not left to your discression. Although God has given us all the right to choose, choosing whether to obey the word of God or to out-right reject it, was not what God actually had in mind.

It's dangerous to pick over and to sift through the word of God, choosing not to apply certain parts of the scripture to daily living. Real smart people attempt to literally dissect the word of God, citing the diversities of cultures and the generational time lines that divide the living styles of people in the bible; relative to the lifestyles of people of today. But let me encourage you to look just a little closer, and you will see that the cycle of life is gravely parallel, as people are people.

We are in fact living in another day and time, but that does not allow for another definition to what is still sin; for what our cultural standards have determined to redefine, for the present lifestyles of people, who want to change the truth of the word of God, into what is clearly a lie!

I have come into contact with many people in the church, who are determined to take on the true armour of God for all of the right reasons, and for the right purpose. I think that it is actually remarkable to hear the people of God preparing for spiritual warfare.

Many of the same people often bring up the questions; of why it is that God did not provide any armour for the back side of an individual? Some have even become reluctant to put on the armour because they feel that in some way or another, the armour is severely incomplete, because, in while they were reading the word of God, there was no instructions mentioned for a back piece or a plate of some sort to be placed on the back.

You must understand that whenever you are properly dressed in the spiritual clothes of the bible to begin with, it's not possible for there to be any areas of involuntary exposure concerning you. Therefore the armour should be considered to be a bonus, or the final layer. While it is true that we are in a spiritual battle everyday of our lives, the truth is that every second and everyday of our lives is not spent fighting.

One of the greater reason for the high volume of sheep

231

attacks, is that everyone is only pre-occupied with the armour, with which in itself enables the mindset for battle. Some Saints never stop swinging even though the battle that they were engaged in has already been completed. When you can't see that your enemy has been downed already, you instincts tell you to just keep on swinging no matter who it is that you are swinging at? Like A Gang Fight!

Christian warfare was never intended for the people of the churches of God, to be battling against each other. It doesn't please God for the church to be so divided as a result not properly discerning the enemy.

I see you with your armour on, but who is it that is really on the inside of the armour? Are you properly clothed underneath the armour? Unless you are properly clothed and prepared before you ever acquire the armour of God, your armour may become more of a danger to work against you, in that you won't practice the proper behavior, while brandishing your bright shining armour.

The armour is relative to a hard shell and a covering. You can be hard shelled on the outside, but naked underneath. It is just like people to care more for the outside, than they do care for the inside, simply because others can't see on the inside.

The armour of God, is often spoken in retrospect to the likeness in comparison to a Halloween costume, or a uniform that is worn in a sporting event. A football player who is fully uniformed on the outside may not in fact be in total support of the team? An individual may know how to put on the uniform, but in reality they do not even know the rules of the game, or the execution of the team plays.

Looking good, does not win the game or even score points. Even though we need the armour, and in many instances in the natural we need the uniforms and the wardrobes, we need also to understand that there is absolutely no performance in the armour or the uniforms. People want to look good, they don't want to be doers of the word of God.

The true fact is that most people have not even put on the armour of God, they have put on a stiff form of religion, that may often be as hard as the metal of the armour, but religion in itself is not the armour of God. Most forms of religion; are not even pure, they are only repetitious practices in a cycle of outward expressions that are purposefully made visible for others to see.

Don't you sense the feeling of many people of the local churches who are religious, but have never truly been saved and washed in the blood of Jesus, being unprotected, as a result of this reading material?

Perhaps you think that too late is a bit too slow to catch up to you? Well, I would not wait around in the vicinity of procrastination waiting for another tomorrow or another time to prepare, because time is also very slippery and unrevealing.

Time can also be un-telling, in that there will be no communication to actually let you know just what might be riding on the back of time, as it makes its approach to your circle of living. If you share the same sentiments that I do, you know how it feels for a visitor to show up to your residence unexpected at a time when you are not even dressed.

At times when you were almost naked, casually lying around the house prepared to go nowhere, you may have even been resting, and nevertheless, someone showed up at the door unexpectedly.

So it is with time, it most likely will bring uninvited guest to visit in the time of unexpectancy. Everything that will come your way in this life will not always be trying to get in, there are some things that will truly come your way for the purpose of getting you out! Like striking you out at the home plate, while you were up to bat! Or, to the likes of knocking you out in the middle of the boxing ring, in a fighting match!

But most severely, there are certain things that are sent from the devil that are designed to get you to step out of the will of God; that somehow looked like they were sent to you from the Lord.

The scouts always had a motto that we were required to remember for the rest of our lives, which says; *"Be Prepared!"*

Get dressed now and don't ever get caught unprepared. In God; your Preparation is your Protection!

How soon do you think that too late will be for you, if you are not properly prepared and truly saved? Only the enemy will deceive you, causing you to believe that too late came really too soon for you to make the necessary preparations for you to meet the Lord. People need to put their feelings and their emotions out of the way, and get busy obeying the instruction of the word of God.

Too Late, doesn't discriminate! It will show up at your address at every opportunity, if you are determined to lay around basking in the bed of laziness, uninterested in the fact that the meter of time is ever running, allowing time to swiftly run out!

They're Not Ready!

As the shepherd and pastoral overseer of the SPOKEN WORD CENTER, I have often been confronted with people who wanted to perform certain task in the ministry, that they simply were not even ready to get involved with attempting to do them.

Because they had no knowledge or skill in the areas that they were just bursting to jump right in the middle of, they were incapable of even beginning at start for an opportunity to try!

All that they had to work with was an extreme overload in the department of desire. Many leaders applaud the huge heap of incompetent desire, and go along with these individuals for the sake of not losing someone that is at least willing, though they have suffered many disasters as a result.

Others were in fact ready to do whatever you asked, just as faithful as they could be to any ministry. I would soon discover that these same people were very fragile and could not stand criticism or correction after haven done a job or performed a task voluntarily, but had lacked the skill to get the job done right. Their projected attitude was that the job had indeed been performed, and because they did it voluntarily, nothing should have been said if it was not performed with excellence.

The situation was like an individual cleaning a large plate glass window pane, but leaving a large visible hand print right in the middle of the glass, or sweeping the floor cleaning everything that is in the middle of the floor, while leaving the corners cluttered with trash. Some even desired to clean the restrooms while doing everything possible to avoid cleaning the toilets!

I am not one to receive a half done job simply because someone else volunteered to do it, but did not do the job right. Not being pleased with the work, accepting the effort just because I was not the person doing the job, and saying nothing at all to enhance or to teach the person to do the job right, is not right.

There are so many people who have chosen to sit down on the ministry of the church, simply for the fact that they don't like to take instructions from any one. People feel that the church is the one place where they ought to be able to do what they want to do, in the manner of which they choose to do it!

People often feel that the leadership is wrong to voice opinions of concern, for the manner of which certain task are performed. They are missing the point and the fact that they need to be trained in the proper manner, in an effort that they might learn to please the Lord in the proper manner, according to the word of God.

The church is the only place where people come to work, refusing training and supervision. They feel that they ought to be given opportunities to prove themselves, no matter of the outcome or the greater damage that may be caused, as a result of their lack of experience and knowledge.

People who desire to busy themselves around the church, that are truly unknowledgeable, but yet teachable; will always be the more productive persons in the ministry. We need teachable people that are willing to follow instructions, which are the only persons that are going to ever be called the "Sheep of His Pastures."

There was a television show which aired back in the sixties and the seventies called the "Untouchables." Elliot Ness, was the boss of well trained police detectives, whose mission was to find and to arrest Al Capone, and the members of Chicago Mafia; and to bring down all mob ties. They went after the enemy with deadly intentions, but also with the skills to get the job done.

On the other hand, too often we are plagued with a group of unqualified zealots; of which I would like to refer to them as the "Un-Teach-ables." These churchmen are foreign to the idealism of the destruction they are capable of, and subject to cause.

Brethren, my heart's desire and prayer to God for Israel is, that they might be saved. For I bear them record that they have zeal of God, but not according to knowledge. For they being ignorant of God's righteousness, and going about to establish their own righteousness, have not submitted themselves unto the righteousness of God.
Romans 10: 1-3

And beside this, giving all diligence, add to your faith virtue; and to virtue knowledge; And to knowledge temperance; and to temperance patience; and to patience godliness; And to godliness brotherly kindness; and to brotherly kindness charity.
II Peter 1: 5-7

Learning and instruction; for those persons who desire to be in the forefront of the ministry, should be desired more than their necessary food and breath. It is not okay to move about the ministry of the church clue-less; and dead from the neck up, and expect to accomplish your given task.

People, are well informed at the point of being hired to do a job and continually aware of the prevention of job promotions and sometimes demotions and pay cuts, and of course ultimately being terminated as a result of being illiterate concerning the task that they have been assigned to perform. It is also understood that there is a certain amount of job safety and security involved in the necessary training, and the understanding to acquire the skill for the job position.

This new generation of people in the church, feel that they are definitely more spiritually informed and biblically astute than the leaders of churches, that have been ministering in the word of God for many years, and for some they have been ministering adequately, for several decades now.

Hurry up, And Get Dressed!

For We Wrestle Not......Eph. 6:12

Eleven

WRESTLING. Catch as Catch Can Style.

For The Cau$e of CASH *Christ*

Yea, they are greedy dogs which can never have enough, and they are shepherds that can never understand: they all look to their own way, everyone for his own gain, from his quarter. Come ye, say they, I will fetch wine, and we will fill ourselves with strong drink, and tomorrow shall be as this day, and much more abundant.

Isaiah 56: 11-12

Then one of the twelve called Judas Iscariot, went unto the chief preist, and said unto them, what will ye give me, and I will deliver him unto you? And they covenanted with him for thirty pieces of silver. And from that time he sought opportunity to betray him.

St. Matthew 26: 14-16

A Bishop then must be blameless, the husband of one wife, vigilant, sober, of good behavior, given to hospitality, apt to teach; not given to wine, no striker, not greedy of filthy lucre; but patient, not a brawler, not covetous; likewise must the deacons be grave, not doubletongued, not given to much wine, not greedy of filthy lucre;

I Timothy 3: 2-3, 8

Perverse disputings of men of corrupt minds, and destitute of the truth, supposing that gain is godliness: from such withdraw thyself. But godliness with contentment is great gain. But they that will be rich fall into temptation and a snare, and into many foolish and hurtful lusts, which drown men in destruction and perdition. For the love of money is the root of all evil: which while some coveted after, they have erred from the faith, and pierced themselves through with many sorrows. But thou, O man of God, flee these things; and follow after righteousness, godliness, faith, love, patience, meekness. Fight the good fight of faith, lay hold on eternal life, whereunto thou art also called, and hast professed a good profession before many witnesses.

I Timothy 6: 5-6, 9-12

Betrayal From the Inside!

*M*ost everyone can identify with Judas; the betrayer of our Lord Jesus Christ; being the very self-serving, back-stabbing sneak that he was. For centuries now, we have always reflected on the misbehavior of one of the Lord's own chosen disciples.

In Sunday school, the thought of disgust and mental anguish has been brought into focus, upon the inquisition of how could it be, that any man could bring themself to betray the savior of the world? How could he do that? It is often suggested, that he should have been more mindful of the fact that he was dealing with Jesus; the only begotten son of God.

I agree, that Judas was indeed a nasty mess in the church of the Lord. He, in my opinion, should have been dubbed; "The SideWinder!" There was nothing at all straight and forward about the dealings of Judas Iscariot. While he may have indeed stepped up to the position of being the treasurer for the church, it was only obvious, that he had another sideline ulterior motive working.

Judas; must have had some kind of pride, in that he was sure that he could do what no one else could possibly do, which was to deliver the Lord Jesus; to the Romans. Judas, was sure willing to betray the Lord!

He was ice water smooth, and calculative! He moved among the brethren with precision, in that he never gave himself away, to any of them. He moved like a snake of the wild in the wilderness, in thrust for the kill of a prey.

Perhaps the movement of Judas was as such, whenever he would step forward to volunteer to do certain things among the brethren. Whenever it came to serving the master, perhaps he was Judas-on-the-spot? The Lord already knew who Judas was, and He knew his motives and his purpose.

The Lord never removed Judas from the company of the fellowship of the disciples, for the sake of teaching the other brethren, what it was that they really should have been in observation of? Jesus watched the others, as they missed the fact that there was indeed a snake among them, who behaved like they did.

Whenever Jesus taught the twelve, He was teaching Judas also! As the others watched, as Jesus performed miracles, Judas was also there! Whenever Jesus walked on the water, Judas was in the ship! When they went to the other side of the sea to the coast of the Gadarenes, Judas was with them, when the demoniac ran forward to worship Jesus!

Judas, witnessed as Jesus set this big confused, demon possessed man free from demons, and from the chains that had him bound. Judas, witnessed the mental restoration of this once mentally-deranged man.

As a result, Judas was sure that this was the lord Jesus

Christ, that he was betraying. He would not deliver the wrong man to these angry Roman officials. Judas was on the inside, he knew everything that Jesus was, and he knew everything that the Romans were looking for in this Jesus, of whom they were seeking to arrest and to destroy.

Judas had managed to get close enough to the Lord, to know Him on a personal basis. It wouldn't be difficult to say to the Roman officials; "I KNOW WHO YOU'RE TALKING ABOUT. I KNOW HIM VERY WELL!" Judas, had patiently observed Jesus over time to the point that he even knew what type of food He enjoyed; he even had an idea of His sleeping patterns.

The individuals who get to know you best, are the most dangerous to your spiritual welfare. They are the ones who can and who will, deliver you to your detractors. Our captors of today, may have very different purposes and means for destroying us, but know this, the enemy in them is still trying to crucify Jesus!

The message got back to the captains of the enemies, that even though they had succeeded in crucifying Christ; on the cross of Calvary, they literally failed! Somehow or another, this Jesus, whom they cricified, mysteriously, HE GOT UP OUT OF THE GRAVE, and there have been reports of Him being seen walking around. HE'S ALIVE FOREVER MORE!

In the natural, whenever an individual pass on from living to death, there is usually another successor to step up to take the helm of the leadership. But, after only Three Days; Jesus is up from the grave giving orders again and running His church, changing the minds and the lives of the people of the world. People were being influenced to follow Jesus now, even more so, than they had before He was crucified.

Perhaps the Roman; and Jewish; officials had begun to

feel as if they paid Judas for nothing!

Just as you are beginning to comfortably comprehend my dialogue, relative to Judas' betrayal of Jesus, how that He sold Him out for money; cash; thirty pieces of silver; I have to inform you to buckle up for the real ride that we are about to take.

The Church On A Roller Coaster!

What Judas did to the Lord Jesus Christ, had an adverse affect on the other remaining eleven apostles. They were spinning with anger and perhaps even with a sence of confused rage? Maybe if Judas hadn't committed suicide, one of the others might have killed him anyway?/!

The devil had entered the church of Jesus Christ through Judas, one of the leaders, and they hadn't been filled with the Holy Ghost as of yet. People do different things that they are not otherwise responsible for whenever they are in grief. The disciples were indeed grieving over the death of their Lord.

At this point and time, I believe that it was the beginning of the unstable roller coaster like ride for the church? Through history, people would hear and read of the ingenious criminal behavior of one of the leaders of the church, and would be fascinated or even enticed to behave themselves, just like Judas!

Ever since the time of Judas, someone down the line of the leadership establishment of the church, has developed the same selfserving tendency within themselves, to launch after the person at the top of the ministry. The shepherd; is always a target of certain persons in the ministry, to the point that it is often better for the pastor to keep few people around their inner circle.

This behavior has placed the church on an even more devastating roller coaster ride. Whenever there is fighting among the leadership of the church, the societal reflection of the church is on even more shaky, ground. Many of the churches in the community are often up and down, year in and year out.

People come into the local churches and become members, and they leave the same churches by the droves, which always places a sence of concern in the minds of the people who should not even be concerned, being that they are not even interested in Christ. People want to know what's wrong with the church; what is the problem that they can't seem to stabilize in the community?

Many leaders have been seriously injured spiritually, and painfully scarred emotionally, as a result of being shafted by someone they trusted to be a supporter of their ministry. Sometimes it has happened more than once or twice!

Whenever a leader gets scarred, there has got to be someone to minister to the hurts and the pains of that leader, to ensure that they will get better and not bitter. However, most people are very quick to tell us, to get up and go ahead and get over it, which is indeed what we need to do.

But! Getting over it is not always that easy to do, knowing that the persons that caused the heartache and the pains that a leader may be going through, might have been as close to the leader, as Judas was to Jesus?

People don't always know that the pastor is dealing with the betrayal of a minister or a leader, that they, themselves had publicly endorsed and received as an anointed individual of the Lord. They had let their guard down in an effort to allow this person, or those persons to assist in the affairs of the ministry.

Often, allowing scandalous individuals to get too close to

the money, and the financial business records of the church, has been the mistake. It is not always easily detected early on, that an individual is in the ministry of your church only for the money, until they discover how much the pastor is getting for a salary, or if, whenever they may discover that the ministry is struggling financially, whereas there can be absolutely no benefit for them, financially. They discover that they could never be on a salary.

Viscious; And Vivacious!

*M*any leaders of the churches, who have the power of influence of the people, also have the temperament of rattle snakes and wild boars when it relates to the financial gain that is associated with their careers, as the pastor of the church.

Pastors, have locked horns with each other like large Wild Bucks and Rams at mating season, over an opportunity to get paid, and for contigious prestige. They support one another, as long as they are on equal grounds relative to the money. As soon as one finds out that the other is getting more money than they are getting, they change like bad weather.

Many of the leaders, appear to be very sincere and focused, until it comes down to the money. They know how to conduct themselves in the presence of other prestigious figures of the community, and carry themselves like respectable leaders in the society.

When seen out dining or having lunch, they project a very religious ora, and of course sometimes they may even seem to project a lifestyle of holiness. They know just how to entreat other individuals, to cause that person to feel good, if not even better about themselves, as a result of haven spoken with one of the very vivacious leaders of their city or church community. To talk with them, you might leave their presence feeling as if they are truly respectful of yourself, and others as well.

What draws the line in the sand, is how dishonest many of these leaders are as it relates to doing financial business? They will smile big like a crocodile, and glare right into your face with eyes wide open like an owl, and lie to you about financial matters, as if their life depended on it!

They make business deals concerning the ministry, sometimes signing on the dotted line, and still have the nerve to renege on the deal. It doesn't seem to matter if you cite their dishonesty as being ungodly, they are usually undeterred with your findings!

I have witnessed pastors who have squandered business dealings, take the pulpit on Sunday morning, and air their versions of how it all went down to draw the people in to pity them, and for support. They are masters at getting ahead of the report of their own ungodly behavior; even as it relates to bad business deals.

Whenever things change, most people want to know what happened. They want to know why things are not as they were purported to have been. The people know that they had indeed put the money into the ministry for a particular project, but what they don't usually understand, is why things are not manifesting as they should have!

In past times, many of the leaders would emerge wearing new suits, and driving brand new cars, or even moving into big brand new houses? What's more, is they never hardly gave any credible accounts for the money that was given for the project in the ministry.

St. Matthew 6: 24

For The Love Of Money!

*M*ammon- is an English word; that is not often used in
the daily varnacular among us, but we who are of the body of
Christ, and are bible readers, we know the significant meaning
in it's definition.

Mammon- derives from the word - *mamonas* – a common
aramaic word for riches; akin to a hebrew word signifying to
be firm; steadfast. *"that which is to be trusted"*;*(or to be relied
upon)* Gensenius; regards it as deriving from a Hebrew word
signifying *"treasure."*

For the love of mony is the root of all evil: which while
some coveted after, they have erred from the faith, and
pierced themselves through with many sorrows. But
thou, O man of God, flee these things; and follow after
righteousness, godliness, faith, love, patience, meekness.
Charge them that are rich in this world, that they be
not highminded, nor trust in uncertain riches, but in
the living God, who giveth us richly all things to enjoy;
That they do good, that they be rich in good works, ready
to distribute, willing to communicate; Laying up in store
for themselves a good foundation against the time to
come, that they may lay hold on eternal life.

I Timothy 6: 10-11, 17-19

The word of the Lord does not lie! So many of the
brethren of the body of Christ are extremely remorseful and
desperately regretful of the fact that they allowed money to

247

rule and reign as Lord of their lives and ministries. Many of them cannot even tell you where they initially got off the track, where they stopped trusting in the Lord to be their only source?

Love not the world, neither the things that are in the world. If any man love the world, the love of the father is not in him. For all that is in the world, the lust of the flesh, the lust of the eyes, and the pride of life, is not of the father, but is of the world. I John 2: 15-16

Far too many people standing on the platforms of leadership, are in love with money! Lots of them love money more that they love their spouses and their families. Money comes before their own parents. Everything in their world has to line up and stand behind their money.

They will do anything, and everything, just to get a hold of the almighty dollar! Many will not even preach a sermon that does not *center* or *land* on the topic of money in one way or another. They seem to have lost their sober minds!

They have selective seating arrangements for the people of the congregation that are known and regarded as rich or even at least wealthy. They have totally disregarded the scripture, and pushed the anointing into a corner, unless it appears to be driving the people towards the offering table.

There are all types of schemes and tricks that are played right in the sanctuary of the churches during what is supposed to be worship. Many people have been belittled simply because they did not respond to what the leader called direction from the Lord, telling them to give a certain large amount of money.

Now we do know that many people of the churches are still in need of being taught to give and to trust God with their substances? Most people still feel as if all the church needs is a dollar; while everybody else in their world needs hundreds and thousands of dollars. So stay with me as I speak to you relative to those leaders who have fallen off the wagon, for a dollar or two, or maybe even millions, down on the ground.

The story that I am about to tell is true! However, it is not true of every minister that is called to the office of the Prophet. Please be strong, and understand that this story is relative to the individual that I traveled with. This is not a story about anyone else!

Back in the 80ˢ I travelled with an evangelist who went by the title of a Prophet! Believe me; he was more, FOR THE PROFIT! He phinagled many people out of their money in the service with the trickery of his craft. He made promises to the people for a price, for which the people were desperate to buy what he was selling.

As a matter of the fact, in order for him to get me to travel with him on the road, before we left, he called my wife and myself out, and told us to sew a $50 dollar seed. He profit-lied to us as well; he told us before the people in the audience; "THE SPIRIT SAID THAT YOUR WIFE IS ABOUT TO HAVE A BOY!"

My wife was quite pregnant, she was very big! So the people showed excitement over the fact that he had called us out with such confidence, it appeared anyway! They applauded and gave more money themselves, since it appeared that if his musician believes in his prophecy, they thought, then they knew that they could believe him?

After the service ended, he paid me very poorly, but I didn't complain because we were at home preparing to leave in just a few days. The promises started immediately following the service when he profit-lied to my wife and I, about our daughter being a boy? He said; "DOC"; WE WONT COME UP SHORT

ON THE ROAD, I'M GOING TO PAY YOU GOOD, I'M THE PROPHET!"

Well, I came back home after about 8 weeks with less than $250.00 in my pocket to a pregnant wife that would go in to labor and give birth to our only daughter, within two weeks. I had taken off my job for what I had thought should have been no more than a week or two at the very most! I lost money all the way around. He promised me that he would still take care of me for being away from my job and my family. Well 24 years later and counting, I can't even say that it was even a promise that was never honoured. He Lied! In The Name Of Cash!

He told the people during his services, to put a certain dollar amount of money in an envelop with one penny, and a note with three things that they needed from the Lord? He told them that he would take the prayer request and literally sleep on them that night, on a special pillow, and that he would pray over them until they got what they had asked the Lord for.

He took his sweet time raising the offering, which probably took about an hour and a half. The people came forward, some out of curiosity, some of out sheer despair; they were hopeless and needing the help of the Lord fast, and of course some came forward because they are naturally faithful givers and sowers?

Mind you, that as the people came forward to give their money, they would receive a profit-lie; or what he referred to as a prophecy! Many of the people would be so excited that they had received a word, though some of them looked puzzled, as if they were confused relative to the word that had been given to them. Some of those people would stop and ask questions right there in the aisle of the church. A few of those people seemed to show disbelief in what they were being told altogether.

Anyway, in the name of cash, he entertained some, amused others, and the rest of the people, he totally confused them, or he just took their money and passed them on.

We went back to the hotel, with a briefcase filled with envelops, that had been packed with money and prayer request. We hardly settled down in the room, before he asked me to begin taking the money out of envelops. I asked him what I should do with the pennies and the prayer request; his reply was one that I will never forget.

When I asked him what to do with the pennies and the prayer request, his exact words to me were; "just throw that in the corner on the floor, housekeeping will pick it up tomorrow!"

I am very serious about the people of God, so I was rather concerned that the faith of those people in that church had been betrayed? I had been on the road with him for several weeks and I had never noticed any special pillow on his bed. I ask him; "when do you pray for the people like you told them?"

He cursed me out, and told me that it was none of my business what he did! I was rather amazed at his reaction to my questions, especially since we were traveling together and spending the bulk of our time in the churches conducting meetings.

He kept me on the road with him, for a solid 8 weeks, promising to pay me better. Whenever he would take in a large sum of money the night before, somehow he would get a call from his wife, supposedly telling him that they had an urgent need for the money. He would rush out to Western Union, to wire the money home.

Upon returning to the hotel, he would promise me that if

I would just stay with him for the rest of the week, that he would raise an offering for me to send back home to my family. The next night in the revival, after he had already drained the people again, he would tell the people that he needed to raise an offering for his musician. He raised about $85.-95.00 dollars for me.

He would come to me and say; "Im' so sorry, I don't know why the people didn't respond better for your offering? I have another revival next week, and you just watch, I will personally take care of you!"

My wife was back at home in Texas; expecting a baby girl any day now. I desperately needed to make money to support them, and he knew that for sure.

He loved money so much, that I saw him do some things on the road so detestable, that I promised the Lord that if He would get me out of that situation, that I would never be caught in that kind of a mess ever again!

He showed me many times, that he would do anything for money. He never opened the bible to deliver his talk, or to perform his show, he talk from prepared notes in a binder. During the day he would have people come to the hotel and pay him money for a psychosomatic; spiritualistic experience? Perhaps something that he could not have done during the service the night before?

Pay Per-View

$\mathcal{S}$eems like I would have known better than to have gone on just a few years later, to become the Minister of Music for a show church?

There was a prominent church in the community that I would frequently visit for many of the very best musical concerts in the metro-plex area here where I live. At first there were only concerts, and then shortly aterwards they began recording albums. They were an "off the hook" excellent music department.

For a while it seemed that most of their singers were from the throne room of Heaven? There were awesome soloist everywhere you turned. Many members of that choir, were of the most unassuming demeanor in their appearance, but, they knew how to deliver a song.

Whenever I was asked to take the position of minister of music, I initially thought that it was only a joke? I know now that even though I was fascinated and impressed with that particular church, taking on the position of minister of music, was definitely a big mistake for me.

The people seemed to receive me with open arms. To my own surprise, the music department that I thought would be there when I arrived, had just been broken up and demolished. A great portion of the choir was still there, but they were seriously scarred over all that had previously taken place, just prior to my coming there. Of course, it was the brokeness of the music department that brought me there in the first place.

The leaders of that church, were so full of themselves, that they just knew that everybody had to have been familiar and associated with their Sunday Morning performances. Their initial expectation of me from the jump was truly unreal! They felt that I should have known their methods and their worshipful atmosphere, just because of who they were? They were on the map as one of the more thriving ministries in the metroplex, and it didn't seem to matter that I had never attended any of their morning worship services.

There were some good times, and many of the services were powerful until the "Big Daddy Pimp" and pastor of the house would get up and come forth. Whenever he would take the floor, most times, he would either talk or hoop with the organ blaring behind him for about 20-30 minutes, and the rest of the service would be built around an extensive, massive, offering!

He once took an offering for 2 hours & 45 minutes tops, no exaggeration! He would have one line on this side of the church, and another line on the other side of the church, while others would just stand behind the pews at their seats.

He would raise an offering at a choir rehearsal, or a prayer meeting. It appeared that something would go off in his mind in the company of at least 5; or maybe a few more people in the sanctuary. I believe that he could smell money in the sanctuary, and he was not going to allow anyone to leave with money if he could get it from them.

In a lot of the churches, the people with the most money received the longest ministry, while those with just under the amount that the others were giving, get less, and the others standing receive a corporate prayer so that they will be standing in the aisles to give the big money the next service time.

Many times, the service would begin with a large crowd, but by the time the service had ended, much of the crowd and most of the choir had already left during the offeratory portions of the service. There would even be officials who had initially come up to the front to receive the offering for the ministry, sometimes they would not even be there by the time the offering had ended. They had left the service and gone home!

In the hype of the offering, every single time, he would tell the people that God could take the little bit and work miracles. But all of the time during the offering, he was literally trying to get it all; he was not going to settle for the little bit! He would never be satisfied with the initial pass of the plate. He wanted the whole heaping pile of cash!

He was a very gifted preacher, and he was very knowlegeable. But, he was not willing to show forth the pulpit edicate of his training, or to release the intellectual wealth of his understanding for the purpose of enhancing and edifying the members of his church, all he really seemed to want was the money!

I had been to many churches like that particular church, whereas, after they had finished draining the people in the congregation financially, they would announce that they were selling food in the church's fellowship hall following the service. They wanted you to stop by the fellowship hall and spend some more money.

I'm talking about thousands of dollars, many times in the multiples of tens of thousands being raised during the services! Somehow that still wasn't enough to share the food and refreshments that had been prepared in the kitchen, for no charge at all. They still wanted more money!

Yea, they are greedy dogs which can never have enough, and they are shepherds that can never understand: they all look to their own way, everyone for his own gain, from his quarter. Come ye, say they, I will fetch wine, and we will fill ourselves with strong drink, and tomorrow shall be as this day, and much more abundant.
Isaiah 56: 11-12

What I'm describing here, in no way represents the message of financial security and the spiritual excellence of sowing seeds in the Lord, relative to the teachings in the bible. Some people might take the occasion to suggest that my reference is to the ministers of the body of Christ that have been anointed and ordained to teach the people of the Lord that we do not have to be broke just to live Holy.

Too often the word of God is taken out of context, and twisted when often the message in itself is clear and infallible to the word of God. God forbid that anyone take this written topic of discussion from this book to use it against any of the anointed ministers of the body of Christ that it does not even apply to. Many of the shepherds have vision that cannot even be brought into fruition, without the necessary financial support from the members of that ministry.

God sends a specific group of people to a particular ministry to support the vision of that ministry. The problem lies within the fact that too many of the people are landing and docking themselves in ministries to which they were never ordained or even led of the spirit to be a part of in the first place. Lots of people are choosing ministries based on the feelings and the motivational reports of their family members and their friends, who are excited about the cosmetics of the building or the good-looking leader.

Some people are only over stimulated by the building orrifice, and the colors of the carpet and the unique style of the pews. Most people are proned to look down front of the church, to check out the pulpit furniture comparing it to other ministries in the area, or over the television. People are also facinated over the large beautiful chandeleres hanging from the middle of the ceiling.

Taking; But, Never Delivering!

So many times an offering had been taken up in my own name, where I could see certain people come forth to bless me very freely, it appeared. Some of the people would approach me after the service to inform me that they had reach into their resources to bless me dearly, because they felt that I deserved the blessing. They told me how much they had given to me personally.

What they reported to me, of their own personal gift to me in the offering alone, was more than I had received for the total offering.

FOR AN INSTANCE: the Sunday evening that I preached my very first message, a very good pastor and friend of mine and his wife had sown a seed of $200 in the offering for me. The total offering that I received for the evening was only $92.00 and some change.

I went back to the pastor to ask him what happened to the rest of the money? In his reply to me, he said; "the rest of the money was put away in the bank to buy books for your ministerial training."

Do I have to even tell you that he lied to my face? I have never to this very day, ever seen one dime of that money. And the only book that I ever received, was given to me that night immediately after my initial message. I received a Thompson Chain Reference Bible, which had already been purchased.

Over the past thirty years of my life, I have way too many of these types of mishappenings from the leaders of the churches to even talk about. It doesn't even make since to try and complain to any of the over-seers of the churches, because they support whatever the shepherds under their leadership do.

The leaders are quick to remind us that we shouldn't take the matters of the church before the unjust judge. But, the law is for the lawless! I truly regret listening to the leaders of the church, as they admonished me to just let it go, when others owed me money! They told me to let it go and laughed behind my back with the other pastors that owed me the money.

Sometimes I got word back from another individual that was not even in the meeting, and neither were they a member of the ministry where I had the financial problem, telling me that the ministry in question never intended to pay me from the beginning. "They just said that they were going to pay you!" They intended to use me from the beginning! Many of the other saints would tell me; "be faithful, the Lord will pay you for what you do." And I'm sure that He will, but it did not help the fact that my family was still in need!

If I had all of the money that preachers owed me alone, I'm sure that I would be in better position financially! Many of those pastors have died and are buried in their graves. It's evil and it's very ugly, to mistreat the people of God. Some of the pastors that are still alive, see me and smile great big and shake my hand and tell me how good it is to see me, as if they never did anything wrong to me at all.

We were always taught that if we forgive an individual for wronging us, that we should never say anything about the situation, ever! Even though the persons who did us wrong, don't even have the courtesy to say to us that they are apologetic themselves for the wrong that they had done to us! When they are forced to see us in a crowd at the church somewhere, they put on the show for everybody to see!

Galatians 6: 10

Have you ever gone out to a restaurant with the pastor of the church, or an evangelist after they had just bled you and everybody else financially during the service, and you discovered that you didn't have any money left to eat, because you had just given it all during the offering?

I have! Many of them were so arragant that they never showed any concern for the fact that they had invited me out after the service, knowing that all of my money had been given during the offeratory portion of the service.

Some acted as if they were even outraged at the fact that I had agreed to come out with them, after haven given all of the money that I had available at that time. Perhaps I should have refused the invitation to dine out with them? Most likely, some of them would have even said that I thought that I was too good to go out to eat with them?

What I have come to know relative to the experiences that I have had with these types of ministers, is the fact that many people have confidence with these ministers and they listen to their opinions of others, and respond to the people according to the reports that they have received.

People are influenced with what looks like the blessings of the Lord in the lives of the people in the ministry. It doesn't matter to them that the money that they are slinging around the town, came from dishonestly bleeding the people of the Lord.

All it is that most people seem to be taken away with, is the cars that the leaders are driving, and houses that they are living in. People pay close and strict attention to the name brand clothing that they wear. They are fascinated with the gold rings, Rolex watches, and the other things that the average person may not be able to afford?

Most of the common people accept arrogance and haughty spirits as being the expected behavior of the rich and the more successful people of the church. Only, what is more detestable than the blindness of the common people, is the determination of these types of leaders to keep the people blind.

Didn't Set Well With My Spirit*

$\mathcal{I}$ have been ousted and driven away from the said fellowship of these types of successful leaders of the church, because they say that I am too believing, and too trusting in the people of the church? In so many words, I have not yet become a game player on their teams. They don't take well to the fact, that the very people of their congregations that they have stepped on, I have reached down to try and pick them up spiritually. I have been accused of being meddlesome in some instances.

God won't wink at the foolishness of the leaders, in that they are willing to lead the church astray through the deception of their faith. The average person in the church will look at another person that may be praying their way through to deliverance from a poverty stricken lifestyle, and count them out as a true believer, or they may even discount them as truly being saved?

I had already been operating in the office of the prophetic dating back to March, 1985; even while yet being the minister of music for many of the minisries. Certain pastors would not acknowledge me as a prophet of God in order to keep the people of the ministry from respecting me as a prophet?

You may think that you have successfully pushed the anointing into a corner, but, you have only fooled yourself into believing that you have exerted control over the anointing in your church.

Several of the people in the church, had gotten word that the "OFFICE OF THE PROPHETIC"; was indeed in operation in my life, and they passed the word on to the pastor. I will say; that this church in particular was rather title struct, and they were walking around the church saying; "He's a True Prophet!"

I was use to being called out over the public address systems in the churches, though I hadn't yet realized that the pastors that were recognizing me publically, weren't all real concerning me. At first, I would always feel as if the leaders of the ministries were endorsing me before the people when they would begin to say that I could do everything!

Some would call out all of my accomplishments and abilities, from preaching to playing musical instruments, cosmetology and so on? I would often look around within the room to see if there was someone present, of whom I did not know, that I needed to get acquainted with. I almost never saw anyone that would be important to my future, as far as I could see anyway?

I began to enquire of the Lord; about being called out like that, and I began to ask the Lord what was the big deal that I was a prophet, while the same people that were always publically calling me out, would never get up under me to give me a lift in the ministry, or why they would never push me financially even though they were aware that I was indeed on the move for the Lord; even as they were themselves?

I thank God, for the engrafted word of God, which is able to answer our questions, and to solve the situations of our complexities. The spirit of the Lord reminded me of the Apostle Paul, and Silas; as they went into the temple at the hour of prayer, in the 16th chapter of The Acts of The Apostles.

And it came to pass, as we went to prayer, a certain damsel possessed with a spirit of divination met us, which brought her masters much gain by soothsaying: The same followed Paul and us, and cried, saying, These men are the servants of the most high God, which shew unto us the way of salvation. And this did she many days. But Paul, being grieved, turned and said to the spirit, I command thee in the name of Jesus Christ to come out of her. And he came out the same hour.

The Acts 16: 16-18

The Lord said to me; "The preachers are not approving of you, they are making the people aware of you, to destroy you. They are even making the other preachers aware, that you are the one that they had been talking about!"

After this experience with the Lord, many of those pastors began to show me their true colors. They would see me out and act as if they didn't see me, or they would turn and go in the opposite direction to avoid me altogether.

Mind you, that at that time of my life, while I was hired to be the minister of music, I was not driving the best car, and a couple of times my car even broke down on the church's parking lot. The pastor was very arrogant (on sterroids), he didn't want the people looking to anyone else for anything in the ministry other than himself. Sort of understandable?

Over the pulpit address system one Sunday morning, he made the statement in the midst of a full house, he said; "IF YOU ARE THAT MUCH OF A PROPHET; IF YOUR PROPHECY IS THAT

ACCURATE; YOU OUGHT TO PROPHECY A NEW CAR FOR YOURSELF!"
Many of the people shouted "Amen" out loud in agreement to
the pastor.

He and his wife drove a pair of Mercedes Benzes, so of
course the people were taught to believe that what you have
materialistically, proved where you were spiritually in the Lord.
People still believe this today.

Most people are not even aware of the fact that many
people of the world believe that the church is for the losers of
the world who don't have the where-with-all to make it
financially in the society. Lots of people who are even rich, feel
that they don't need God, or salvation; they feel that they have
enough money to meet all their needs!

So, the perception is that God is only needed, to help the
people who are truly helpless. Many who are rich and living
on the outside of faith in God, are often deceived and gravely
unaware of the fact that God is not in poverty, neither is He
only for those in poverty and He certainly is not in need of any
materialistic substances.

But That's What They Wanted!

*P*eople, are looking for a church with a "CASH
ADVANCE!" They don't even want to be associated with a
church that may have a need for financial support, they think
anyway! I have found that many of the people today want to
be in a church where they can network for business hook-ups,
and for advancement opportunities in the areas of their careers
with the other professional business persons in the congregation.

The people of the church, as a whole, have been deceived

about receiving from God, in that all they want from the Lord now, is cash! They don't even want to be forgiven by Christ anymore, unless He's coming with some cash! Many of the people of the mega-church, have become so nasty in the manner which they entreat other people in other congregations or in the church communities. Their noses are so high in the air, that if the wind were to blow strong enough, it would burst their lungs! (FIGURATIVELY SPEAKING)

This is all based on the fact, that the officials have announced to the congregation, that the church has finally reached the status of financial stability, and in some instances, they have reached fanancial superiority to many of the other churches of their own surrounding community. Sometimes they even announce that they won't be fellowshipping with certain churches that they had fellowshipped in the past, because they have financially outclassed them.

To speak with some of those individuals, about the move of God that is taking place in your congregation, their attitude is to likes of saying; "YOU HAVE GOD; WELL; WE HAVE CASH!"

Sometimes you can't hardly get a word in about a testimony of the power of God, before they begin telling you about how the people in their church are receiving financial blessings and career advancements, new cars, and bigger houses. Material blessings!

They have a way of letting you know that they believe that if there are financial struggles in your church, that God must not be present in your church? People are deceived, but, they don't believe that they are deceived; truly. God has been turned into a cash register, or a slot machine based on the amount of money being given in the offering.

Other churhes have allowed deacons and even the church's

secretary, who sell drugs on the streets in the community, to operate in the business of the church. The lay-people of the church are aware of who these individuals are in the community, and they know that they have not been delivered. But, because they have cash, they are allowed an indellible portion in the affairs of the ministry, which can only be a mess!

I met a Deacon, who was known among the brotherhood to loan his money, only to find out that he was a full blown loan shark! There was no wonder that he had so much money to loan? He would have loaned me $500.00 for $750 in return, in only a two week turn around. Too many people in the church believe that this type of dealing is acceptable.

I talked with this gentleman for a while on the telephone, and he told me that he had been a deacon in his church for more than thirty years, and that he had always done business this way. He said to me that he had also loaned money to many of the pastors, who supported his methods. I asked him if he had ever read the scripture about his business dealings, and he told me out of his own mouth, that he had not!

I shared the scripture with him, and he has never spoken to me again. I shared this scripture;

Lord, who shall abide in thy tabernacle? Who shall dwell in thy holy hill? He that putteth not out his money to usury, nor taketh reward against the innocent. He that doeth these things shall never be moved.

Psalms 15: 1,5

You would think that people would shy away from these types of churches, or at least from these types of people in the church? The truth is that these are the churches that the people flock to in great numbers. According to the brother that I spoke with, the attitude is that of saying; "If the pastor supports what I do, it must be okay!" He didn't seem to understand why his behavior did not agree with my spirit. I believe that he felt that I should go along with his methods just like the other pastors did.

Hollywood; talks frequently about the Pimp turned Rev. Pimp, Dr. Daddy-Day-Care; in care of the flock of the church. The media also talk of the Hustler, Con-Man who adds REVEREND OR DEACON to his name and moves the scheme of his trade to the church, to hustle the people of God out of their hard earned money.

There can never be pimps, without people who are willing to prostitute themselves, to be pimped. There is no hustler that is successful without the people that remain in the company of these skillfully slick con-men to be hustled.

I can't say that I will always blame the crooks for being as crooked as they are, even though they are extremely damaging to the people of the church in the areas of their faith. It's these same people who are being raked over like a pile of fallen leaves, that keep the hustlers in operation!

Too many people are willing to take their eyes off of Jesus, placing their focus on the man or the woman in the pulpit, just like Peter took his eyes off Jesus and began to sink while walking on the water.

Though these leaders may have a very desirable presentation of themselves, as a result of the fact that they work out in the gym to keep their bodies tight; they wear expensive suits, and always smell good because they use good expensive colonge; they are wolves in sheeps clothing. They sport name brand shoes and eat at 5 star, premium classed restaurants. Many times they are rotten to the core, but the people don't seem to care; all because of the cash!

We can no longer afford, to overlook the fact that that's

exactly what the people wanted! We are beyond the day of blaming the shasters for leading the people astray! It's time for the people of the churches to be reprimanded, if there is such a thing to be implimented, for encouraging and enabling these tricksters to increase in the presence of such a needing world. These days, most people know that the people of the world need to see Jesus, but they have opted to show them the schemes of cash instead.

Today; if you ask a person a reason for being a member in the church where they are presently attending, many of them will tell you how that their church helped them to pay their bills or how they gave them money when they needed it, or maybe even they bought them groceries. Some are so carnal minded that they will tell you how successful their pastor is, and what type of an automobile they drive. These things come out of their mouths first, before they even attempt to talk about the presence of the Lord, and the vision of the ministry, if they know it?

Many people, have a tendency to think of the anointed preacher of today who live holy, that won't adhere to the low-life schemes of the devil, as CORNY AND OUTDATED. People believe that they need a flashy dressing minister adorned with the ora of flambouyance, and a silver tongue in the pulpit. Whether they know God or not, is usually not the important issue. When they are chosen, as the pastor of the church, many of the people want to know, how much money they have presently in their own bank account? Their financial status is too often the key factor in being chosen.

For what is a man profited, if he shall gain the whole world, and lose his soul? Or what shall a man give in exchange for his soul? For the son of man shall come in the glory of his father with his angels; and then he shall reward every man according to his works. Verily I say unto you, there be some standing here, which shall not taste of death, till they see the son of man coming in his kingdom. St. Matthew 16: 26-28

Never forget the fact that Jesus is coming back for His church! I know that many people are teaching different things about the imminent return of Jesus Christ; but I urge you to believe the word of God! Jesus won't be coming back for your cash!

Naked came I out of my mother's womb, and naked shall I return thither: the Lord gave, and the Lord hath taken away; blessed be the name of the Lord.

Job 1: 21

WE NEED CASH TO LIVE HERE ON THIS EARTH, especially if we intend to live in peace. There is almost nothing that we can do without money.

Jesus is the miracle worker, but, at the time of tax season; He commanded the disciples to go and catch the fish with the money in it's mouth. He did not recreate more money, rather He used the money that was already in the earth. Jesus only commanded the fish to swim to the bottom of the water to get the money that was already there.

Notwithstanding, lest we should offend them, go thou to the sea, and cast an hook, and take up the fish that first cometh up; and when thou hast opened his mouth, thou shalt find a piece of money: that take, and give unto them for me and thee. St. Matthew 17: 27

Even Jesus knows that we cannot live here free of charge! But Jesus also instructs us not to allow money to become our main objective for living, moving about our daily affairs, or for being alive.

Lay not up for yourselves treasures upon the earth, where moth and rust doth corrupt, and where thieves break through and steal: But lay up for yourselves treasures in heaven, where neither moth nor rust doth corrupt, and where thieves do not break through and steal: For where your treasure is, there will your heart be also.   St. Matthew 6: 19-21

People who are obsessed with money, are evidently possessed with the desire to have money. This is the reason that the people that have been described in this chapter, act and behave themselves in the manner that they do. They are out of control, and many times they are not even aware that they are.

I, spoke with a pastor once, who was dealing with a money shortage in his ministry, who said to me that he had been advised by a senior pastor, who said that he did not have the money that he needed, because he had not developed a strong enough desire for money! He said to him; "You Don't Want It Bad Enough!"

D. J. Rogers; wrote a song back in the seventies, that said; "stress and strain, is hard on the brain; worrying about money will drive you insane. Living is all that matters!"

Obsession, will lead you to do anything and everything to get money. You will always find your self outside of the will of God, trying to obtain money on your own without God. Don't even be fooled into thinking that it is going to please God for you to bring the money of your own blood guiltiness, to offer it as an acceptable sacrifice to the Lord.

Giving money and finances don't impress God. God is not sitting on the throne saying; "WOW; Look at the amount of money they are bringing to that church!" You will never have the money that God has, or the resources to make the money, or the hills and the trees to make the money. God has more than all the world put together.

We are all personally acquainted with just a few people that are known for being very selfish and greedy. Are you so confused, that you believe that men on the earth, are responsible for dividing and dispersing money throughout the common wealth of the entire world?

Only God; is responsible for money being in every continent over the face of the planet. If it were not for the Lord, only a hand full of the people on the earth would ever have any money, were it left up to the decisions of man. So you can stop right now, acting as if you don't believe that God wants you to have money. **HE DOES!**

Money doesn't rule in the kingdon of God. Some people are only elevated to places of authority in certain ministries, because they have money in their bank accounts. That's alright for the business matters often times, because you don't ever need or want broke people handling the money of the church; it can be a temptation too tough for them to handle? But, that individual's money doesn't have anything to do with the anointing. Some people still think that they can purchase a move of God; a miracle; an anointing; a church or anything else that is on the inside of the kingdom of God.

And when Simon saw that through laying on of the apostles' hands the Holy Ghost was given, he offered them money. Saying, Give me also this power, that on whomsoever I lay hands, he may receive the Holy Ghost. But Peter said unto him, Thy money perish with thee, because thou hast thought that the gift of God may be purchased with money. Thou hast neither part nor lot in this matter: for thy heart is not right in the sight of God. Repent therefore of this thy wickness, and pray God, if perhaps the thought of thine heart may be forgiven thee. For I perceive that thou art in the gall of bitterness, and in the bond of iniquity. Then answered Simon, and said, pray ye to the Lord for me, that none

of these things which ye have spoken come upon me.
The Acts 8: 18-24

I am awfully afraid that many people of the churches today are in danger of the wrath of God, for the sake of seeking the almighty dollar instead of seeking God!

Just a few days ago, the whole country was comtemplating the possibility, of moving about without cars in this modern American culture, because of the extreme rise in the price of gasoline.

With war in full progress, if the Lord were to allow it to be so, we could all be scrambling for food and shelter, with no clothes to wear on our backs. Just because the American soil is not the present battlefield, we should not be enticed to forget the fact that God is everywhere also. The mid-east war may not be here, but God is here! God; is not sitting on the throne with His back turned to the world. I'm not even sure that God even has a back to turn!

We are not moving about in and throughout this world behind God's back, in any form or fashion, just as we don't watch a movie from the back of the movie screen, or from the rear of the television.

Many people, who are still in the sanctuary of the churches, have put down their swords for a Hundred dollar bill. They have even stopped tithing and sowing seeds in the ministry of the Lord. It is dangerous whenever the pastor stops giving and tithing, because they believe that everything that comes into the church, belongs to them.

Most destructive leaders, keep on going in the wrong directions until they hang themselves, and cut their own throats; (FIGURATIVELY SPEAKING).

Saul was told to destroy the Amelekites and to destroy

everything that they possessed. But Saul; saw that there was cash? in the camp; (spoils), he thought that it would be alright to disobey the orders of God, because all of the good stuff that they found in the camp of the Amelekites, could be used to give offerings, and to make sacrifices to the Lord. But his greed was the end of his ministry, and leadership as king over all of the tribes of Israel and Judah.

> *And Samuel said, Hath the Lord as great delight in burnt offerings and sacrifices as in obeying the voice of the Lord? Behold, to obey is better than sacrifice, and to hearken than the fat of rams.*   I Samuel 15: 22

The moment most people come in contact with money, big money; they think that they have graduated from the need of God! The more things people seem to acquire that are of any value, they seem to believe that the volume of the pricier things that they have, makes them more blessed than everyone else. Many of the wealthiest people, might have forgotten the fact that all things are subject to the destruction of fire and water, and they are subject to being stolen.

Pastors right here in my city, seem to have forgotten that Jesus is Lord and savior of the people. They seem to have also lost the fear of the Lord. Alcohol and drugs have found it's way into the lives of those individuals who stand in the pulpits as leaders of the churches, more openly and frequently now.

Preachers, are not only using drugs, they are actually supplying drugs to the members of the congregations. I knew of a pastor that would give money to drug dealers to make their large buys, and the drug dealers would return, twice as much, or more money to him? It was often reported that he was seen in the crack houses doing business with the dealers. The dealers became so comfortable, that they walked up on the church campus with a large brown paper bag of money, and asked someone to give it to the pastor.

A young man in my city confessed to his family that he had bought his first marijuana cigarette from the pastor of their church! It's not worth establishing the pathway to Hell for someone else in the church, just because you are demonically driven and enticed to have more money.

It has become aware, that the message which admonishes us to take hold of money without allowing money to take hold of us, has been silenced! Someone forgot to remind most people that no matter what they acquire and accomplish in this life, "Only What You Do For Christ, Will Last!" No matter how rich you become with money and assets, you can't take it with you.

It is sad to realize, that some people are so taken with their riches, that they are even buried with it. Some people have been buried with large sums of cash. Others were buried sitting upright in their favorite automobiles. Some people have had their gold literally fashioned into the coffin to which they were to be buried. The coffin was actually put in the ground with them! Too many people have been deceived into believing that they would be just as rich in death as they were living.

HERE IS A CLOSING FACT FOR YOUR MIND :

In death you can neither be rich or poor! The very state of being rich; or even the state of being poverty stricken and poor, is a state of reality that is based on what you are able to know and to accomplish while you live! There have been people who have walk the earth that were rich but never knew it because someone kept them from that knowledge.

Many people who are very poor, their actual state of existing, is not always easily detected based on their personal demeanor, and the spirit of their attitude about life and living. Any poor man or woman on the face of this earth can think themselves rich! Not, fantisize themselves to be a rich person, but they can alter and even enhance their own ways of thinking and eventually become positively, productively, and financially, rich! Legally!

For as he thinketh in his heart, so is he:
Proverbs 23: 7A

There is no one in the grave, that is having a heart attack or stroke, a brain aneurism, or suffering with cancer, that already killed them, dying all over again as a result of being broke now. Believe me, they are not in the grave talking to the Lord about their financial status. There is not a single bank executive that has gotten a telephone call from the grave to inquire about the status of their saving, checking, IRA, stocks and bonds, or any other accounts for that matter.

Some Christian denominations, teach that we should never read or refer to the old testament of the bible. Let me tell you that those individuals that don't want to give respect to the old testament accounts, of the reality of God, will never be able to come into the full knowledge and the complete truth of God!

The same people that preach and teach that we shouldn't even touch the old testament, don't observe the same respect for touching old money! Many people have not even been made aware of the fact that it is the factual precepts and the principles of the old testament, that allow us to even be prosperous today.

Only the old; can produce or be responsible for the new! People have lost their sober minds, in that they allow themselves to believe that they don't need to respect that which came before their time.

With all of the money that you may have right now, if

you leave the presence of this world unchanged and unchained from the love of money; in Hell you will discover that your money won't be able to buy you any relief, or a way out of the torment of the fire. You can't buy air conditioners in Hell; as a matter of the fact, I'm not even sure if there is any air in Hell at all!

Don't be stupid enough to fail God over a dollar! Money can do a lot of things, but, God can do anything!

Who Cares?

The adorable appearance of the church, as we have always known of the church, has begun to dwindle away for a more user-friendly model that is less offensive to the sinfully determined individuals that despise the idea of change. People will literally curse and throw a punch if you insist on showing them the error of their ways, a true shepherd can be no wimp.

As long as people are giving lots of money to the church, certain leaders are protective of these persons. They don't want these types of people disturbed or upset, so they refuse to be proactive against their agenda to willfully sin, while remaining active in the church.

There are some people who need to literally be cast out from the presence of the people of the church, because they are going to cause even greater damage to the people in training to be the leaders of the church, as long as they are allowed to hang around.

People who give large amounts of money in the church, oftimes, feel that they have a voice to say how things should be run around the church. It doesn't even matter that they have not been converted; they refuse to be silent about the matters of the church because they feel that they have bought their way into the business affairs of the church.

Others like to feel as if the pastor ought to be dangling on a string like a puppet, for receiving the large amounts of money from those persons. We have all witnessed pastors who have been bought out by certain people with lots of money. It is easy to be bought when the reason for being in the ministry is only for the purpose of supplying an individual's financial needs. They want the money!

PASTORIAL, THEOLOGIANS; tell bible stories to the congregation while skipping over the biblical guidelines for daily living, so that the people who support the ministry financially will not be offended if they are told the unadulterated truth, as is told, in the word of God.

What people feel now whenever we tell the truth over the pulpit, won't even compare to what they are going to feel should they die and end up in Hell!

Your Cash? Or Christ***

For We Wrestle Not......Eph. 6:12

Twelve

WRESTLING.   Catch as Catch Can Style.

Divided Instead of Divine

*We are **Not** called into purpose;*
*We are called **Because** of our purpose!*

William Thompson, Jr.

According as he hath chosen us in him before the foundation of the world, that we should be holy and without blame before him in love: Having predestinated us unto the adoption of children by Jesus Christ to himself, according to the good pleasure of his will, To praise the glory of his grace, wherein he has made us accepted in the beloved.

Ephesians 1: 4-6

To Be; Or Not To Be; That Is the Question!

*P*erhaps, the stories told of the churches of yester-year, probably sounded to the people back then, much to the likes of which they sound to us today? To be honest with you, the idea of the future church here in America; is a very scary thought to me, simply because of the damage that has been done to the comprehensive design and the actual prototype of the church.

Everywhere you look, and everywhere you go for a time of worship, you soon discover that most everyone has developed their own idea of what they feel the church ought to be. This of course includes the standing shepherds of today that have come forth to establish their own gathering places for the new fangled scope of worship, that many times have nothing at all to do with Jesus Christ, according to the word of God, in the King James bible.

Of course, it does make good sense that the church would progress with the ages to a certain degree; but the progressiveness of the church should not be relative only to the creative drafting designs for the upcoming building projects of these opening ages.

The scope of change surrounding the church, should have never been an attempt to alter the true identity of God, and a total redefining of the written word of God. Many people of today are questioning; what's the church really all about? Is it the most brilliant financial scheme in the history of time? Is it the most likely place for sociably gathering to find a partner or a mate? Whether the mate is a soul-mate, or only a sexual-mate; as people often refuse to seek the Lord for a spouse?

I have often asked myself, as many others who have been in the church for a while have ask the same questions that I do; why it is that people are not taking the church as seriously as they used to, just a few decades ago? The new generation is quite satisfied that the church is less apt to influence real visible change, demanding accountability to accompany any verbal confession of Christianity.

We might as well play Putt-Putt in the aisles of some of the churches, and watch major sporting events and play X-BOX video games on the large jumbo-tron monitors in the sanctuaries for viewing the activities of the service to the mega crowds in attendance. Most people get more spiritual enlightenment and excitement from a sporting event than they will ever experience at many of the churches nowadays.

Far too many people of the church, are better acquainted with the power of the ball and the rules that govern the game, much more than they will ever know about the power of God on any Given Sunday! People go all out for a game in their dress and their behavior, but they prefer to show up at the church looking like they just stepped out of the shower, or as if they just left the park after playing ball themselves.

Whenever you hear an athlete give an interview to a journalist, they say; "the noise of the crowd makes all of the difference in how the game is to be played." They feel that the noisy crowd shows a sense of appreciation and support for the team.

Don't forget the fact that many of the noise makers in the crowd at the game are the same people that frequent the pews of the church on a regular basis. Many of these same people are so turned off with the actual purpose of the church that they become paralyzed and they seem to develop laryngitis every time they show up at the church for a service, where they should be a participant.

Many people prefer the role of the spectator at a sporting event, rather than to be a participator during the worship service at the church. Here's why : While the benefit of being a worshipful participator is far greater and much more rewarding for all of the persons in attendance; the spectator enjoys the feeling of control, in that they are free to express themselves in almost any way possible that they choose to do so.

Bending the rules and going beyond the limit of discipline as a spectator, is often a defining factor that makes a statement that their involvement of boosting their own team is necessary for their team to clench the victory?

Spectators prefer the high of a beer, and God only knows what else they might choose to indulge themselves prior to the start of the sporting event, that gives them the push to go beyond the better reasoning of their own intellectual reasoning, into the embarrassing realms of spectatorship, where there are no limits or rules. The same persons likewise despise the power of God and purposefully separate themselves from the activities of true praise during worship.

At best; all I can say is, get out of the way and stay clear of the outrageous behavior of spectators who feel it necessary to express themselves at the game! But by the very same token, watch them whenever they enter the church for a worship service, while of course we know that they are aware of the fact that the behavior of the believer is to be purposefully altered for the benefit of every true worshipper.

You almost wonder, what it is that they have chosen to show up at the church for? The church is not just an alternate choice of places to go for a different type of weekly entertainment.

As children, most of us were taught that we needed to be on our best behavior everywhere we went, while being impacted to adhere to the fact that as a believer, our behavior should be the same everywhere we go. We were made aware that we would attend many different places that require different levels of our behavioral respect, but we needed also to realize that no matter where we are as a believer, that no building or sporting arena is to alter our commanded behavior, as a worshipper.

My wife coordinated an outing to a sporting event for the young people of our church. Being a small church, we needed the parents to chapperone their children. You may or may not be surprised to know that the children sat there like little trained soldiers, while their parents acted as if they were hired cheerleaders and dancers straight from the ghetto, which was definitely embarrassing, as well as compromising to our position as a ministry and a church. They took us by surprise, because they never acted so wildly at any other time!

Well Who's To Blame?

*I*t seems only obvious, that people would be liable themselves; they're to be blamed for their own behavior in the church that is less than honorable and truly thankful to the Lord, just as they are responsible for how they conduct themselves at any other setting.

The shepherd has been called by God to teach and to instruct the sheep in the ways of the Lord, teaching them to know how to conduct themselves as believers, enabling the impacting repose of their righteous disposition, for the rest of their lives.

I have seen so many people outraged and totally disgruntled at the leadership of the church whenever it comes to constructive criticle teaching. There are leaders that choose to disregard the necessary teaching for spiritual welfare and the practical application of the word of God for daily living, while opening up to listen to the rhetoric of the rebellous congenators of the faith.

People are ignorant of the pre-ordained purpose of the church, because they have either truly ignored the teachings that explains and reveals the actual purpose of the church, or they have been misinformed through faulty teaching that caused them to be deceived as a result of erroneous directions that are totally to the left of the purpose of the church.

All who have taken the platform of the shepherd are not called by God in the first place. They have established their own guidelines for the church relative to their own flaws and failure to follow the written path in the word of God. Show me the direction of the head; I will show the exact direction of the body! As the head cannot go in a separate direction from the body except that it has been severed from the body.

As much as everyone desires for their analogical position to be the right path for the church to follow, the fact is that only God is right and the church is only on the right path whenever closely following Christ. People are led into areas of unrighteousness and rebellion to the word of God, by any leader's influence, who hasn't been influenced themselves, by

God; and filled with the Holy Ghost!

The average person of the church cannot even give an elaborate definition of the true purpose of the church when called upon to do so. They feel that they are only supposed to know that the church is the place where people come to worship God, which is totally incomplete to the actual purpose of the church.

We that are truly a part of the church from a born-again perspective, have the understanding that whenever we wake up to a new day that we have indeed showed up for another opportunity to worship and to glorify God, on the exact same day that we have been given to live again.

Many shepherds, of diverse denominational, persuasive spectrums, that are determined to adhere to their own coorporate ways of thinking, should realize that every time they approach a new day, that they have indeed showed up again with spiritual padlocks, chains, and fetters, as a prison guard at the gate of their own chosen mental facility for Christian's separation and Biblical amputation, to ensure that the body of the Christ is yet divided at every connecting joint, severed from the adjoining true-vine.

While the only reasonable explanation for the denominations to segregate the people, is for the benefit of distinction relative to social statuses and racial barriers, the pastors under the umbrella of the denominational organizations are usually so engulfed with their own agendas to promote themselves to higher positions of status, that they don't realize that they have been sent to spiritually blindfold the people, to keep them from knowing God's true will and purpose for His church.

Many churches have become nothing more than social

clubs and civic centers for the benefit of city government and a lawful aid to connect with the lawful code enforcements of the city, so that the people of the church might be forced to lend their support to the cause of the city government, which could care less about the spiritual welfare of the churches.

Divided Or Diverted!

I will never play, concerning the truth! People usually do know what the real truth is concerning the welfare of the church. However, diversionary tactics are used to purposefully sidetrack the mental focus of the people.

Perhaps the reasons for these less than genuine activities of the leadership of the church, is for the purpose of sheltering oneself from the possibility of being exposed? It is one thing to instruct people in the ways of the Lord, and to coach them into the practical application of the knowledge that they have acquired, but it is all together a totally different thing to actually be an example of the lesson that you give to the persons under your teaching.

There are persons in leadership positions that should not have been in position simply because they are not ready to assume the responsibility to lead. They were never really prepared to know the seriousness of leading other people. Perhaps they may have been overwhelmed with the idea of being out in the forefront?

Popularity is not the only benefit of being the leader. It always feels good being in the front when everybody is applauding you and speaking your name, as long as there is no stigma attached to your name! People like the feeling of being on the top of things, but the feelings change whenever the circumstances of the things that are associated to you reverse in position, and now everything is on top of you!

Not everyone want others to know that they might have lost control of the situations, or that just maybe they were never prepared for being blindsided by an unexpected blow. Guess what? No one is ever really prepared for being broadsided from the blindside of their ultimate expectations. But, what will make the difference, is when the leaders take the necessary precautions to insure that they will be able to bounce back from the element of surprise that took them down, but not necessarily out.

Because of pride, many people are never going to admit that there has been a problem, as if they are exempt from ever having any problems. They send up a smoke screen to camouflage the true reality of their struggles in the ministry of the church, which only further damages their positional strength and the tenure of their leadership in the church.

The local church is consistent of imperfect people from all walks of life, which will never allow the visibility of the local church to exist without the appearance of any problems or negative situations. The powerful ability of the church to affect change in the lives of the people associated with the church, is relative to the culpability of the people who readily surrender their will to the will of the Lord.

Leaders divert the reality of what has indeed taken place in the church whenever they feel personally responsible for the behavior of the people that they are suppose to be leading. It's time for leaders to step forward and begin to tell the truth about the behavior of the people who are indeed rebellious to their leadership, because these disobedient people don't relegate the truth of the actual purpose and the power of the church, as was preordained of God.

Just because people don't follow, it doesn't render the leader incapable of leading the people in the ways of righteousness. If we are not careful, the need to impress other leaders and laymen alike, can fester to a progressive rage to fuel the fires of falsehood, relative to the assignment of the churches of America and the world at large.

I had a conversation with a very good friend of mine about the call of the ministry. His actual statement to me was; "it used to be that people were called to the ministry just a few years ago. Now it appears that every time we speak to a minister of the church they are talking about how they are going to the seminary to become a minister or a pastor."

If God don't call you to the ministry, you could attend Fifty Theological Seminaries, but that doesn't make you qualified to be a minister of the Lord Jesus Christ. Your strong desire to be in the front of the ministry, does not equate to the actuality of the call of God. You may be intelligent, but so is every other sinner, although the sins they are committing don't shed any light on the fact of their intelligence! Smart is not what the Lord is necessarily looking for to lead His people in these latter times of the church.

> *For ye see your calling, brethren, how that not many wise men after the flesh, not many mighty, not many noble, are called: That no flesh should glory in his presence.*

> I Corinthians 1: 26, 29

Native Romans, and Greeks; were always carried away with intelligence and allowing the mind to take flight free of any boundaries or restrictions. Your mind will do just whatever you allow it to do! It will run away with you, while leaving you to believe that you are actually going with the impulses of your mind.

The smarter we become, and the more we are determined to follow our minds instead of following the leading of the Lord in the church, the purpose of the church becomes more and more distorted and fragmented to the point that most people who were not raised up in the church, are divided in their heart and minds about what the church ought to be, and what the church ought to be doing in the community?

Too many people are reading books and not the bible for the welfare of the church. We all learn from the experiences that we have had while in the church, at least we all should learn, but our experiences don't merit the attention of the church so that the bible is no longer needed.

Classrooms and CDs, tape series and group studies can never take the place of fasting and prayer for an understanding of the word of God, for the purpose of leading the people of the church.

Look in the word of God and nowhere else for the actual purpose of the church, or else somebody is going to be gravely misinformed and led astray based on somebody's feeling and emotions about the word, and how it is to be applied to our daily lives.

Mine Is the Divine!

I am determined to mimic David who said in Psalms 121: "I will look to the hills whence cometh my help."

My church went through the most tumultuous times of

the 7 year history of the ministry of The Spoken Word Center. We suffered a great loss in every since of the word! People are not very easily figured out, and they can be very unpredictable.

My purpose is to have a church that mirrors the very image of the God who made us all. I don't believe that God intended for us all to be alienated even after we have come into the knowledge of the truth of Jesus Christ our Lord and Savior. The Father's love has drawn us to Himself; of which the very same drawing effect remains even after we have come to Him, and it is the binding tie of the global church, universally. Though it is necessary to have multiple houses of worship, relative to the mass number of believers of the one self same purpose, there should be no racial differences, or biblical divides relative to theological understandings.

I have always set the stage for a ministry that is to be diverse in terms of the people that attend and become an avowed part of the ministry. There will always be one message delivered in the Spoken Word Center; and that message is the message of the gospel of Jesus Christ. Make no mistake about that issue! Our church began with Black, White, and even Hispanic; though it was predominately Black.

It has been like a revolving door as people come and go, all races of people have chosen to attend, for any number of reasons. It's my endeavor to make people to feel welcomed without compromising the message of the gospel. I felt that there were people in the ministry that had been there long enough to understand my vision, but to my surprise, the people that I thought really knew and understood my vision, as it related to God's people, were the very people who walked out of the ministry whenever diversities really came about.

The people who walk out of the ministry, were not the

individuals who caused the devastation to the ministry at all. The very people that stayed and falsely embraced me as a man with a mission that only God could give to a leader were the very same people that hit me below the belt, to my face.

I made the mistake of believing in others who are called of God, to the point of allowing them to go forth in the ministry without prejudice or fear of being undermined as a leader and deceived by a friend that I embraced as a brother.

We were struggling our way through the ministry financially, but with the hopes of soon coming out on the top of our financial woes. We have always had plans to minister to the community in every way possible, but were not yet financially stable to put forth our hand as a ministry to the community, still we did responde wherever the need called. Our minds were made up to stay in the race, fighting to win the battle.

We were fighting with the shield of faith out in the front of us, believing that the war that we were fighting was also in the front of us. But, to our surprise, the real fight was just in the midst of us! We were being stabbed in the back from behind us by a friend we thought honestly stood behind us! The very persons we trusted were the same people who caused our ministry to be busted up the middle!

People walked out of the ministry without any real legitimate explanations to our leadership? They disregarded the hours and the personal time that we had given up for them. They made us feel as if the teaching and the training that we had giving to all of them was nothing at all, even though they had communicated to us that they were being taught in the word of God, as they had never been taught before?

I'd been feeling like a real failure and a loser in that I was not able to keep the ministry afloat despite the fact that I had run all over town seeing to the needs of many of the people in the ministry, and had spent hours counseling and listening to the problems of the people, along with all of the times that I had the people over to my home for bar-b-que, and we also had several picnics to build the relationship of our church family?

I have prayed for and have ministered to countless people and have given away my money. But, to my big surprise, all of the things that I had done in the name of the Lord and for the sake of being the pastor, still did not keep the people around. I made sure that everything that I was doing, was being done from my heart and not for the purpose of having a string to attach to the people that I had helped.

Prior to entering into the pastorate order of the ministerial call of God upon my life, I ministered in the music department of many churches working very close to some of the pastors who openly discussed the fact that they were not going to help people in the ministry without a commitment from those persons, saying that they would stay with their church. Some people were indeed denied help for refusing to commit to that ministry.

I witnessed the treatment of many people who had been helped by certain pastors, how they were made to feel inferior to them simply because they had helped them.

I witnessed people being belittled from the pulpit by the pastor during the morning worship services, when the pastor told the congregation that they had helped those persons, and told the reasons for helping them. Of course I have also witnessed people get up and leave the ministry because of very similar circumstances and never come back to the ministry.

I think the picture of my determination to treat the people of the Lord right, is coming into view. (Galatians 6:10) Some things that I had witnessed concerning the treatment of people is unmentionable, or rather I would prefer not to mention those degrading things?

Whatever I do as a leader of the church, should leave the people looking back to the Lord with an even greater determination to live for Him, knowing that there is really someone in the church that is living true to the word of God, and can be sleighted as a true Christian that is not only a talker of the word of God, but a doer of the word of God!

I purpose to show the people Christ; not just to tell the people where to go to find Him in the time of need. Though my heart has been ripped, I place it in the hands of Jesus, because He knows the good that has come out of such painful experiences for me. My bleeding heart could never compare to the bloody cross of Calvary! I realize that I only bleed for my losses, But, Jesus bled for all humanity that would last through out eternity.

Neither Hot Or Cold**

*N*owadays, the church as we know of the church at large, all over America, is out of order. Don't get me wrong, lot's of people are still coming in to be a part of the societal front of the church in the communities, which only allows the people to continue as they were before they came.

What many people refer to as acceptable church attendance, is simply pausing from their daily routine to sit underneath the voice of a man or woman behind the pulpit, to hear a prepared sermonic babble story; usually altered itself, for the benefit of the working class sinners, who feel that they are actually doing the church a favor with their attendance?

A great percentage of today's leaders do not even consider themselves to be shepherd's over the Lord's flock. Perhaps the fault for such detached accountability of the leadership, is by way of the Seminary? I have heard many of the Leaders refer to themselves as Hired Servants of the church; they rarely refer to being called of God to lead the church in the first place. It's all about the paycheck, and the benefits! They have become enslaved to the board of trustees, of which often they are very careful not to upset the members of the board.

Over the years I have noticed that many board members have good business sense, but they also lack the spiritual connection and biblical understanding that makes for having a good relationship with God, in an effort to really care for the people. For this reason alone, the board members are apt to watch the behavior and business conduct of the pastor at every step, assuring their obedience to the bylaws of the church, and the requirements of the board, while it matters least to them that the pastor may be impotent to lead the people in the ways of the Lord by example.

The local church is not likely to be anything more than it is, when we have people leading the congregation from such a subverted position. One of the requirements of today's church leaders, is to maintain limited interaction with the people, for which the board makes sure of that, and rightfully so............?

Notwithstanding the fact, that many leaders have been caught up in the wringer of negative media spotlight for having misbehaved themselves so detestable, that their grotesque demeanor has marred the perported exemplary aspect of spiritual leadership, and the endeared portrait of the church all together;

Weak, fearful leaders, who have no fire or a vision, must operate from beneath the divided spectrum, looking at the world, or even looking to the world for the direction to move the local church in the community? What has not been revealed to leaders who obey the men of the board, and disregard the master of their calling, is that the media which rapidly reports the misbehavior of the people of the clergy, belong to the world.

Everytime that I see another minister in the media, whether they are found innocent or guilty; I hear the media saying to the rest of the standing members of the clergy;

"We will do the same thing to you! You are not that special; so you'd do better to stay behind the walls of your churches. You may entertain the people of the church, it is acceptable even if you amuze them from time to time; but, never take it upon yourself to influence the people of the society to believe your God, or the Holy Bible, over and above what is in this world of our's." We're watching you too!

Those who have never been spotlighted in the media, whether they are misbehaving or living examples of the truth of the word of God, many of them have been spooked by the media, to the point they have begun themselves to prefer very little interaction with the people who make up the congregation where they are the pastors. They are distant in every since of the word.

The duties of the pastor are often many and very time consuming, whereas, pastors would often have little time to themselves, in the past anyway? Today's pastors have taken unto themselves other ministers in their churches and ordained them as pastors, and have divided the responsibility to the others to do the work, in representation of the overseeing shepherd. Mind you, that all of the credit goes back to the one that should be doing the work in the first place.

It is not the common practice of people to work for absolutely no pay, and little recognition. More often, the situation is that the other workers of the ministry will rise up to reward themselves, causing all sorts of caos among the people of the congregation, futher extinguishing the flames of the fire in the church. Any disgruntled worker may have the ability to influence the people to believe that the pastor is not doing his job, because its being done by them!

What is even more detrimental to the cause of the disgruntled worker, is that they have the people to back them, citing that, the pastor never showed up to care for their need; The other person came instead of the pastor. Although the people of today are getting use to the absence of the shepherd among the flock, they are likewise as equally disappointed and outraged at the thought of the pastor to which they are supporting, never being available to touch them in the time of their need? People don't always want to talk to someone else other than the shepherd that is feeding them in word and doctrin of the bible.

While it is my position as the pastor to point the people in the direction of Jesus, it is also my purpose to lead them that will follow my leadership, to the presence of God; being the first to get there. As the shepherds of these times have lost the fire of God, they have also lost the warmth of that loving feeling that drove them to see to it that the people of their ministries were being properly ministered unto.

It doesn't really make good since to allow others to front

the ministry, when their heart could never be the heart of the ordained leadership of the church. A true shepherd is set on making it to the destination that they had been called and ordained of the Lord to lead the people. An assistant to the shepherd, just may be apt to take another turn in the process of fronting the ministry, citing the insurrection of their own vision as a method of leading the people.

Let's start out with a pitcher filled with ice water, and a fire pit filled with hot coals? The pitcher of ice water would be cold and refreshing. Just over a short period of time, the water would even be colder than it was before, because of the consistency of the ice. The ice is still there! Even if the ice in the pitcher of water would all melt away, the water would still be very cold and refreshing to drink as a result of the ice that had been there to begin with. The focus is the ice cube!

The ice has to remain in the pitcher of water, and even be replenished when necessary, in effort for the water to remain cold. Just a bit of intelligence should keep us in mind of the fact that the water is never to be left unattended, to become luke-warm; as result of the ice that would have already melted, whereas the temperature of the water could not remain the same without the element of the ice to bring the temperature down from being hot, or from being luke-warm, to being cold and refreshing.

In a very different scenario, the fire pit that has been filled with burning coals, is qualified to serve whatever the purpose intended. The one thing that we know for sure is that the fire must not only be hot enough to serve the purpose, but it has to remain hot enough to finish the cause. When the coals are left burning on the fire until they are burned out, the fire in and of itself will likewise remain hot, until it burns out. Whatever the recepticle that housed the fire, it will also remain very hot to the touch even though the flames will have gone out. The focus is the coals!

I'll show you the subtlety in the deception of division: We know that all Ice is cold. It is not really the ice as much as it is the volume number of ice cubes that changes the temperature, as one block Ice cube does not make the pitcher of water cold. But, fill the pitcher with ice cubes, add water, and the temperature conditions of the contents in the water pitcher immediately change.

If we pour a glass of water from that same pitcher of water, whereas several of the ice cubes also fill the glass, we have a cold glass of water. Just because the pitcher being filled with ice and water, has cold water as a result, that doesn't mean that we could take a luke-warm or a hot glass of water and separate maybe one or two of the ice cubes from the cold pitcher of ice-water, adding them to the luke-warm or the hot water, to make the water in the glass cold.

Standing alone, a single ice cube, or a pair of ice cubes can slightly effect the temperature of the water in a glass or even in a pitcher filled with water. But, being divided and separated from the rest of the ice cubes, they are not strong enough in temperature, to sufficiently effect the pre-stabilized temperature of the water enough to make it cold.

Should we continue to divide the ice cubes even from the water pitcher, one by one, or two by two, eventually the cold water in the pitcher itself would begin to change temperature and become warmer, not having enough ice to sustain the cooled condition of the water. Collectively, the ice cubes temperature stand in strength to keep the water cold; divided they lose the ability to effect the desired change and the refreshing condition of the water.

Likewise, the fired pit is also very hot as result of the volume of the ignited coals. One burning coal does not have the heat intensity to sufficiently prepare the fire pit for the intended usage. As long as the coals burn together to heat the pit, the purpose will be sufficiently benefitted. There are times when even a well lit fire might need the aid of a poker to stir the coals on the bottom of the pile so that they might be properly ventilated and burn sufficiently.

Should we begin to take away one or two of the coals from the fire, we would not immediately notice a difference in the heat level, because the strength of the temperature of the fire is yet in the volume number of the coals burning in the pit. We knew from the beginning, that it would take plenty of coals to make the fire hot enough to sufficiently heat the pit for the intended usage.

But, should we allow the coals to continue to be alleviated from the pit, we would soon notice that the temperature of the fire would have drastically cooled. Together the coals stand to sufficiently heat the pit for the intended usage. Coals burning with intense heat, once being divided from the rest of the coals in the pit, is rendered impotent to the exact purpose for which it was initially ignited.

> *I know thy works, that thou art neither cold nor hot : I would that thou wert cold or hot. So then because thou art lukewarm, and neither cold nor hot, I will spue thee out of my mouth.*
>
> Revelation 3 :15–16

That which is either cold or hot, must be married, in comittment, to the cause of being either cold or hot! God never makes an empty promise, to which He never intended to fulfill. God neither likes, nor ordains that which is only lukewarm, because it is most assuredly indicative of indecisiveness and confusion. There is no way to tell what was originally intended, whether to be hot or cold!

God says; I WILL SPUE THEE OUT OF MY MOUTH!

Initially, I'd like for us to understand that lukewarm, is a bad taste in the mouth of God. But, it means that God will neither speak with you or to you any more, as result of the attempt to mesh that which is hot with that which is indeed cold.

Doesn't that sound just like the churches of today? The leaders of the churches don't want the church to be too offending to the sinners of today, they want to make the church a desireable place to be, so they set the spiritual atmosphere conditioners to comfortable, so that the sinners and their demons can feel at ease in the sanctuary of the churches.

My friend, this is also the reason being that many of the churches segregate themselves from other churches that demand excellence and accountability with the association of their confessions of Christ. God intend for us as the church to be on fire! While the churches need to fellowship with one another, it is imparative that we understand that there is absolutely no fellowship with those who are of the darkened work of Satan, among the churches.

You would have to show me in the scripture, where God is calling for the church to create an atmosphere for Satan and any of his followers? All sinners are not to be associative to those who primarily instinctively strictly follow after the works of Satan. Don't get it twisted, the church is the place for the sinner to come to be saved, but, the sinner must find the hot spiritual invironment, powerful enough to connect them to the power of God through repentence.

The installed boundaries of righteousness are eternally installed for us in the earth. Many clergymen have been detrimental to the cause of Christ in that they have not been strong enough in the Lord to uphold the standards of the pre-installed landmarks. Many have thought of the church as being too stern in it's stance against the sinfulness of men, so they chose to establish their own church atmospheres, so that the ungodly would no longer avoid attending.

You have never, ever been rejected until you have been rejected by God! King Saul, is a perfect example of what I am saying. When God shut him out, there was no one anywhere that could get a word to Saul from the Lord, because God wasn't speaking to Saul anymore. Samuel went down on his knees, in prayer and fasting for Saul, but to no avail. God asked Samuel; How long are you going to lament for Saul, seeing that I have rejected him from being the King over all of Israel and Judah? (I Samuel 16 :1)

Almost immediately, God said to Samuel, get up from there and wash your face, I already have another man for the job. Whatever God says is right, and He's right the first time!

Anyone that doesn't know how to behave themselves in the presence of the people of God, should not lead the people of God in the first place, being that they are out of control, and in need of deliverance themselves.

Common sense, should tell every luke-warm leader, to pay attention to the media for the purpose of notating that the media often stray away from the leaders that are truly on fire for God, as long as those same ministerial personnel don't take advantage of the media to move the message of Christ to the masses.

Don't make the mistake of associating the idea of religious broadcasting with the general media across the board? At large, religious broadcasting is to the likes of giving a dog a bone, once all of the meat has been stripped from the bone. The true reaching ability of the television media will not be known through what we know of as religious broadcasting, even though religious broadcasting signals have been allowed into the airways of many foreign countries now.

Once we get in to the airways, to actually take advantage of the broadcast programming, what the people are actually hearing and possibly seeing when they are experiencing this religiously divided, American smorgasbord, that has been so stripped of the meat elements of the faith, is that the portrayal of the church is neither hot or cold! The church started out hot, on fire By God, with God, and definitely for God. Now God is the least likely thing desired in many of the churches now. (Hebrews 12:29)

The church is styled as an entity to meet the needs of humanity in the present communities, and abroad, even though people are required to get a job and work to individually meet the financial requirements for the benefit of their families, and for the benefit of meeting the needs of the ministry and the body of Christ.

These things we know of even from the stand point of our government. The failed system of government welfare should have sent the message to the church, that helping people is not really beneficial unless people are willing to help themselves first.

A divided church that is now sleighted to be multi-faceted, in that it offers many different types of sociable opportunities to the people, leaves the church looking to the common wealth of the people for a sense of purposeful fulfillment as a church, especially when they have allowed the light of the fire of God to go out!

When the power of the Holy Ghost has departed the atmosphere of the church, it has become nothing more that a civic organizational gathering of people no matter what is being taught across the pulpit and in the classroom sessions of that church.

Division, in and of itself, is often subtle, though at times it has been caused by a catastrophic circumstancial devastation of some sort. The division is often not what we focus upon, it is however the soon visible damage of spiritual relationships with God through Christ Jesus, and the Divine purpose of the church, which might have been allowed to fade away, that is quite visible.

We need Powerful Prayer N'
The Churches!

For We Wrestle Not......Eph. 6:12

WRESTLING.   CATCH AS CATCH CAN STYLE.

Thirteen

Grace In The Battle!*

GRACE–GOD'S UNMERITED FAVOR

The Lord is my light and my salvation; whom shall I fear? The Lord is the strength of my life; of whom shall I be afraid? When the wicked, even mine enemies and my foes, came upon me to eat of my flesh, they stumbled and fell. Though an host should encamp against me, my heart shall not fear: though war should rise against me, in this will I be confident. **Psalms 27: 1-3**

No weapon that is formed against thee shall prosper; and every tongue that shall rise against thee in judgment thou shall condemn. This is the heritage of the servants of the Lord, and their righteousness is of me, saith the Lord.

Isaiah 54: 17

Seek ye the Lord while he may be found, call ye upon him while he is near: let the wicked forsake his way, and the unrighteous man his thoughts:

and let him return unto the Lord, and he will have mercy upon him; and to our God, for he will abundantly pardon.   **Isaiah 55: 6-7**
And the God of peace shall bruise Satan under your feet shortly. The GRACE of our Lord Jesus Christ be with you. Amen.   **Romans 16: 20**

Don't Fear; Face the Grace!

So often, we're afraid of the unknown outcomes in the traumatic experiences that are hurled against us. As a result of being unknowledgeable of the origins and the reasons for the horrendous attacks against me, I've found myself, most unsettled!

The females of my immediate family, were very emotional, so whenever unfavorable things would take place in the family, they would sound off in response to the attack and counter-act against the culprit as a result of panic, which is a form of fear. They were usually prone to re-act, rather than to calculate their responsive actions, according to the word of God.

To offend my family was like setting off a nuclear reactor on the battle field in a war. An offender knew very shortly, that they had possibly done a bad thing to push the wrong buttons.

The inner workings of our awareness was to the likeness of professional boxing; we were counter-punchers. It doesn't matter how fast and skillful another boxer might be, whenever they get a shot off, the opponent responds almost faster than the puncher at getting their fist set to throw another punch.

They had already been hit, and sometimes knocked out, before they were even aware! Counter punching might be a good thing for a boxer; or a fighter, but you would soon discover, that you would always be found fighting or at least always fighting back, with such a mind set!

As I matured, through reading the word of God, I discovered that the reactions that I had grown accustom to, were the direct results of fear. I began to realize the actual manipulative power of fear, and how it is that fear will have you spiritually spooked and distrusting of most everyone, and of everything.

I have always been one to examine the surroundings around me. Through examing my own family's atmosphere, I could see that we were going about some things in ways that perhaps were not in the best interest, to bring about the desired results for the life that we'd planned to live in Christ.

Our family was relatively alone, living without the relationships of the extended family on both the maternal and paternal bloodlines, although my parents had come from fairly large families. I believe that we were so responsive to an attack, for fear of the fact that we were alone as a single family unit. Other family either lived too far away from us, or it seemed to us that they just simply were not interested in us.

We were never blessed with the company or the presence of relatives, growing up around us to assure the bond of family living. We never had other relative's houses that we could go to spend the weekend or to spend the night with any of their children. Believe me, we were alone.

We made friends at school and in the neighborhood, and we had the extended family of the church, who were not always real in their dealings with us, but, they were there.

Our parents didn't believe in allowing us to spend the night at the homes of other people who were not our family members anyway, so we were left to make the better connections with each other. There were seven siblings living in the house, and we had a good time amongst ourselves.

We're not often perceptive of the fact that people have been alone in their life for any period of time, or that they may be feeling that they are alone daily. Although they are surrounded by scores of people, doesn't mean that their behavior is easily understood.

Rather than to live on the love and peace of life, which is the grace of God; most people prefer to exist on their skills of survival. Though we were faithful members of the church, had family prayer, always taught and encouraged to bless our meals, thanking God for the provisions, we weren't always aware that God was in the midst of situations with us.

We felt that we were being punished and persecuted, just for being alive and for being born to the family of which we had no choice in the matter. It was very difficult being disliked just because others felt like it. Other families in the neighborhood and in the church would pick at us, and talk about our family, pushing the painful knives of rejection in even further than they had been already.

We were literally forced into fist fights at the church, in the neighborhood, and at school, just for being someone that others did not like. I really doubt whether our family could even be qualified as a dysfunctional family? I know for sure, that Satan did not want us to survive the attacks of the people who surrounded us, but he lost that battle! We made it by the grace of God!

I am crucified with Christ: nevertheless I live; yet not I, but Christ liveth in me: and the life which I now live in the flesh I live by the faith of the son of God, who loved me, and gave himself for me. I do not

frustrate the grace of God: for if righteousness come by the law, then Christ is dead in vain.
    Bold italics added   Galatians 2: 20-21
(Or Christ died in vain, William Thompson Jr.)

The greater frustrations in the middle of any battle, are the feelings of being inferior to the attack. Whenever we feel impotent to successfully fight back, or to ward of the offending attack of the enemy, it is possible to begin to feel useless to the cause of living. We frustrate the grace of God; in these situations, whenever we overlook the presence of God's grace in the midst of our battles.

You could actually be strong and yet be impotent to exercise the strength that has been given to you for the fact of believing that you are weak. Whenever you determine in your own mind that you are weak, it becomes a reality.

Fear magnifies weaknesses and inabilities to perform at any rate, for any reason. Simple oppositions can evolve into the likes of an all out war against you, if you allow yourself to focus on the fight or even the fighter, rather than to focus on your faith.

Many people are determined to finish the fight, for the reason that they feel that their opponent would only be left to return at a later date to finish what they had started against them, ensuring defeat the next time. If ever you feel, that you are truly too weak to handle the fight against you, find someone in the body of Christ that is stronger than you, to stand with you in prayer, to defeat the enemy.

We then that are strong ought to bear the infirmities of the weak, and not to please ourselves.
                                    Romans 15:1

I have emerged victoriously, through the mercy of God, to encourage those who may feel that there is no way out of the battle, to realize the actual power of grace, and the grace in the power of God. Most people only refer to the grace of God as being the strength of salvation only, but there is a greater grace that has been set and released for us after we have been saved!

Whenever we ask God to help us, He will not do so because of pity, feeling sorry for us, or because He feels that we are too inadequate to help ourselves, He helps us because He already knows that we are incapable to win our own battles and to conquer our challenges without His provisions initially set in place. You must always remember that God has got a design with you in mind!

Do you really believe that God would get the glory out of watching the enemy stomp you to the ground, to annihilate the total existence of your faith in God?

Never develop the loser's mentality, feeling that it is the Lord's purpose for your life, if you never conquer a battle. Lately I've heard ministers preaching to the people in the congregation; that, "GOD WANTED THEM TO FAIL!"; as if God needs mankind to be repeat offenders to the cause of Christ. Ever since man fell in the garden, it has been God that put a cushion under mankind by His undenying grace. God needs for us to succeed!

As it is written, For thy sake we are killed all the day long; we are accounted as sheep for the slaughter. Nay, in all these things we are more than conquerors through him that loved us.

Romans 8: 36-37

The thief cometh not, but for to steal, and to kill, and to destroy: I am come that they might have life, and that they might have it more abundantly. I am the good shepherd: the good shepherd giveth his life for the sheep.

St. John 10: 10-11

You've got to have confidence in the sacrifice of Jesus Christ, and believe that God is on your side. You can trust and depend on Jesus always, no matter what your circumstances may be.

Fear forces you to run for cover, but I was always taught that a dog couldn't even chase you unless you ran! The devastation of fear, will literally have you running when there is nothing and no one even chasing you. Whenever we allow ourselves to fear, we open the door for every emotion to be stirred and exploited by the enemy. The enemy would love for you to be caught bundled up in a corner crying your eyes out, for reasons that may not even be clear to you.

Through most threats of major storm disasters, for the sake of fear, many people will almost empty their bank accounts, and charge their credit cards to the maximum, preparing for the disaster, as a result of panic.

Over and over again, I have seen many people with egg all over their faces, when what they feared didn't happen! Don't you remember the Y2K scare; at the entrance of the new millennium; in the year 2000? Probably 80% of the world braced themselves for a Twilight Zone like disaster to happen when the world's computer systems would fail.

Many who were supposed believers, panicked and gave in to the hype and the hoopla of the news media. Most either forgot, or either they failed to face the grace of God! Some still have the rationings in the basements of their homes, and locked away in storage facilities.

What shall we then say to these things? If God be for us, who can be against us? He that spared not his own son, but delivered him up for us all, how shall he not with him also freely give us all things? Who shall lay anything to the charge of

God's elect? It is God that justifieth. Who is he
that condemeth? It is Christ that died, yea rather,
that is risen again, who is even at the right hand
of God, who also maketh intercession for us. Who
shall separate us from the love of Christ? Shall
tribulation, or distress, or persecution, or famine,
or nakedness, or peril, or sword? For I am
persuaded, that neither death, nor life, nor angels,
nor principalities, nor powers, nor things present,
nor things to come. Nor height, nor depth, nor
any other creature, shall be able to separate us
from the love of God, which is in Christ Jesus
our Lord.
                          Romans 8: 31-35, 38-39

Since God is for us, who or what could even be successful
being against us? Nothing and no one is greater that our God!
Therefore we have absolutely nothing and no one to fear.

A Winner From the Start!

*I*n our Western; English speaking culture, we read, write
and even understand from the left of the page to the right side,
and from the top of the page down to the bottom. In other
words, the only comprehensible explanation for us is to start at
the beginning and to proceed on to the finishing end, in forward
progress. That's usually all we need to understand.

We relate to starting from the top and going down to the
bottom. We don't dive in to a swimming pool, a lake, or the
ocean from the bottom of the deep because it's impossible. We
must enter in at the surface, on top of the water and make our
decent to the bottom no matter how deep we desire to go.

Upon entering most buildings, we are accustomed to
entering through the front door and moving on towards the

back of the room when necessary. Sometimes, we enter at the front door entrance and are required to exit at the rear. So, where we are allowed to enter, is not even the same place that we are given as an exit. Then on the other hand there is one way in and only, the same one way out.

God; on the other hand, He starts from the finish, and completes the finish the moment He starts. God establishes the bottom in an effort for the top to have a place to rest. He completes the story before He ever allows it to be written or read. Jesus fought the battle of the crucifixion, because He had already won it! He never had to win! *(Revelation 5)*

God is not like us, but, we are to be like Him; if we can believe that we are, according to the word of God. We as people, just need to know that our likeness to God is spiritual and that it is not attributed to our natural forms in any way.

Because of the grace of God; your battle is already finished even before an attack could ever be levied against you, even before a single punch could be thrown at you. The problem is that we are so in love with life and living in this world, that we are threatened and alarmed at any sign of opposition that might endanger our livelihood and possibly end our lives here on the earth. We've been spooked with the idea of death, even though we refuse to make the necessary preparations to face dying.

As dreadful as it may be, we know that a war means death for someone, and it often means death for many! We are in a spiritual War! Instinct tells our survival skills, to step up to the home-plate to bat for our lives, that we might win another chance to remain alive and in the land of the living.

We fear, as if death itself is the uncertainty, but it is living that is uncertain in that we never know what being alive will bring to us from day to day. Death is coming to everyone for sure; all you have to do is just keep on living! You will participate when the time comes for you to die!

In order to win in the end; you have got to develop the conquering behavior of being a winner, right now. It is ordained of God, that we know the victory of defeat over every enemy in our lives. No enemy, or weapon will ever be excused to pass through God's hand of protection, and successfully attack you and conquer you, as long as you remain under the grace of God.

> *No weapon that is formed against thee shall prosper; and every tongue that shall rise against thee in judgment thou shall condemn. This is the heritage of the servants of the Lord, and their righteousness is of me, saith the Lord.*
>
> Isaiah 54: 17

The only reason the enemy is winning in the lives of the people of the church, is simply because they believe in their minds, that they are losing a battle that literally has already been won through Jesus Christ.

I have ministered to so many people who will not grasp the reality of the fact, that Jesus has done it already, alike the Jews in the book of St. John; they still seek a sign. They want God to perform another miracle so that they can see something even more incredible than what has been recorded in the books of the bible.

Most people who claim to be believers, don't really want to possess the power of the Holy Ghost to the point of being powerful themselves, rather they desire to witness the power of God on open display before their own eyes, working through someone else.

I am determined to be a direct docking station for the power of God, so powerful that every miracle and blessing that could possibly ever flow through me, for the benefit of the body of Christ, will be ever present and available through me at every need! I am a conduit of the powerful movement of the spirit of God.

People desire to be, what God has already ordained for them to be! They are already whatever they desire to be in the Lord, but it has not been revealed, for reason of the fact that the warfare to which they have been thrusted into, has served the purpose of taking away their rational thinking, simply because they are focusing on being the victim, and never the victory over the warfare!

Somehow, we are triggered in our thought process to believe that we need to keep our focus on every move of the enemy, even though we often cannot see him, and neither are we aware of the hidden places of his entrenchment? We give away the precious moments of our thinking capacity to think on those things that are causing us pain, and all of the negative things that hinder our faith. That which may indeed be hidden from us, is never hidden from the all seeing eyes of the Lord, and they could never escape the presence of God, so give it to the Lord and let Him work it out for you. *(Philippians 4: 8-9)*

Gracefully Thinking Grateful!

The manner in which we allow our thoughts to flow through our minds, ought to be graceful. Our minds really ought to work in the like manner of the movement of the spirit of God, that has the power to transcend all boundaries and barriers. Turn on the fluidity of swiftly passing thoughts on through and out of your mind, at any given moment of the day or the night. Absolutely nothing and no one have the power to stop the thought process of your mind, as long as you have a mind to think on the Lord.

In any passage way, as long as the opening is clear of trash, filth, and junky clutter, whatever is supposed to flow through can and will do so without any hindrances. The mind of any believer, should never be clogged with worries and the concerns of spiritual warfare, because it diminishes the ability to properly exercise faith to the maximum potential. Our faith must always be in the optimal working order to reach up into the throne room of the grace of God to retrieve the provisions of God, and to keep us gratefully thinking on the goodness of the Lord.

It's up to every individual to be sure that the arteries of the mind are not clogged. Whenever the arteries of the heart get clogged, usually a heart attack follows. You may not have considered the fact that the mind also has an attack, whenever the arteries of the mind get clogged. The mind has a tendency to blow out of shape and out of the proper mental order.

All heart attacks are not fatal, or even permanently debilitating. So just because you didn't lose the total control of your thinking capacity, that doesn't suggest that you are ok to think on the things that don't bring glory to the name of the Lord, and peace to your mind.

Thou wilt keep him in perfect peace, whose mind is stayed on thee, because he trusteth in thee. Trust ye in the Lord forever: for the Lord JE-HO-VAH is everlasting strength.

Isaiah 26: 3-4

Let the wicked forsake his way, and the unrighteous man his thoughts: and let him return unto the Lord, and he will have mercy

upon him; and to our God, for he will abundantly pardon. For my thoughts are not your thoughts, neither are your ways my ways, saith the Lord. For as the heavens are higher than the earth, so are my ways higher than your ways, and my thoughts than your than your thoughts.
Isaiah 55: 7-9

You just can't allow yourself to think anyway that you choose, because no one knows what you're going through. I have been through things that I could not successfully articulate to any of my friends, even in the ministry. But by the grace of God, He never allowed me to charge God foolishly in my thinking.

Many times the devil wanted me to think that God hated me for things that I had done in the past. But, I always remembered the grace of God, in that He had already forgiven me and washed those things away, even from the bondage of the memory of my past. With God; it is as if it never even happened! So often I had to battle that kind of thinking, even based on prior erroneous teaching about sin and God's ability to forgive sin.

As long as I focused on the sins of the past, I had no peace, and for certain I had no victory over my past. But whenever I began to think on what God has done for us, in the person of Jesus Christ; immediately I began to have peace of mind, and I began to experience a quieting in my spirit. Right then and there, I knew that I had the victory and an even greater power to defeat the enemy from now on! Glory to God!

The greater detriment of my plight, was that I allowed the warfare against me to linger too long before deciding to praise and to worship the Lord. Many times other people honestly can't help you, but for the better part, most others could care less about you and what you are going through. It doesn't matter to them whether you sink or swim, live or die, succeed or fail, or even if you disappeared from the face of the earth.

So many people have others that they have endeared to their hearts, for something that that person had done for them sometime back in the past. We frequently hear the statement made; *"I will never forget what they did for me!"* The things that they did, are things that other people could have likewise done, if they would have?

We have a natural tendency to be grateful for the things that were done for us by people that we can see, while we have a problem or just simply choose not to thank the Lord Jesus whom we cannot see; for all of the things that He has done for us! Somehow we overlook being grateful to the Lord!

To neglect the grace of God, is to forsake the victory of the win. God who looks through the portals of time, He knows the joy of being victorious, winning the battle against any enemy.

It stinks in the nostrils of God, whenever we determine in our hearts, to identify with the natural flesh of man, as being the provider of the things that we needed the most, rather than to identify with God who is a spirit; but, He provided those things for us before we ever even came to the earth.

The breath that we breathe, is already available for us right out in mid-air, it was not placed hear by any man or any one group of people, anywhere!

Did anyone ever tell you that God is a provider? Well, He is the provider of the things that are necessary for us to live from day to day. Should you ever need to survive, as the result of any tragic circumstances, you would discover that God had already provided the substance that you needed.

Undeserved Blessings!

*M*aybe you struggle to understand just how it could be possible for the Lord to provide in such adverse situations, as in the times when we'd suffered horrendous attacks from many diverse sources and directions? Most people choose to ask the questions; *"If God loves me, then why would He allow these things to happen to me?"*

It is understandable, that confusion about pain may cause you to be momentarily stunned. Is it not necessarily the norm to think through the pain of suffering for most people. However, I am determined to speak to the sheepfold of the body of Christ. It is more than just a probability, that I was asking the wrong question, in the time of a tragic situation, it was a reality.

Mary and Martha, the sisters of Lazarus both said to Jesus very painfully; *"If you had been hear, our brother Lazarus had not died!"* They spoke those words in direct reflection of their pain. It is very clear to us as we read the word of God, that they were in severe pain at the loss of their brother, but also they were feeling that they had been denied the help of the Lord Jesus Christ, in whom they had a very close and personal relationship.

They were very passionate about their feelings because Lazarus died! But, what they might have missed for sure, was the fact that they did not even know the end of the story! They only wanted Jesus to heal Lazarus so that he would not die. But, God had a greater plan which carried a more exceeding weight in Glory. He allowed Lazarus to die and to even be buried in a grave.

Whenever a person has been buried in their grave, it is understood to be over completely; all hope is gone, and every possibility of any kind of a change in the situation has concluded in grave disappointment and grief.

For a brief moment, Martha spoke through her pain remembering who Jesus is, she said to Him; *"I know that even now whatever you ask of the Father, that He will give it to you!"* Martha stepped away from her pain just briefly enough to FACE THE GRACE OF GOD.

It's not about how long you and I, may live here upon the earth; it's all about the fact that Jesus is alive and well and that He is alive forever more. The power of His grace, is ever present before the cries of the people of God. We must not worry that the warfare may take too great hold of us, even too much for the Lord to deliver us from any gripping defeat.

Most shepherds would have turned and walk away from the presence of the people, had they gone to see about an individual and the family members said that you had just showed up too late, and that it was probably your fault that their loved one had just died! I don't know that most of us today would have been focused enough to follow through with the greater miracle that God had already provided.

Don't get me wrong, healing is great and it would have been great for Lazarus. By the way; do you think for one moment that death hurt Lazarus any more than the sickness in which he had been suffering?..........................

No; I don't think so at all, because death as we understand it, is definitely the end of suffering from pain and sickness. In a sense, death was a form of healing for the sickness that had gripped the body of Lazarus.

Healing was good, but resurrection was an even greater exploit and show of the Lord's grace in love! Mary and Martha; preferred the healing of their sick brother, but God preferred to give Lazarus brand new life all over again; and to use Lazarus' resurrection to move the doubters and the unbelievers, to believe on the Lord Jesus Christ; *and it worked!*

You might want to consider the fact that they didn't even deserve that kind of a blessing from the Lord, because He is God; and God is sovereign!

God wasn't wrong in that He allowed Lazarus to die, any more than He was when He allowed our loved ones to leave the presence of this world. Don't ever neglect to think of the fact that many of the mourners that stood by, had also lost loved ones, that would never be resurrected until the rapture, if they believed God, and confessed Christ.

Perhaps now you could rethink your position about what you feel that God has allowed to come upon you, and begin to thank Him for all that He has not allowed to come upon you?

As a member in the body of Christ; what have you allowed to come upon your church, as a result of never interceding for the body of Christ? Do you even have a clue of the things that have slipped through the cracks, since you failed to pray for the body of Christ? How many people have died in the church that you never would even pray for? How many members in the body of Christ have suffered the loss of their homes and their possessions, as a result of the fact that you are not dedicated to prayer?

How many church doors have closed since you slept and filled your own belly with fine dining, and cared for the needs of your own house, and paid the utilities for your residence, exclusively?

Since you have such a problem with the amount of money the church might receive, was it also your better judgment to only give the church a very minimal offering, even in light of the fact that the cost for living is at an all time high? How many other families has your church been able to assist?

Perhaps you thanked God for your job, in that your company has not had to close the doors; but you never see the need to pray for the other people that have been laid off of their jobs indefinitely?

Maybe you have been like other members of the church who drive nice cars, but whenever they saw me walking, they made sure that they blew the horn and waved to me, while they yelled out my name, but they kept on driving wherever they were going? Maybe they were in a hurry to get to wherever they were going, or maybe that fact is that they did not want me to ride in their car? Only God Knows!

Grace Never Stops!

I'd had very negative experiences in the building where our church was located. I had the neighbor from hell, docked next door to the church, that had her business in that same shopping center for about 2 years prior to us coming there or maybe even longer. Whenever I went to the shopping center to enquire about moving the church into the shopping center, I went into her business to meet and to greet this particular tenant.

Upon meeting her for the first time, she was quite approach-

able and kind. We spoke for a few moments about the ownership and the tenants in the strip center. She asked me what we
were bringing to the center, and I told her that it was a church.
She mentioned to me that she was a Christian and that she was
a member of one of the more popular churches in the metroplex;
but then she said in an almost whispering tone of voice, that
she did not want another church next to her business. I heard
her, and I assured her that we would not be disturbing her business, and that we only came to have church.

I told her that we did believe in making a joyful noise unto
the Lord. Not just noise; but joyful noise unto the Lord! I
parted and went on to establish the church in the strip center.

We had a previous situation of real-estate fraud while
attempting to acquire another property for our church. We
hired an attorney and filed a law suit to get back the money
that we had sank into the property.

During the process, the city division gave me the blues
over changing the usage of the building, the parking, the plans
for seating the people, and anything else that they could think
of.

After a 6-month grueling battle with the city we knew
that we would not be successful at placing our church in that
building. Upon choosing to move on, we lost the greater
following of the people who had appeared to be excited about
our ministry, but as we moved on God blessed us tremendously.

We shared the sanctuary with three different churches
before finding this building, so you should know that we were
excited to finally find a place for our ministry to call our own
place of worship. The city inspectors; all of them; signed off
on their inspections all in the same day, and by the weekend of
the next week we were having church in that building.

As we began to have our services, we also began to experience problems with our neighbor just next door to the church. We moved the Hammond organ and the drums, and the piece of a PA-system that we had into the building along with about fifty borrowed chairs.

Going forward with the church seemed to anger the woman next-door to the church, in a way that was definitely demonically influenced. None but the devil; could wage a war on the church like that, and cause that much grief. I bent over backwards to work with her even whenever she would open the door to the church or begin beating on the walls, saying that we were disturbing her with our services.

If at anytime, I might have personally felt that we may have gotten a little loud on a Wednesday evening Mid-week service, I would always apologize and listen to her sarcastic remarks about our service. The nicer I tried to be to her, the angrier she became.

We were in the building working on one particular summer day, my children were there with me and they were having a good time, until she yanked the door open and begin to yell at myself and my children as if she had lost all reasoning of her sober mind. You might have even thought that she was drunk or high on some type of a drug.

I was not going to tolerate her yelling at my children, as if they were a bunch of dogs or animals in the zoo. So, I responded and took charge of the situation very quickly, but still I made an attempt to be as peaceful as possible. Boy; that did it for her, I guess that meant war!

The following week, during our mid-week service, we were in the midst of praise and worship, singing *"Jesus is the light of the world!"* And of course we were putting on the praise kind of heavy. She burst through the door right in the middle of the service began yelling; *"That's Too Loud!" "You Don't Have To Play That Organ Like That!"*

I kept on playing the organ and I motioned for someone else to handle her and to remove her from our service, but out of all of the people who wanted to be in charge of the different things in the church, absolutely no one would move to get control of this woman. She walked over to me and knocked my hands off of the keys on the organ while I was still playing the song that we were singing!

I leaped from the organ and began to rebuke her in the name of Jesus; and I told her to never ever walk up in the midst of our service and show that kind of disrespect ever again. She tried to cause me to put my hands on her but I never touched her, she acted as if she wanted to fight me. She had already set the stage for an out of control confrontation; but the grace of God held me and kept me from shaming the name of Christ.

We won that battle in the name of Jesus; but the war was just beginning to heat up. She began calling the landlord on the church to cause us problems. Each time that she would call on us, the landlord would respond to her complaints, and he would warn us that actions would be taken against us if the problems persisted. He never once tried to hear our side of the issues citing the fact that she had a long lease with the company and they did not want to upset her.

She began parking her cars in front of the church and allowing her customers to park in the front of the church even on the days that we would have our services. Our people had to park a little further away from the doorway to the entrance of the church.

She began confronting the people of the church; she would

stare them down as if she were Mike Tyson, or Muhammad Ali! As we would have sidewalk sales and car washes to bring in the money for the church, she would tell her customers not to associate or to participate with whatever we were doing.

This woman, in my own opinion, she was FULL-GROWN EVIL! She wasn't missing a beat on causing the church as many problems as possible. Don't forget that she told me that she was a member of a Christian church that was supposed to have been spirit filled?

She started calling the police on our services, of which the first few times fizzled out like a "Fourth of July" dud.

We began putting down carpet, and hanging heavy curtains and we even went to Sam's Wholesale and bought cushioned chairs for the sanctuary as an attempt to muffle the sound, but there was not going to be any pleasing the situation. This was the work of the devil!

She is close friends with the postman that delivered the mail to us, and she began bothering our mail delivery, which is a crime if it can be proven. The only problem was that no one was willing to listen to our complaints, as if people in America don't commit crimes against the church.

Other pastors treated my complaints about the woman next door to the church, as a make believe story right out of WonderLand. They didn't seem to believe me, and they didn't express a desire to join me in prayer over the situation. I later found that some of the pastors wanted me to deny the gift and the calling of the prophetic on my life! If I would take a more inferior role to them, they would help me; so rather, they sort of gloated at the severity of the warfare against our church.

February 7, 2003; we had our first praise and worship explosion, where we invited other churches to come with their praise teams and do nothing but worship the Lord with us, in song to our Lord.

The same day of this event, we had carpet installed in the sanctuary, which this person watched all day as we went forth to finish out the place for worshipping. Her business hours for closing were @ 7:00 pm. However, she stayed over because of the progressive working going on, and a large number of people began to gather for the service, which was on a Friday evening.

She waited until about 9:00 pm the same evening of our service, and began calling the police complaining about noise. The police came out the first time that night, and stepped right up in the service, as if we were a bunch of criminals, or as if we were having some type of wild party, where people were hanging on the outside with their alcoholic beverages or drugs.

A few of the members spoke to the police and they asked us to lower the sound in a 2,900 square foot room that had been filled to the capacity with believers praising the Lord in the beauty of holiness.

Believe me the police knew the difference whenever they approached the building, between people having church and people having a party. As a matter of the fact, there was a club just up the sidewalk from the church, of which by the way no one had ever called the police on the club! *Now isn't that amazing!*

She wasn't satisfied with the actions of the police, so she waited until they left the premises, and as soon as we got cranked up again she called the police again, and this time they came demanding to see me so that they could write me a citation for noise, and they did!

I told the police, that if we were going to be cited for having church, that they might as well get ready to return because we were going to raise it high. Of course they did not return that night. Out of about 15-25 times of having the police called on the church whenever we would have our services, that was the only citation that was ever written.

Several of the officers who responded to the call against the church, reported to us that she cursed them and threatened to bring charges against them for not citing the church for a disturbance. But it was the officer's job to determine whether or not a crime had been committed. Most of the officers who responded to the calls would often apologize to us for such major distractions.

I set the ticket for court, because the citation carried a fine of $385; if found guilty as charged; we were not guilty of making noise, we were having church. Just what is to be expected from about 200 plus people in a service making a joyful noise unto the Lord? We don't apologize that we are not of the more silent sectors of those who claim to be Christians.

It is our philosophy that we didn't play with sin and our sinful ways, therefore we will never play around with praise and the worship of our God. We knew how to do this and not cause an infringement upon anyone else's right to worship whatever it is that they choose to worship.

There is also a cult located in the strip center, who by the way has moved into the unit just next door to the rowdy neighbor where our church had been located, but they did not use instruments or a PA-system equal or even compatible to the system that we used. She has never called the police on the cult!

We found that the officer that wrote the ticket that night, wrote a citation for DISORDERLY CONDUCT; which meant that in some way or another, we had to have been outside of the building disturbing the peace. This was a false accusation against the church, because we were never disorderly.

It is evident that we disturbed the devil and his followers greatly that evening through worshipping the Lord!

Here is the grace of God working through that situation. Each time that citation had come up on the docket for a court hearing, our individual case would have to be reset for a number of reasons. The case was literally reset 5 times.

Five is the number of God's grace. On five occasions the case could not even be heard; I believe they wanted to hear the case but they couldn't. The grace of God will provide a defense for you when you don't even have any one to defend you in a court of the law. We never had any of the pastors that were present in the service that night, to stand with us in court. They left us that time also, but God had a hand on the court and the judge!

The very first judge to hear the case; asked me to explain the details to what had happened on the night in question. He was sure of himself, that the situation had taken place at a residence. He thought that we were having church in our home and had gotten out of hand and caused a disturbance to our neighbors.

He asked me on three occasions if we *lived* at the location of the church. I explained to him that this was a building that had been inspected and passed by the city. I said to him; "Your Honor; we were having church!"

He dropped his head and looked down at the desk of the bench where he was seated, and said to me; "Pastor Thompson; "I'm sorry that this happened; we will reset this case for a hearing at a later date!" Through an inside source who worked at the court house, we were told that this particular judge told the officers in the area where the church was located, not to ever write anymore citations against the church.

The officers told me, that anytime the woman called next door to the church, that they were required by the law to respond to the call and come out to the location. But we never received another citation even though they were called on many occasions and did respond! There is a record of these calls at the city of Fort Worth, this story is no lie!

I was embarrassed as the leader and the shepherd of the house of God; about receiving a citation in the presence of all of my guest, of which none of them seemed to understand how a citation could be written against SWC for having church on the inside of the sanctuary, which is designed for that purpose alone. I have been in the church all of my natural life, and I had been a witness to certain situations that might have warranted having the police come out to the church, but often they were never called.

We spent the better part of $2^{3/4}$ years dealing with this particular issue. More unfavorable situations took place by the way of our neighbor, that I would have had to dedicate the entire book to write about them if I had chosen to do so. Each attack that we encountered should have taken us out and shut down the operation of the church, but the grace of God always provided a way for us to stay in the building.

Grace Anyway! In God We Never Lose!

I remember the time that my church was going through financially and another pastor suggested to me that I should allow him to help me come out from under the financial pressure. I agreed to allow him to host a service at my church. He said that he had several pastors and their churches that he would be bringing over to assist my little church and to help us catch up on the lease on our building.

In the process, I spoke to several other pastors, who gave me their word that they would indeed be in attendance for the service to help my church. We had just over a month to plan for the service and to come together for the purpose of knowing just what it was that my church needed. We were on the verge of being evicted, as a matter of the fact that landlord had already filed a case against us that was pending. I believed that this pastor was genuinely going to help us to come out of the jam that we were in financially.

One of the pastors that I had asked to come, had located that building for us and he told me about it. We had been using his church for our services after their services would end on Sunday afternoon @ 2:30 pm. He agreed to be with us, but said that he would probably be late. Nevertheless I looked for him and for the rest of the people who were supposed to be coming over that Sunday evening to assist us.

On the day of the event, the pastor that asked if he could bless our church, called me to tell me that a very well known evangelist was in town and that most of the other ministers and their churches that he had asked to participate in the service were planning to attend that service, but not to worry because his word was his bond and he would be there no matter what.

As it turned out, none of the pastors or their churches showed up to assist us, not even the one pastor who said that he would be there anyway. He did not come to the service; and of course I did not even hear from him until two months after the fact. One pastor did come by the service with a $100 dollar offering of which we were most appreciative. I really wanted to give it back to him since none of the others had showed up, because what we needed was so much greater, but I also didn't want to be rude or to appear ungrateful. We needed several thousand dollars to catch us up from the rear.

Well, we went to court anyway the same week following the failed service on Thursday morning October, 2003 and the judge of course ruled against us and ordered us to vacate the premises within five days.

My daughter went to court with me at 8:30 am that day, but she had to be at work by 10:45 that same day to open the restaurant. Our name was not called on the docket until almost the last. I suggested to my daughter to go ahead and leave me at the courthouse, and I would later get a ride to her job to pick up the car. *Well, God had a plan!*

After going over the case with the judge and the landlord, we were dismissed from the court. The landlord noticed that my daughter had left the courthouse, and he determined that I needed a ride. Look at God! Mind you now, we had just lost the case before the Judge and we were given five days to be out of the building and off of the premises.

But, from the courthouse to my daughter's job, God began to work on the heart of the landlord; in that automobile. I had been unsuccessful at reaching the landlord by phone, so he took it upon himself to enquire of the situation with the church, and he asked me what he could do to help us with the situation so that we would not have to move the church. We talked and came to an agreement disregarding the decisive action of the court.*

We were given an extended grace period even though we were already three-four months behind on the payment of the lease, to come up with only a portion of the money, and the rest of the money could be brought in at a later date.

The other pastors left us thoroughly disappointed; the judge vehemently disapproved of us, but God; miraculously provided for us. God showed out! He did it anyway! The money began to come in and we met the need of the building. I posted a sign in the parking lot of the shopping strip where the church had been located that read; *"In God we win, and we never lose!"*

We wanted money to pay the bill, but God; wanted to establish a relationship between the church and the landlord, who had been just sitting on ready to have us removed from the building. I was grateful for what God had just done for us, in that He allowed the doors of the church to remain open for another miracle, deliverance, and for other souls to be saved and set free.

The Unexpected Miracle of Grace!

*B*elieve me; I am not a liar! The situation really took place against the church. Each time the police were called to the church; people would leave the ministry and never return to worship with us. Not even the visiting churches would return to share with us in worship.

Whenever people leave the church, so does their financial support. Whenever we would begin to grow again the trouble would start all over again. The property was sold un-be-knowingly to the church which meant that we had a new building landlord. He did make an attempt to handle this woman and to give the church a better opportunity at having our services, but the woman would not stop calling the police on the church.

We complained in writing to the landlord and his response was identical to the prior landlord. "The woman has a long contract with the property and we are not going to disturb her because we don't want to lose her."

We took the initiative to push on forward with the business of the church. I spoke with a number of attorneys who were always suggesting to me that the woman was within her legal right to protest against the church and that we should be especially careful not to allow her to physically engage any of us to battle with her in a fight; and of course primarily with me, as the pastor!

She approached me, on three different occasions as if to start a fight, but each time I would go inside the building or get in my car and leave. Being pastor doesn't mean that I've forgotten how to fight, by the grace of God; I never had to fight! Pastor Bill Thompson never went to jail for fighting back. I would not have been responsible had I given her the fight that she so desperately thought she wanted?

Only, Grace; stands between all of us who have learned to let Jesus fix it for us; and those persons who are locked away in jail and on death row. It's not for any goodness of my own; it's by the grace of God that I was kept with a sound mind and a determination to keep moving on.

Grace can keep you through every battle that you encounter. By grace, we've been given favor of the power of God. Rather than being left to choose from the carnal weapons of destruction; throwing blows with our fist, feet, knives and guns to handle our situations.

For though we walk in the flesh, we do not war
in the flesh: (for the weapons of our warfare are
not carnal, but mighty through God to the pulling
down of strong holds;) casting down imaginations,
and every high thing that exalteth itself against
the knowledge of God, and bringing into captivity
every thought to the obedience of Christ; and
having in a readiness to revenge all disobedience,
when your obedience is fulfilled.

II Corinthians 10: 3-6

Finally, my brethren, be strong in the Lord, and
in the power of his might. Put on the whole
armour of God, that ye may be able to stand
against the wiles of the devil. For we wrestle not
against flesh and blood, but principalities, against
powers, against the rulers of the darkness of this
world, against spiritual wickedness in high places.
Wherefore take unto you the whole armour of
God, that ye may be able to withstand in the evil
day, and having done all, to stand. Stand
therefore, having your loins girded about with
truth, and having on the breastplate of
righteousness; and your feet shod with the
preparation of the gospel of peace; above all,
taking the shield of faith, wherewith ye shall be
able to quench all the fiery darts of the wicked.
And take the helmet of salvation, and the sword
of the spirit, which is the word of God: praying
always with all prayer and supplication in the
spirit, and watching thereunto with all
perseverance and supplication for all saints;

Ephesians 6: 10-18

In short; we have to work with grace, gracefully; in order to get what grace has indeed provided for us. It is necessary that we use the tools of faith provided to win the war against the devil, and all of the individuals that agree with the evil spirit of the devil.

You can never use the devil's weapons and win the battle against him, because he knows how to use those weapons against you. Don't be deceived into thinking that you want to fight the devil on his own terms and own his own battle ground. Stand on the word of God and win from the start of the battle. Stand faithfully armored to face the challenge of the enemy knowing that whatever he uses, won't prosper.

March, 2005; we finally decided that we had enough of the drama and the merciless warfare, from the neighbor next door. Although people left the ministry, new people came that were even more supportive than many of the people that had left earlier. Through all of the warfare, we began to experience progress in many other areas.

I have learned for a truth, that you have to take the bitter with the sweet, and the good with the bad. It would be wonderful if we could always have the ups and never the downs. The laws of physics states; "What goes up must come down!" There were times whenever our church was almost filled to the capacity, but the finances of the ministry remained under attack. A lot of people don't necessarily mean that a lot of money is coming in to the ministry.

People have different ideas about the ministry based on the size of the building or the membership base. When the church is small most people believe that the pastor will take all of the money and live on it. Whenever the church is in a large building people feel that the pastor will take the money, as much as he can get away with, to live as luxurious as possible. It appears that they hardly ever believe that the money is being used for the utilities and for the facility.

Although people would walk into the rest room, and there is the essentials that a person might need, there were Kleenex-tissue, and other bathroom essentials. We kept cleaning supplies, office supplies, printing supplies, printed envelops and stationary for the ministry, somehow they seemed to forget the fact that these things don't come free.

The people could see where their money was going into the ministry, but as a result of the spiritual warfare, they were still reluctant to give to the cause of the ministry.

Again we began to struggle financially and were operating from the rear relative to our lease payments. Other ministries will assist another ministry with just so much of it's financial weight, for just so long; which is not very long at all.

The ministries that did respond to the needs of our ministry, either gave or loaned us percentage wise from 25%-48% of what we may have actually needed. So if ever we returned to request further assistance from them, we were told that we weren't lining up with the word of God, because we still hadn't come to the point of standing on our feet financially; 100%.

Once again, we were facing a day in court to be evicted because we had fallen back on our commitment to the property. This was one of the times that no matter what we tried to do absolutely nothing seemed to workout for us. We kept on praying and seeking God to help us to keep the doors of the church open, but to no avail it appears. Nevertheless we kept on believing that God would do it again.

In the midst of all of this turmoil and confusion, my wife was invited to minister for three nights, as the keynote speaker at a women's conference. That week, she developed flu like symptoms and became heavily congested in her chest. Nevertheless she spoke on "Love" and the Lord used her. I stepped in to minister to the people after the message had ended, the anointing was very heavy in the room. There were no more than 30-50 people present.

The spirit moved so richly that no body wanted to leave after the blessing of the benediction, dismissing the service. One of the persons in attendance of whom I had never seen prior to the service that night, approached me after the service had ended still speaking in tongues and blessing God, with her bible in her hand and began ministering to me.

What I am about to tell you next will bless your socks right off of your feet. We went on home feeling blessed and encouraged to go on knowing that in one way or another God would fix the small matters; that didn't seem small to us at the time.

The very next day I was shoveling dirt in the front yard of my home, when the Constable of the Sheriff's Department, drove up in his car with papers in his hand that stated that we had until 6:00 am, the next day to be out of the building or we would be forcibly removed, and that all of our equipment and property would be set out in the parking lot. He said to me, pastor you know that we do not want to do this to your church, we are just doing our job; see if you can work something out?

I went into the house to show the documents to my wife, and I left it with her and I went back out in the yard to finish spreading the dirt. After finishing the work in the yard, I went back into the house and my wife said to me, "you just can't let them come in and take all of your stuff and throw it outside for everyone to take it from us!"

This was to be the second day of the conference, and I was going to have to step in and speak, since Sharon wasn't feeling that well. We called the members of our church and decided to remove our stuff, and put in a call to the church where we were scheduled to speak, and informed them that we wouldn't be able to attend the service that night. The pastor's wife came by our church to offer her truck to us for the purpose of moving some of the things.

When she came in she could see the place in total disarray because we had begun taking the place apart, we decided to dismantle the ministry. The pastor's wife went back to the church or either she went home and began to pass the word on to the people that were to attend the service, that we were in a crisis and would not be in attendance for the service.

The little woman who ministered to me the night prior, at the end of the revival service, phoned me at the church. When I heard the phone ring at the church my first instincts were not to answer the phone. But I picked up the phone anyway, and I wasn't very pleasant when I answered the phone; because I had allowed myself to get into the flesh and begin feeling as if we had been denied the help that we needed?

I heard the woman's small voice over the phone as she said; *"Prophet?"* I answered;'Yes, what could I do for you!" I knew that I didn't recognize her voice, and I was sure that someone else was calling on the church to help them and we weren't going to be able to do it; I thought to myself! She knew that I sounded disturbed over the phone, she asked what we were doing, and I told her that we were dismantling the ministry because we had to move out.

She said to me; "Prophet, don't dismantle another thing! God has spoken to me, to give whatever you need for your ministry!" She asked me what we needed; she wanted the exact dollar amount of what we were being asked to pay. I told her the exact amount that we needed; and she said to me; "You have to be at church tonight because you have to minister to the people of God."

We stopped what we were doing; my wife had just taken

a load of things to our house, upon returning to the building I told her to sit down for a moment. I asked her; "Would you believe that God has just blessed us with every dime that we needed?" Sharon knows me; and she knew that I wouldn't lie to her about God moving for us, and neither would I be joking at a time like that. I told her that the woman of God said that she would meet us at the church.

We went on to church and we arrived just in time for the service to get started, they were entering praise and worship. We ministered as we were scheduled. Shortly following the service, the woman asked if she could escort us to the building where our church was located. We rode with her to the church and we went inside to speak with her.

She prayed for us and handed us a check for the total amount of our need, and instructed us that this was not a loan! "It's a gift!" "You do not ever have to worry about paying any of the money back, God told me to do it!"

We went on with our church and even starting our school of ministry afterwards. God blessed us with two semesters of the school before moving out of that building. The membership again flourished and diversified in terms of the attendance of the people who came from far and near. People got delivered and set free from drug addictions, and alcohol addictions, smoking cigarettes, and some were even healed of cancer.

People confessed, that they had never felt the power of God before, until they came to the SPOKEN WORD CENTER. Many people who came to the services had never been in the presence of God before. Some of them confessed that they were always told that God wasn't real. They were told that a ministry like that of my own ministry was a sham, and that they should never be found in attendance of such a spectacle.

OH, BUT IT'S REAL!!!!!!!!!!!!

No matter what you have to go through, God is there for you! The only way to get through, is to go on through! God; is so awesome in His infinite wisdom, He has provided for us even when we didn't deserve it! You can make it through every battle, through any storm, and in spite of every mountain!

Trust The Grace Of God!

For We Wrestle Not......Eph. 6:12

WRESTLING.   Catch as Catch Can Style.

Fourteen

In Your Face

Yea though I walk through the valley of the shadow of death, I will fear no evil: for thou art with me; thy rod and thy staff they comfort me. Thou preparest a table before me in the presence of mine enemies: thou anointest my head with oil; my cup runneth over. Surely goodness and mercy shall follow me all the days of my life: and I will dwell in the house of the Lord forever.

Psalms 23: 4-6

Come and See!

THE LORD IS ON MY SIDE

*H*ad it not been for the Lord; who was, and is on my side; there is no telling what my enemies would have been successful at doing to me! I have tunneled through many hard places, escaped traps that were set by people that I called friends, and I have stood the test of being lied on. I always thought that I had many friends because there were always lots of people surrounding me.

People kept me around, but, not necessarily hanging around me; for the purpose of seeking fringe benefits, if there were any?

I can truthfully say that I have always been a lover of people, especially to those persons that were in my own chosen circle of friends. Though I was careful and painstakingly selective, I was forced to realize that I only had a few real true friends. I enjoy laughter and just plain old good clean fun. I enjoy living, but, to my dismay, I learned that the same people that were laughing with me all of the time, were really laughing at me most of the time!

For some reason or another I seem to have that stamp on my forehead that gave the impression that I loved to be mistreated? I don't think that my so called friends realized that I could appreciate receiving from them to the same magnitude of which I enjoyed giving to them.

I choose to believe that the teachings of the church back in the days of my youth were not at all in error, teaching us to help one another. And neither do I believe that most of the people of the church were really listening with the intent to

342

hearken to the teachings. People listen to the teachings of the church for the purpose of entertainment and not always for the instruction to guide daily living.

I might have been one of the few persons listening on my end anyway, to the teaching that instructed us to be helpers of one another. I was so inclined towards being a helper to my brothers and sisters in the body of Christ, that I failed to realize for many years of my own life that I had been called and ordained of God to be a leader.

Until a few years ago, I continued to believe that sooner or later some of the people who were of the like teaching persuasions as myself, would remember the teachings of our former leaders and lend the support to me that they knew that I would give to them if I were in their like positions to do so.

WatchThat Friend In the Middle!

*M*any people who crossed my path, back in the day, applauded me in my face and often times they would verbally acknowledge my presence upon entering the room. Whenever I would enter the sanctuary of the church they would single me out over the PA system telling everyone that I was there, but they kept the knives in my back as soon as it was turned.

People from the inner circle would come to me to report a lie that may have been in circulation with my name attached to it and they would reveal the responsible culprit and their motives. I learned often that my good friend was also my best enemy and the good friend of the enemy that was causing me the problems.

Of course you know the drill, they would say; "Keep this between you and me", or "Just keep that under your hat!" and finally; "I'm Your Friend!" My mother raised us on a principle; "The dog that brings a bone, carries a BONE!"

We are not always aware that people are only talking to get information to take back to our enemies. There are more people that are filled with the spirit of the devil who thrive on opportunities for scandles and gossip, knowing that such behavioral patterns are usually detrimental in every possible way, rather than there are people that are truly filled with the spirit of the Lord, who seek to bring peace to the present atmosphere and glory to the name of the Lord.

I was often considered a misfit in school and even in the church. Often considered to be nothing; just a spot in creation until certain people discovered the multiple talents and skills that I have. People are usually willing to take a second look at you for the benefit of themselves.

Once it seemed as if I might just be a valuable commodity to boost any undercover scheme that certain people might have had, or to enable a motive to get more money or prestige in the church, they seemed to want me around. God has blessed me in many ways to ensure that I would be a blessing to the body of Christ.

People who are not from your inner circle will often be more apt to realize the gifts or the talents that you display and they will verbally compliment you. This usually seems to excite a spirit of envy and jealousy in the people who think of you as nothing. They seem determined that you would better serve their cause if they kept you in slavery to the bondage of their negative critism of you.

I have always had a determination to succeed; All of my

life! Although I might have allowed certain people to stop me from doing certain things, afterwards, I cited those things to be both very miner and unimportant. The things that were indeed important to me that were not in error to the word of God, I made it my business not to allow anyone to stop me!

Believe me, I could write another book about hinderances and the people who set themselves as stumbling blocks in my life to thwart my plans for success. But, to their own surprise, I'm still going on in the name of Jesus! By the grace of God I'm still here!

I'm not crying the victim here, because, I don't feel unique in that maybe something happened to me that has never happened to anyone else.

Judas Iscariot, kissed the face of Jesus and delivered Him to the Roman captors for a little money that he later did not even want. He threw it away! Many of us have discovered and are willing to admit that since we have walked into the callings of our ministries, we all have also had a Judas who showed up in our lives as well.

That friend in the middle is the most dangerous to your welfare whenever they are proven to be your enemy! Because, they are the persons that you may feel most confident to share your heart with. Just because people look at you in your eyes while you talk to them, doesn't mean that they are genuinely caring of you. They hear you and they can usually repeat what you have said to them. But, more often than what is truly comfortable, you may find yourself asking the question; "Why did I give them all of that information?"

I'm most effectionately referred to as "Bro. Bill" by most people who know me, and those who have known me on a more personal basis, refer to me as "Bill." Hearing my name in the middle of a conversation, I learned just how popular my name was? A couple of people were having a conversation about something that they had heard concerning me, in my presence, and did not even know who I was! They were really dialoguing about the things that someone told them, of which I have to tell you were not even true.

I soon realized how blessed I was not to have been put into the position of the lime-light to be targeted by the POPULAR-RAZZI of the church, too soon. These things starting happening to me when I was very young in the church and in the Lord. My so-called superiors seemed to be rather intrigued with the fact that certain people of the church had taken a very negative interest in me, so I had to learn to deal with situations like this, on my own, with the Lord.

Too Confident to be Cocky!

It had often been determined by many people who really didn't know me from a personal perspective, that I am over confident or even very cocky! For the simple fact that no matter how things seem to stack up against me, I am always determined that I am going to make it no matter what!

They seem to realize that I've never gotten the message that I couldn't get beyond their hold over me? Although they may not like the fact that I will never quit, I have determined that it's their problem! They only think that they have been upset with me in the past, they will definitely blow a fuse when they see what the Lord has done with me!

I have a very present hope in the Lord. My *now*; can

never be *later;* but my later on will always become my now! Though many of the things that I believed God for right now, never seemed to manifest until at a later time, I can't afford to allow the time of the manifestation of things to push the expectation of my hope into the realm of "Maybe one Day!" I believe God! God is now; therefore everything that I believe the Lord for is also regarded as now!

The Lord is my source, I never find a reason or the strength necessary to believe that things are impossible for me to accomplish. I believe that there is nothing that God can't do, so by the same principle I believe that there is noting that God won't do, through me. It is my duty to just keep going even though people don't seem to be influenced to assist me in my endeavors.

I haven't gotten the memo from the Lord, saying for me to just hang it up because it doesn't seem likely that the people of my surroundings are going to support me in my vision.

I have found an over abundance of people who have determined to inform me that the expectations of my faith, relative to the word of God are unrealistic and way out over the ocean somewhere. Often the same people will make uncanny efforts to convince me that they, themselves are faith people.

Some feel that I should mix a little faith with a lot of my personality, and develop scemes and work them to abate people to sympathize with me and open up their finances to me, no matter what. They don't seem to care if we as men of the cloth compromise our integrity and destroy all possibilities of the faith that people have in God!

Many seem to be determined to ensure that the people believe in them whether they be holy men of God or just men of political influence in the community. They work over-time to convince a congregation that they are able to get their sons and their wayward spouses out of jail, but they skip all together every opportunity to preach and to teach to the point that those same family members would escape hell and even stop going to jail.

I am confident that teaching the word of God will keep us all, both out of jail and out of hell! The opposition has come from those who are supposed to be doing the same thing that I am doing. I've been told, that I tell the people too much, that I should leave them ignorant and to let them find what ever they need in the word of God by themselves.

My problem is that I am hooked on telling the people the truth and teaching them the mysteries of the word of God, as it has been revealed to me by the Holy Ghost. We are called to enpower the people of God for such as the times that we are living, right now.

Too many people of the church are standing at awe when situations arise in their lives, not knowing what to do. They are handicapped and impotent to effect change in their own situations through faith in God and patience. Many are teaching the word of God with the mind sets and the principles of giving just enough to keep the people coming back for more. Oftimes, that is only a fraction of the information people need to be successful in their walk with the Lord when they have left the four walls of the sanctuary of the church.

My people are destroyed for lack of knowledge: because thou hast rejected the knowledge, I will also reject thee, that thou shall be no priest to me: seeing thou hast forgotten the law of thy God, I will also forget thy children. Hosea 4: 6

I am confident that the ministry to which I have been

endowed by God, is for the benefit of the body of Christ, else the anointing never would have been given to me. It's one thing for the people to reject the knowledge that has been given to them, but it is a totally different animalistic behavior to refuse to give the knowledge to the people that has been given to us as leaders and shepherds.

It takes a very heartless individual to see that the sheep are hungry, but refuse to feed them. Although I have been victimized often as a member of the church, I can never afford to stand before the people of the Lord as a bleeding and wounded victim of religious circumstances. It doesn't do the body of Christ any good, niether does it benefit the testiment of the power of God, to carry ourselves as if we have wounds that will never heal.

I have learned that sympathy is only good when others sympathize with you, and yourself with others! When absolutely no one else besides you can feel what you feel, your sympathy is null and void to the cause, and the body of Christ. Thank God that I have discovered that I don't have to carry myself in and throughout my day, as if life will never be productively blessed for me.

Jesus came to this world to die, so He sent me here to the world to live! I choose to live; I have made a life long decision to stay alive and to live while doing so until the Lord calls me home to be with Him. As a child in the church choir we use to sing a song that said;

> Everyday with Jesus, sweeter than the day before;
> Everyday with Jesus, I love Him, more and more.
> Jesus saves and keeps me, He's the one that I adore,
> Everyday with Jesus, I love Him, more and more.

Many feel the pastor should be blessed, until he is actually being taken care of by the congregation? Many church people tend to love pastors who carry themselves as if they could careless about the people of the church. They seem to want to give their right arm to a pastor who still drink alcohol, and smoke cigarettes. People appear to prefer a pastor that is not too holy in their daily walk with God?

Pastors who seek the Lord for direction and guidance to lead the people of the church, will often come under terrible scrutiny concerning the financial gifts that they are receiving from the people of the church.

The Prepared Table!

PREPARE- To make by a special process.

*E*verybody wants to be appreciated for what they do, although in the church many people do things grudgingly, especially when those things are done for the pastor. People stretch their hands to aid the pastor with an eyebrow raised, expecting the pastor to sign their life away, with the expectations that they will lighten up on the message of the gospel.

The attitude at best is that of saying; whenever you catch me in the wrong from now on, don't forget what I've done for you? Turn in the opposite direction of me when you find me to be in error.

Many project themselves as being the one who spreads the table for the pastor and their families, which is one of the more stressful and degrading attitudes for any pastor to have to deal with in the ministry.

Take a little time to get a clear understanding about the meaning of the *"Prepared Table."* In this always and forever hungry society of this western hemisphere, when the average person even hear of a prepared table, their minds usually leap to the spread of a banquet, breakfast, lunch, or a dinner table.

Food and dining is what seems to capture the focus of the average person. Whether people are chronic dieters or gross over eaters, the thought process relating to the table is basically the same.

I concede to show you that perhaps we have missed what the Lord is saying to us, whenever the reference is made to the prepared table. People of God, there are so many different tables to be taken into consideration.

FIRSTLY: ask yourself if God would only be concerned with your appetite? What makes you to believe, that God's ultimate concern for you is your gut?

Perhaps the very reason that the average American is over-weight is because they feel that the number one reason to even be employed is for the purpose of being able to put a meal on the table. While there is a very significant difference between good food and bad food, from this moment on remove food from the top of your list of necessary things regarding this reading material.

God has always provided food for the people of the earth. In the garden of Eden, of the things first mentioned to Adam, were the foods that he would be allowed to partake of and eat in the garden. The one thing that God is sure that you and I could not live without is food. Good Food! God is concerned about our health, so in His infinite wisdom; He knows better than we do , that we can't eat bad food and have good health.

David said; "THOU PREPAREST A TABLE BEFORE ME IN THE PRESENCE OF MY ENEMIES."

Notice that he did not say which table was being prepared.

The fact is that many of your enemies are not trying to stop you from eating, perhaps they are trying to prevent you from successfully bringing your next major business idea to the table, where all of the financial heavy hitters are seated?

I intend to show you that you are already seated at the table of success. The real problem is not your enemies, it is however, your lack of spiritual perception, and your determination to continue to look in the wrong direction on a consistent basis.

Stop looking at your enemies! As I have stated earlier in this book, the enemy of all of the children of the Lord will have us looking in the direction of each other, suspecting one another of being the enemy. Allow me to repeat my statement of conviction on the matter; The devil is <u>OUR</u> enemy! Even the persons that you have found yourselves distrusting for whatever the reason, the devil is their enemy also!

So even though we may have been, or though we yet may be skeptical of certain people, we are to be assured of the fact that the devil is certainly the enemy that would love an opportunity to over-throw our prepared table, if it were possible.

The deception of the enemy will have us focusing on the wrong individual and in the wrong direction while he totally destroys our possibilities of success in life.

Has it ever appealed to you that certain people were attempting to write you off and to count you out of the inner success of your surroundings?

"Table of Contents."

*F*rom the Introduction, to the Conclusion of the story

of your life, it has already been written and completed by the Lord.

You need to understand the fact that God did not allow the help of anyone else to assist in writing the story of your life, so the final say on whatever your life will be has already been given. If you look deeply enough into the story of your own life you will find these two powerful words sealing the facts of the history of your life; you will find already written and eternally sealed into place, the words; "The End."

The story of my life is already complete! Every chapter of my life had already been written without the consent of any person on the face of the earth. God is not worried about anyone desiring to see me fail. I have discovered that God is not pacing the floors of heaven, and ordering troops of angels to come from heaven to watch over me because the enemies of what might be perceived as my success, are about to change the story of my life.

There is not a pen, a pencil, or a computer to change the story of my life! The written table of contents, in the story of my life has already been completed. I choose to live the story of my own life! The success of my life has been written into the details of my own story!

Others have tried desperately, to get me to live according to their stories that they had written for my life, and have become gravely dissapointed with me as a result of not conforming to their wishes for my life! If they had it their way, I might already be in a grave with a LARGE TOMB STONE? I can imagine that some might have even visualized one of the largest funerals in the history of the DFW Metro-plex area; with me as the guest of honor; or dis-honor?

I can't think of many who would have planned for me to

have been extremely successful. Else they themselves would be successful and they would have put forth the efforts to assure my success.

I could write a list of the people who would like for me to succeed as long as they are in control of the success and could reap the benefits and take the credit for any ability that they may cite as note worthy, and capable of leading the way of success for me. But, because I know that that wouldn't even be necessary, I will purposefully omit to do so.

God is the only responsible sourse of my success; all that I am, is all because of Him!

"Communion Table"

*Y*ou might be surprised to know of the people who feel that they are capable of preventing you from having sweet communion with God. Some people have been refused the communion service in the churches, because someone else felt that they were unworthy to receive.

You need always to be the only person concerned with how you partake of the Lord's Supper. When you partake of the Lord's supper in sin, the consequences are against you and no one else.

The interjection of partaking the Lord's supper in a worship service, was for the purpose of opening up the doorway to your understanding. There seems to be nothing more sacred and holy during the worship service, than to see the Communion Table adorned and decked as if the Lord Jesus Christ is coming in to the service to sit at the table to dine with the saints.

Have you ever looked at the word communion? Look at-

Come-Union! Or come and unite with me; and I urge you to never see it as if the Lord is saying to only have a <u>common-union</u> with other people of the local church! The table is to be perceived as an already prepared place for this union to take place. Long before anyone else could see that you were moving in the direction of communion with the Lord, God had already prepared the table just for you to come-union with Him.

If you know of the beauty of the communion table in the worship service as I do myself, then you can imagine the beauty of communing with God, one on one. The table is set with your name in place at the exact seat for you, at a table that no one else can approach but you. As you dine and sup with Lord, the Holy Ghost will wait on your table. He will serve you at the table.

The saints used to sing a song during the testimony service which said; "COME ON OVER HERE, THE TABLE IS SPREAD, FEAST OF THE LORD IS GOING ON." Until you get the revelation that the table that is indeed spread has got your name personally applied at the place setting, you may be more apt to stay away even longer that you have already?

Look through the eye's of your spirit and you will see the opened door, the person standing in the doorway with their arms extended beckening for you to come is the Lord Jesus Christ. Every since the cross of Calvary, Jesus has never lowered His Arms, and He is still saying to us to Come.

Yes; according to the scripture, Jesus is seated at the right hand of the Father, but, try not to focus with such a humanistic perception, and you will be able to understand that being seated is relative to a positional status of our Lord. It is also relative to the fact that His purpose is fulfilled, in that He did everything that He came to the earth to do. When He finished, He did not cease to exist!

Jesus being seated, is relative to the analogy in the scripture which suggest to us that the Father rested on the seventh day, after He had finished creating the world and all that is in the world as we know of it today. Had it been so that the Father ceased to move another finger, or to be involved in the affairs of the earth, as a result of resting, you and I would not have our Lord and savior Jesus Christ to save us from the destruction of sin and self.

"Operating Table?"

No need to worry at all about the sickness in your body, God; is The Healer. As it relates to sickness and diseases in the human body, the enemy shows up in many different forms.

"Thou Preparest A Table Before Me, In The Presence Of Mine Enemies."

If you can be consistently reminded of the fact that the table has already been prepared, you might not be so apt to go ahead and worry yourself to death over your physical condition and die!

Sometimes the enemy may be family and friends, or the doctor and their medical staff, all of which are consistently discouraging you from believing God for your healing, through faith. I have personally been in service at many different churches, where the pastor or a minister in the pulpit is instructing the people in attendance that God is not going to heal everybody. That might not include you!

I believe that there is one reality for the believer an another reality for the unbelievers, altogether. God will do anything but fail; and He will heal anything; and everything; but, DOUBT AND UNBELIEF! If you die as a result of the sickness in your body, you ought to go down in your grave with the testimony that you were indeed seeking the Lord for healing every step of the way.

Doubt; never pleases the Lord, so you don't want to come before the presence of the Lord stinking of doubt and unbelief, because that smells just like the devil! I wouldn't be too quick to follow after a leader, who through their message to the church, is saying to us to just go ahead and die if you get sick, because God may not heal you anyway!? ! ? ? ? ? ? ??.....Or Will He?

God may not have healed everybody that has ever gotten sick in their bodies, but, don't ever forget the fact that He can! If God had created sickness, He never would have created healing for the purpose of getting the sickness out of your bodies. Everything that God created was for the purpose of remaining or being constant in the realm of humanity.

For the lack of spirituality; certain people give a lot of hairbrained explanations for sickness and diseases, that come upon people. You don't need explanations that taint your faith, you need God, in the name of Jesus to heal you quickly. I have prayed for many people who have gotten healed from sicknesses and diseases, who had even been diagnosed, giving only short time spans remaining, to live.

God healed those people and raised them from their death beds. What if I walked among the very people who needed me to pray for them, believing that God is not going to heal everybody?

Faith in God won't fail you!

Most people of the churches are quite familiar with the story of the woman with the issue of blood, how that she went where she heard Jesus would be passing by. If you will allow me; SHE SEATED HERSELF AT THE WELCOMED TABLE!

She knew that the master surgeon would be operating on her condition today; she must have thought in her own mind? Bear in your mind, that there were people who did not even want her there in the way, as Jesus passed by. I thank God that she didn't get too preoccupied with whatever the people were saying.

The ultimate design of her plan, was to get her healing from the only one capable of changing her situation. This woman started out with only a concern that became an illness, which later developed into an all out five alarmed situation! She tried everything that her money allowed her to try. Her money and her abilities all ran out, as her blood continued to flow.

In her own desperate situation, she was looking and listening for the next sensation to come available, for her condition. But, one day she heard about Jesus, and she prepared to go and meet Him. She didn't appear to be too concern with getting aquainted with Him, speaking to Him face to face, she just wanted to be healed.

Jesus comes with an agenda that is not hidden! JESUS won't heal ANYONE He can't have! Jesus didn't just have a conversation with the woman so that she could be sure that He was indeed the one who healed her, but, the moment He began speaking with the woman, a right relationship was begun. From that moment on, that woman knew that Jesus did not just heal her, but, that He also loved her, and appreciated her touch. That's right, she touched Jesus! You ought to also touch Jesus! Ask Him; "LORD; LET ME TOUCH YOU."

"Examining Table"

$\mathcal{O}$thers have been looking you over for years, checking you out from your head to your feet. I think that it is just hilarious when people think that they know you, and that they have got you pegged, simply because they have observed you for a while.

Most people who look at you never have an interest of being intimately acquainted with you. Whenever you talk with your peers, you will discover that they are not interested in getting to know the real you, because they already have a pre-conceived idea about you that satisfies their curiousity about you.

Some people are looking at you from the perspective of your failed family members, thinking that you must be exactly as they are? It usually doesn't help much whenever we come in contact with people who might have been acquainted with our family history, back before we were even born. You may not even show any of the family traits that they seem to be so familiar with, but they still look at you and say; "THE APPLE DON'T FALL FAR FROM THE TREE?"

Others look at you based on the report that they have received about you, they are usually convinced within themselves that they have got to be right about you, because they heard about you from a reliable source.?.??

There are times when you could be talking to another individual about yourself, and that individual will be looking back at you as if to say that you have got to be lying, because somebody else knows more about you than you. Although it maybe tough to deal with, be acceptably informed of the fact that many people will believe in their informant about you, before they will ever believe you!

Jesus on the other hand, is interested in the real you. He knows when you don't even know the real you, for the fact that you have been answering to what everybody else has been saying about you. This is the reason you don't ever have to be afraid to come to the Lord based on who you might be, because Jesus knows the part that you play, and He knows who you are when you get home and take off the mask and the make-up.

Doctors examine us to find out what's wrong with us when things are not going so well physically, but, Jesus examines us because He already knows everything there is to know about us both naturally and physically, and His purpose is to show us who we are.

In the 32nd chapter of Genesis, Jacob wrestles with a man all night long. He wrestled until the breaking of the day, or until daybreak. In wrestling with the man, he managed to get a hold onto the gentleman, to the point that the man said to Jacob; "PLEASE LET ME GO!"

However, Jacob's reply to the man has caught me by the collar. Jacob said; "SIR, I WILL NOT DO SO, EXCEPT YOU FIRST BLESS ME!" Many of the people that we have held onto in the past, should have been let go of much sooner that we did. Not only were they not impressed with us, but neither did they have the power to bless us! We have a tendency to hold on to people who feel that they have thoroughly examined us and have further determined that we are good for nothing. WE NEED TO LET GO!

As Jacob refused to let go of the man; he touched Jacob and moved the hollow of his thigh. In paraphrasing; JACOB'S HIP WAS OUT OF JOINT. The flesh of the shank of the upper thigh, withered. Jacob's hip was out of joint to the point that what he had indeed been standing on could no longer hold him up. He would no longer be found standing on the effective ability to decieve, as a way of maneuvering through his own life, and through the lives of others.

The shank withered up; which indicates that the tricks of the chosen trade of Jacob were no longer operable in the life of Jacob.   There would be no more strength to perform. The sceme of deceptively influencing others would forever lack the gleaming luster that it once had for Jacob. Jacob was truly delivered first; having the cancerous ills of his own nature, surgically removed by the hand of the Lord.

It has been revealed that the man in this vision or dream that Jacob had was actually an ANGEL, because no natural man could bless in the manner that Jacob had been blessed. Some way or another Jacob had a revelation of this person, and what he possessed.

Jacob was already wrestling with himself, over himself, and because of himself. Internally, intellectually, Jacob is spinning and grueling over his past reputation and the behavior of his own past. He is already wrestling internally in fear of the retaliation of his brother Esau.

In the past, Jacob did his brother wrong, now he's determined to make peace with him. He's very sorryful for having stole his brother's birthright, for a bowl of stew. He sent messengers to his brother to inform him that he is coming to make peace with him. His messengers return to inform him that Esau is coming to meet him with 400 of his own men.

Immediately Jacob took this to mean that his brother was coming to destroy him and everything that he had, even his own pregnant wives? Jacob begins to maneuver his things and his servants around into small companies, so that if Esau attacks and one band is lost, there would yet be others left.

Jacob, at this point and time of his life, he is still behaving according to his reputation, which is relative to the definition of his name. Jacob- means "TRICKSTER OR SUPPLANTER." He is preparing to trick his brother into believing that he has destroyed his stuff should he decide to attack him. Bear in mind that Jacob has always been a deceptive little sidewinder.

The Lord had promised Jacob that if he went over the river Jordon to return to his land that He would not deal with Jacob according to his own wayward past.

It's hard to trust other people when you have been untrustworthy yourself. Deceitful people are always expecting to be deceived by others, and even the Lord. Other people may indeed deceive you, but, there is no deception in the Lord Jesus at all. Jacob didn't have to worry about the Lord deceiving him, but for a short while he was concerned. He was afraid that as a result of what he had done in the past, that that only qualified deception, as being all that he could ever receive.

The moment Jacob heard that Esau was on the way, he immediately turned to the Lord and begin to question whether the Lord had led him to Esau to be killed? So Jacob began sending everything and everyone that was with him, away from him, to insure the fact that he would definitely be the last one standing from his own camp.

Jacob strategically sent his servants and his stuff away in shifts, so that everything would not be lost all at once. HE ALWAYS HAD A SCHEME! He was willing to sacrifice everything else first, so that he could buy time to conjure up another sceme in case the others began to fail.

In doing so, he was left alone in the twilight of the

midnight, where he met and wrestled with the angel of the Lord. God was wrestling with Jacob trying to get him to put down the ability to trick other people and to put away the record of his own past. But, Jacob was wrestling for the opportunity to hold on to who he was with his own dear life! He was doing whatever he thought it might have taken to insure that he would be able to live and not die.

Just back at the river Jab-bok, before Jacob ever sent his servants to his brother, he looked up and saw a band of angels watching over himself, and his entourage. It was at this point that Jacob was actualy on the Lord's EXAMINATION TABLE.

God sees; what He already knows; and not what someone else may be attempting to show Him about you. The name Satan- means "ACCUSER OF THE BRETHREN." No one has been more bent on trying to show the Lord how much you do not deserve the blessings of the Lord, other than Satan!

A Hidden Change!

In Jacob's isolation, he's at a point in his life where he can receive the blessing from the Lord, that has been longed for, quite a while.

God knows that you want to be changed, but often times you may be surrounded with people from your past who are determined to hold you hostage, and run interference to the blessing that will come your way.

While people can't stop the hand of God from actually getting to you, they can effect your ability to receive the handed out blessing from the Lord. Certain people of thc church have a tendacy to act just like the devil. They move about the church or even the church community, dumping salt on your character to sources that they are sure will return to you to report the negative onslaught against you.

When they see that certain people have taken to you, they slither like a snake and meander around behind your back to poison your influence with your well wishers. Whenever an individual will get taken in with the possibility of the negative attention, it also has an effect on the relationship between that person and the Lord. However, be advised that God can't be influenced! If so, no one would ever be blessed! Though some people feel that they are bosom buddies with God, nothing moves God favorably to bless an individual but, obedience to the word of God!

Absolutely no one was left in the presence of Jacob to hinder him from being blessed. God in His infinite wisdom, knows the exact time to reach in to your situation to bless you. It wasn't until everybody had left that God made His move. God wants everybody that you have often erected as powerful people to be removed from your surroundings, so that they will not be able to say that they are responsible for you being who you are.

The very same people who may have vowed to others that you would never change, they would like to be the same people to take the credit for your change. Many times they have already signed your doom! They have told everybody that would listen to them that you will never be nothing! They signed that statement by saying; "Over My Dead Body!"

What is amazing to me is how they actually believe that they have the power and the right to stop God from blessing you!

Looking cosely at the story of Jacob, I noticed that Jacob experienced a hidden change! God has moved on the lives of many people in the privacy of their own homes and cars. Some people went for a walk and had an experience with God that has truly been life changing.

I have heard testimonies from people who were on their way to fulfill a sinful desire, and they ran head-first right into the presence of the Lord. The saints have always sang a song in the church that says; *"I WENT IN THE VALLEY, DIDN'T GO TO STAY, MY SOUL GOT HAPPY, AND I STAYED ALL DAY!"*

No one follows you to the operating room but the doctors and their staff. Could you imagine someone in the operating room telling the surgeon; "Put the scaffle down! Don't cut them like that!" Suppose they didn't like one of the very important surgeons or nurses in the room with you? Could you imagine them trying to remove certain persons, who for sure had the operating skills that you needed in that operating room?

In their own ways, people do make attempts at controlling your deliverance. They don't want certain people preaching to you, or ministering to you one on one. They certainly don't approve of certain people laying hands on you, even though they themselves aren't anointed to lay their hands on you.

Many don't believe that you can be changed anyway! So, perhaps, what you might have been believing was indeed abandonment and isolation, has only been the maneuvering of the hand of the Lord to get you to the place of a passionately, powerfully, hidden change!

Many people of the church feel that if they are not present to see you changed, then it can't possibly be real. Don't you be fooled into denying the movement of the hand of the Lord over your life. As ordained of the Lord; IT WAS NOT THEM; IT WAS HIM! He's the one that delivered you!

We also sing a song in the church that says; "THERE IS NO SECRET, WHAT GOD CAN DO!" While there is no secret what God can indeed do for you, many things that God will do for you, will be done in secret.

Come up, from beneath the guilt of being ashamed that God did something for you while no one else was around? Did you ever notice that God was not ashamed to do what He did for you while no one else was present to see it; not even your pastor? Your pastor needs God's approval, God does not need their approval to bless you!

It is our jobs as pastors to be nurse-mates and nurturers to the people of the Lord once they have been delivered and set free. As pastors, we are always the servants, and we never become the savior!

LIKE JACOB; YOUR HIP MY BE OUT OF JOINT, BUT, GET YOUR BLESSING!

Despite Jacob's past, God brings him back into alignment, to fulfill the promise that He had made to Jacob's grandfather; Abraham! You may not even know of the promises that had been made back several generations before you were born, but God does. Many times whenever the enemy is fighting you with everything that he can think of, it's not necessarily you that he is actually targeting?

The enemy is trying to block the pre-ordained promises of God over your bloodline, before you ever came to be. You be assured that whenever God makes a promise, it will come to pass. You may have to come through hell and high water to get to the promise of God concerning your own bloodline and family name, but by the grace of God you will make it!

If members of the family got out of the will of God and strayed from the presence of God many years ago in the past, whereas, the present generations of that particular family have not been members of the church, the promise is still in effect. God will bring someone in the family into alignment to receive the manifestation of the promise. God Don't Lie!

Many times it's been hard, and the battle has been long, but, don't even think of giving up on the Lord. You may not even know the past promises that God has made concerning your bloodline, but whenever the promise get here, you will know it for sure. God is so awesome that He will never leave you in the dark concerning His promises.

For this reason alone, many people who are now prospering in ministry and in life right now, they fall under the judgment of God because of pride and self-righteousness. You are never the sole reason that you have made it in this life on the face of this earth.

Somebody prayed for you, even before your great, great, great grand parents were even thought of. Somebody came into covenant with God long before you did.

So in order to stop God from blessing you, those individuals whomever they might be, would have to be successful at stopping God. They would have to be able to go all of the way back to the years and the times whenever God made the promise to your ancestors!

Bad News: To Whom It May Concern;

Time is in forward progression always, there is no way at all to go back in time. Even if you did, you would find that God is not back there, He's here right now; in the Now! You can't get behind God, and because of the wrong spirit that you are operating in, you can't get with God right now, and you certainly will never get ahead of God. You're not even fast enough!

When a man's ways please the Lord, he maketh even his enemies to be at peace with him **Proverbs 16: 7**
Thou I walk in the midst of trouble, thou wilt receive me: thou shalt stretch forth thine hand against the wrath of mine enemies, and thy right hand shall save me. The Lord will perfect that which concerneth me: thy mercy O Lord, endureth forever: forsake not the works of thine own hands. **Psalms 138: 7-8**

A Message To My Enemies*

I have never been so blessed as to realize through reading the scripture, that my table is set, and prepared for me in the presence of my enemies, who may even truly rejoice with me over my success. They will be glad for me, even though they will not understand why they've had a change of heart concerning me.

When our ways please the Lord, He will make the hunting dogs, stop hunting us. God will break chains, and curse all of the curses that have been spoken against us. He will dispel the spells, bury the dungeons, and disperse the curses into many fragmented and broken pieces, so that that spoken curse will never be the possession of your enemy for a second chance opportunity at sending it after you again.

In the heat of the wrath of our most fierce enemies, the mercy of the Lord is poured out over us, keeping and protecting us from the wicked will of them who have launched out after our success.

So shall they fear the name of the Lord from the west, and his glory from the rising of the sun. When the enemy shall come in like a flood, the spirit of the Lord shall lift up a standard against him.

Isaiah 59: 19

And we know that all things work together for good to them that love God, to them who are the called according to his purpose. For whom he did foreknow, he also did predestinate to be conformed to the image of his son, that he might be the firstborn of many brethren. Moreover whom he did predestinate, them he also called: and whom he called, them he also justified: and whom he justified, them he also glorified. What shall we then say to these things? If God be for us, who can be against us?

Romans 8: 28-31

My purpose has been preordained by God, there is no way that you could predispose of my purpose, my name or even my existence. I'm here to stay, so you might as well get used to having me around, because I'm not going anywhere until God says so!

I have always taken it personal whenever I realized that someone else had aligned themselves against anything that I was doing. For years I walked around questioning myself, trying to figure out why certain people had dropped me like a hot potatoe, after we had been so close, even like brothers I thought anyway?

About ten years ago, I really began to petition the Lord about the situations, as others seemed to have jumped on the band wagon in opposition of me, the Lord began to remind me of a song that He had given me to write, which simply states; "Let GO!"

Even though some of the people who parted friendship with me felt that they had reasons that were in reflection of me, God has since informed me that it was never about either of us.

God ordained the separation for the purpose of the anointing on my life. I have come to realize that I had not been abandoned after all, they had to leave me!

I would inquire of any the persons that had been at least in my circle of laughs, questioning whether I had offended them in any way, they would give me no reasoning, and would say that everything was still alright between us.

I had to learn to stop dialing their phone numbers, and expecting them to contact me.

Letting go has been so rewarding for me, because I am able to go on forward with what God has called me to do without interruptions and hinderances. Many of our good friends and family members have a tendacy to hinder our progress, by invading our private time with the Lord, though unintentionally most of the time.

Have you ever been studying the word of God or down on your knees praying, and at the very moment that you know that you have made the connection, the phone rings, or someone knocks at the door?

Alike Jacob; when others have been removed and are out the way of your connection, between yourself and God, He moves in and begin to go to work on your change. God is so wise, in that He knows how to get us to the point of being set in the right place and positioned just right to receive His hand moving over, in, and through our lives.

It has always been my desire that God would get the glory out my life. It has also been the desire of most of the people that I ever hung around. At least that's what they have all told me? It is always good to know why others have you around. You may unknowingly, trap yourself in the inferior dungeon, of the projection of what may look like the successful lives of your friends?

Some people are easily removed from the friendship that you have had with them at the admonishing of others who don't care as much for you. Anyone, that is easily removed from you, should permanently stay away from you!

Several years ago, I searched the scripture to see what the bible had to say about friends. The pendulum began to swing favorably for me after reading the word of God relative to having friends. What I soon discovered, was that all along I never really had many friends at all. The other 2% of the people who were friends, they know who they are.

Perhaps, God moved them for me, and He moved me for them? Whatever the reason, at best I know that we are all out of each other's way!

Blessed is the man that walketh not in the counsel of the ungodly, nor standeth in the way of sinners, nor sitteth in the seat of the scornful.
Psalms 1: 1

This is the Lord's doing; it is marvelous in our eyes.
Psalms 118: 23

There is such a thing as being too close to see people for who they realy are. Even though others who know them, know that they are rotten to the core, they will receive a report from those no good people about you, defaming your character as being no good.

Often, they are in pursuit of the people with whom they are sure that you have influence with, to preceed you from positively reporting any true facts of their real character! They are so busy being no good, that they never even realize the good in you, in that you have remained friends with them even though their flaws are often times on open display. Perhaps, they let their hair down whenever they get around you, and they really don't want the others to know.

People who are around us, but, never really in our presence because they love us, will result in us being around the Lord, while never being in His presence because we love Him. We learn the wrong behavior.

The worst advise that I had ever been given, and the worst ideas about myself that I had ever heard, came from people in and around the church. You might want to consider the fact that people don't have to be unchurched to give you ungodly counsel.

If you are like me, you tend to believe in the people of the church, but also alike me, you are in for a rude awakening. The fact is that people are at the church for many reasons other than to seek God. They believe and are governed by books and writings and belief systems other than the word of God.

They had planned all along to pull you down from your place of favor with man and with God, both male and female! They may be successful for a short time, but don't ever forget that it's all about your purpose in the Lord, and your obedience to the word of God, that will subdue and conquer your enemies.

Where Are You Going? Don't Run!

David said; "THOU PREPAREST A TABLE BEFORE ME IN THE PRESENCE OF MINE ENEMIES!" To prepare a table is one thing; but David said that He preparest; which means that there is a perpetual continuation in the preparedness of the table set for me. It always is, it always was, and it always will be set for me!

He promised to do this in the presence of our enemies.

The revelation that is indeed precious concerning this passage of the scripture, is the understanding that you don't have to be in the general vicinity of your enemies every single day of your life, subjecting yourselves to grueling punishment, or putting yourselves in the way of deadly possibilities, in order for the Lord to bless you in the Presence of your enemies.

Be mindful of the fact that you do not always know who all of your enemies are, or of their exact location? Wherever they are, and whomever they may be; the Lord has got a day numbered, and a time set to display you with your blessings of the prepared table, before them.

Remember to get a revelation of the table that has indeed been prepared for you, so that you will rejoice over the right table, and not just any table. Certain stores have thrift tables with low budget items for the persons who choose to buy in that manner. There are tables set out at a rummage sale, often times decked with all types of second hand, used items.

God is neither a thrift store or a rummage sale! But, God is a Well-Fare office, in that when He is finished, you are going to gladly tell all of the enemies of your success, FARE-WELL!

Finally; I would like to say to all of my enemies, Thank You for all that you have done to me, and against me! If it had not been for you, I would have missed out on knowing God for myself, in the fullness of His power.

Thank you for hating me, because you caused me to learn that God really does love me. Thank you for pushing me away from you, because God drew me into Him, into the secret of His Tabernacle! I've found a hiding place in God. Thank you for destroying my name, because I have found a name much greater than every name, and even above yours. The name of Jesus is a strong breaker, and a powerful keeper.

When your firery darts were flying towards me, the name of Jesus was my shield and my protection. Thank you for denying me and often saying no to me, because God said yes to me.

For all the promises of God in Him are yea, and in Him amen, unto the glory of God by us.   I Corinthians 1: 20

Thank you for all of the times that I sat on your instruments, and ministered in your pulpits, and you held back on the financial blessings that were due, as the servant is worthy of his hire. Even when you raised money in my name and kept most of the money and dealt treacherously with me; God has been my rewarder. He's going to repay me right here, right now for everything that you have done to me.

Give and it shall be given unto you; good measure, pressed down, and shaken together, and running over, shall men give into your bosom. For with the same measure that ye mete withal it shall be measured to you again.   St. Luke 6: 38

Since the word of God declared that men would give into my bosom, I always thought that it would be those of you of which I offered my services and sowed into your ministries. Many didn't pay me, and I know that they will never pay me! Others didn't pay me what I was actually due, as if groceries and the gas for my automobile, and my utilities did not cost as much as theirs!

Thank you for blocking my music ministry for the time that you did, and for dumping salt on my character while you shook my hand everytime you saw me, and stabbed me in the back whenever I left your presence; God told me; "THAT MY MINISTRY IS TO HIM WHENEVER I PLAY SKILLFULLY UPON THE

INSTRUMENTS." Though you prefer for me to die, "GOD COMMANDED FOR ME TO LIVE!"

Thank you for laughing at me, when I often thought that you were laughing with me! "GOD HAS SMILED ON ME!" You know, I thought that we had an understanding. When I thought that we were laughing at an inside joke, I later found out that I was the joke all of the time.

It never felt good discovering that when certain people turned away from me, and acted very nasty towards me whenever I saw them again, as if I had killed their dog; you were the cause!

For it was not an enemy that reproached me; then I could have bourne it; neither was it he that hateth me that did magnify himself against me; then I would have hid myself from him: but it was thou, a man mine equal, my guide, and mine acquaintance. We took sweet counsel together, and walked unto the house of God in company. Psalms 55: 12-14

My friend, you may have knocked me down; the fact is that you could not knock me out! Thank God; because of you, I have been forced into a hidden place. I have even learned to appreciate the sweetness in the words of people who hadn't seen me as often as they used to, when they say to me; "WHERE HAVE YOU BEEN?"

I have learned that there is a genuine beauty in absence. My mother used to lead a song in the choir which said; " No Never Alone; He Promised Never to Leave Me; Never to Leave Me Alone." At times we can't even perceive the fact that God is even with us because of blocking friends and family members.

My friend, in the wake of your removal from me, I no longer have any grief. I 've had that funeral, and I have buried the painful grief in Jesus. The Holy Ghost officiated the service, and delivered the Eulogy. God was the undertaker; He resided over the committal of the remains to the final resting place, and pronounced the benediction over me.

Afterwards, I went to the presence of the Lord, to the finest dining hall, where the most elegant table was prepared, and we have dined ever since!

> *He that dwelleth in the secret place of the most high shall abide under the shadow of the almighty. I will say of the Lord, he is my refuge and my fortress: my God; in him will I trust. Only with thine eyes shalt thou behold and see the reward of the wicked. Because thou hast made the Lord, which is my refuge, even the most high, thy habitation; there shall no evil befall thee, neither shall any plague come nigh thy dwelling. For he shall give his angels charge over thee, to keep thee in all thy ways.* **Psalms 91: 1-2,8-11**

For We Wrestle Not......Eph. 6:12

Shepherd's Wars & Sheep Attacks

Grand Finale

The Big Guns

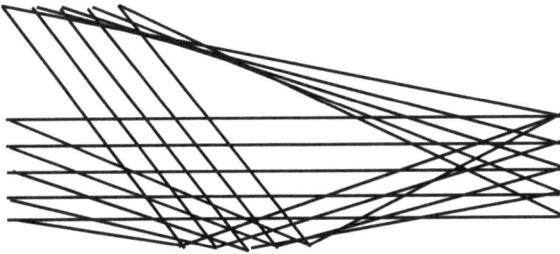

Let the redeemed of the Lord say so, whom he hath redeemed from the hand the enemy;

Psalms 107: 2

And they that shall be of thee shall build the old waist places: thou shalt raise up the foundations of many generations; and thou shalt be called, The repairer of The breach, The restorer of paths to dwell in.

Isaiah 58: 12

We who are of the salvation of the Lord Jesus Christ; we are the redeemed. We have been through the process of being exchanged! We have been bought with a price, that was too great for any man on the face of the earth, or anyone in the entire planet of the cosmos to pay, for the exchange of our redemption.

Those of us that have been ordained, predestined and called to the five fold ministry of the gospel of God; we are not only of the redeemed of the Lord, we are become advocates of redemption. We are the ordained service personel for the purpose of getting the message of the redemption out to the people of the earth.

Adam sold us out to Satan in the garden of Eden; Jesus bought us back at the cross of Calvary. Jesus paid the price and signed the document of our redemption in His own blood. As we spread the message of the gospel of Jesus Christ with excellence, often times without us even knowing that we were selling the rights for redemption, many people have come forward to buy that which had already been purchased.

Ho, everyone that thirsteth, come ye to the waters, and he that hath no money; come ye, buy, and eat; yea, come, buy wine and milk without money and without price. **Isaiah 55: 1**

Only in God, can that which had already been purchased, be bought havng no money or an established price to begin with. It has never been about what you and I could do, because God already knew that you and I could do nothing without Him. It has always been all about what God has already done.

Put those carnal weapons down, and stand up in your calling and the anointing, being the spiritual weapons to which God has endowed you, and rise to the occasion.

Instead of being the repairers of the breach, many have become only fault finders and breach makers around the entire spectrum of the churches. People are walking around with religious magnifying glasses on their eyes attempting to see the hidden things in the lives of their fellow brothers and sisters in Christ, that were never intended for them to see in the first place.

The problem with the people of the Lord is deception! Often deceived about our true identity in Christ. If we continue to feel unworthy to be used by God, and continue to remain insecure about our status before other organized religions, we will never be the powerful instruments of war against our enemy.

We have spent too much time comparing ourselves against each other in the body of Christ. The spirit of envy and jealousy has been impregnated into the spirits of many of the people in the church. Religion has allowed us to take on the spirit of coveteousness, through singing songs like; "There is No Secret What God Can Do; What He's Done For Others, He'll Do For You!"

Most times whatever God has done in the life of someone else may not even be necessary for Him to do in the life of another. He is the same God, but we often have different needs. You ever stop to think that, that is all the others may be getting from the Lord for a long while, simply because that's all they have ever wanted? God has got so much more for those of us that will just continue to wait in patience, before Him.

For our comely parts have no need: but God hath tempered the body together, haven given more abundant honour to that part which lacked: that there should be no schisims in the body; but that the members should have the same care one for another. And whether one member suffer, all members suffer with it; or one member be honoured, all the members rejoice with it. **I Corinthians 12: 24-26**

One of the greatest deceptions of the enemy was convincing the church community of every society, that we are all of a different sort of Christian, but, under the same Christ!

All paper comes from the one same source of trees which grow in the forest or even on the side of the road, even though there are many different types of trees. An envelop is never going to be a notebook. A book is never going to be a dollar bill; though they are all made from one type of paper or another. All of these material substances are made and developed from a natural resource. Trees!

Perhaps the churches have been deceived into believing that alike paper materials, that the churches can likewise be different entities, though they have been brought about by the one self same spirit of God?

There are many different types of trees, so maybe there can be multiples of diverse paper materials. Some paper materials are stronger than the others; however, I'm not sure if that is because of compounding the very same type of paper substance, or if it is because of a different type of tree substance. I like to think that it is perhaps because of the manner in which the natural substances are manipulated and handled in the factory.

Just as you may never closely examine the paper

materials that we are accustomed to using on a daily basis, being able to determine the type of tree it is made from, based on our skills of visibility; you would never be able to know that many churches and the leaders in the churches are Christians; wrought in God.

There is often nothing visible, in what should be the finished product, relative to the disposition of the church that resembles the original source from which they were made. Or; were these churches indeed born from the true sourse?

As we entrench ourselves into the battle, it is important to never overrun the battle, allowing it to spill over back into the ministry of the church where we have been planted, against our fellow churchmen.

If we all kill one another, who would be left to fight the enemy that is indeed fighting against the agenda of the church? Either the enemy is influencing the people of the church, or the people are convincing themselves that the soldiers that are entrenched right next to them in the spiritual dugouts, need to also be destroyed, for the reason of some type of an imperfection of their character.

It's half-past TOO LATE! We who are of the church, we need to get ourselves together, to start helping the people of God to begin living godly lives in Christ Jesus, before we decide that they would be better off dead!?!

In a battle, there are many guns and many skilled personel at using those guns. Certain weapons are only designed to take out one target at a time. Others may be a little better equipped to take out a small band of soldiers in the army of the enemy. A grenade will destroy a group of offensive enemies or maybe even it may take out a particular room in a bunker, or in a hiding place of the enemy.

Any individual that is given the authority to use these weapons, must have an accurate knowledge of the powerful usage of these weapons. There are times when these weapons are not enough for the task at hand. Anyone fighting in a battle has got to know that they need an adequate weapon to fight against the enemy on the battle field.

It's not wise to take a knife to a gun battle; or to take a pistol in a battle against a tank. The obvious would be that the lesser in terms of preparations for the battle would lose the fight.

You, being as spiritual as you are; might say that perhaps I must have forgotten about the battle of David against Goliath? Well if you are as spiritual as you believe, then I know that it has also been revealed to you that David was definitely better armed for the battle than Goliath!

Goliath allowed the devil to deceive him; he believed that he was the biggest and the baddest thing on the battle field. Goliath just knew that he was the big bad bear! He had even convinced the armies of Israel and all of Judah that no one would ever beat him in battle. The Israelites, were convinced that he would take them out one by one. But what Goliath didn't know was that the rules of engagement had been changed right in the middle of the war. Right there in his face on the battle field, the weapons of warfare had changed.

Goliath was soon going to realize that he had indeed taken a knife and a spear, though they were a big knife and a very large spear; he had taken them to a gun battle. He looked at David's sling which was indeed made of wood and possibly a leather strap or some other type of a material, he thought that it was a stick, or rather a pair of sticks?

God; would be taking David's sling and transforming it into the power of a Gun. Goliath looked, but he didn't see what he thought that he saw. He thought that he was looking at the performance of a novice. He was thinking that he would swat David like annoying flies are swatted when buzzing around about our heads. Boy; but wasn't he wrong!

It is always important to trust God with whatever you have in your hand. Whatever you take with you to the battlefield, you want to be sure that the Lord has given an approval of that weapon. David couldn't; you and I can't ever afford, the weapons of our warfare to fail us in the time of battle.

What makes a gun so deadly is the power of the projectile that is realeased from the weapon. Many toy pistols, rifles and guns look exactly like the real thing. But, what makes a toy ineffective is the lack of the power of any projectile.

The lead that bullets are made of are as hot as they are piercing. In speaking to certain persons that I had been acquainted with, after they had been shot, their report has been that bullets burn like fire.

I watched a document once as scientist worked for hours in a laboratory to re-enact the events that must have taken place on the battlefield between David and Goliath. They were stomped at the fact that a stone which had been released from a sling shot, how that it had entered and sank into the forehead of Goliath. To them like most things in the bible, it did not add up to the projections of modern science?

Lead is a natural substance that is found in the ground;

David picked a rock from the ground; as a matter of the fact he picked up five smooth stones. There are usually at least six smoothly shaped bullets in the spin-chamber of a gun. Five is the number of God's grace, for which David chose five stones to reverence God. Six is the number of man. Anytime a person chooses to pick up a weapon to settle their battles against another individual, they are definitely operating in the destructive power of self and the flesh.

Gun powder, is the power of the striking release of the projectile that is fired from a gun. The hammer of the gun has to strike the shell casing of the bullet in order to ignite the gunpoder in the shell, for an instantaneous combustion, to compulsively discharge the projectile from the barrel of the weapon to the intended destination of the target.

For our God is a consuming fire. Hebrews 12: 29

THE HOLY GHOST; is the power of the projection of the rock that was released from the sling shot of David. Alike the gunpowder that causes an explosive release of the projectile, the fire of the Holy Ghost struck the power of the word of God and propelled the faithful release of rock, from the sling shot of the anointed Psalmist, on the battle field.

David had his own gun range; out in the field tending to the sheep, he was in the field trying and testing the word of God, for which God had even allowed him to test the accuracy of those weapons against predators in the wilderness. Don't you remember how David refused to use the armor and the weapons of King Saul, to fight against Goliath citing that he had never proven those weapons?

I believe, that upon physically coming into contact with those carnal weapons, that David's skillfully anointed hands did not sence the power of the presence of God on those weapons. He had the sence enough to pull away from carnal ideology, as the policy and procedure for handling the problems of the church of God, and he refused to go forward with that the Lord had never anointed.

And Saul armed David with his armour, and he put an helmet of brass upon his head; also he armed him with a coat of mail. And David girded his sword upon his armour, and he assayed to go; for he had not proved it. And David said unto Saul, I cannot go with these; for I have not proved them. And David put them off him. And he took his staff in his hand, and chose him five smooth stones out of the brook, and put them in a shepherd's bag, even in a script; and his sling was in his hand: and he drew near to the Philistine. I SAMUEL 17: 38-40

Many of the churches of today, are failing because the generals have taken upon themselves to use carnal manuscripts of the world, to govern the business of the church. Many have left off from following after the leading of the Lord and have never even been filled with the Holy Ghost. They project themselves and their intellectualism as the power to destroy the enemy, even though most of them do not even have a clue as pertaining to who their real enemy is.

Too many of the churches are allowing things to go on that they know that God has never ordained. Just because God may allow certain things to go forth in the church, doesn't mean that God has also approved of the same.

Under these circumstances, more confidence is being shown in carnal things, than in the spirit of God. The things that are fashioned and formed by the hands of man, are often conveniently available to be chosen as an option for handling the matters that surround your ministry. You may even be apt to make the carnal choices that you are making, as a result of the fact that the other pastors of your own circle have also chosen those particular methods of doing things in their ministries?

Even though you have noticed that those methods don't bring the glory of God to the ministry of the church, or that it does not even reflect the righteousness of Christ among the bible believing people of the vast society in the communities, you still choose to follow after that which is common, rejecting that which is spiritual.

Maybe it's that you don't want to be cited as a rebel, whereas the pastoral coalition of your surroundings would probably oust you from the fellowship of their churches, because you choose to follow the Word and the spirit of God; rather than to follow after their god-less methods.

All of the other soldiers, even David's older brothers, fought using the same mehtods of warfare that Saul had presented to David. But thank God, that wasn't enough for David to make the same losing choice of fighting from the methods of their choosing.

Upon David's approach to the battlefield, he noticed that the men of Saul's armies were hiding in the trenches, afraid to come out and face this big giant of a challenge.

NOTE ALSO: there were dead Israelites strewn on the battlefield that had been destroyed by this giant. Alike the leaders of today, I'm sure that many of the leaders in Saul's army were looking at the circumstances saying that Goliath posed a real challenging trend against the movement of the church of God.

There are several simple little things that have been erected as great challenges in the churches now days, that only require the back-bone of the leaders to take a stand according to the word of God, and release the power of the Holy Ghost in the midst of the people to redirect the idealism of the people of the church, and we will see change.

It didn't matter to David that everyone else was doing it that way, when he noticed that the anointing of the Lord was not upon that method, he swiftly abandoned it.

In paraphrasing: David said to Saul; "I'VE GOT A BETTER WAY, A SURE WAY THAT IS PLEASING IN THE SIGHT OF THE LORD. I WILL GO OUT THERE AND BRING THAT GIANT DOWN WITH THIS ANOINTED METHOD!"

Saul and the armies of Israel and Judah, were so terrified that I really don't think that it mattered what method David used, though David had a resume of the experiences he had with the Lord prior to this offensive attack of this Philistine giant.

Some were sure that David would lose his life also as did others, because the giant was out of control and he had the attentive influence of the enemies of the armies of Isreal and Judah. Goliath talked about the God of Israel and Judah, as if there was no reality to our God at all. Even as David came closer to the fight, Goliath was still talking a lot of noise, about the armies of God.

The enemy looked up and noticed that David, being only a little lad; had stepped up to the challenge. Even Goliath made the mistake of believing that the challenge was too much for this ruddy little shepherd boy.

The problem with people who are always at war with you, is the fact that they may see you, but they are often blinded to what you are bringing to the battle.

Don't worry yourself about people sizing you up as

being inadequate to do the job for the Lord. If God has given you the instructions to go forth for what ever the reason, you are more than enough for the assigned task or else God would not have ever given you the charge!

> *And when the Philistine looked about, and saw David, he disdained him: for he was but a youth, and ruddy, and of a fair countenance. And the Philistine said to David, am I a dog, that thou comest to me with staves? And the Philistine cursed David by his gods. And the Philistine said unto david, Come to me, and I will give thy flesh to the fowl of the air, and to the beast of the field. Then said David to the Philistine, thou comest to me with a sword and a spear, and with a shield: but I come to you in the name of the Lord of host, the God of the armies of Israel, whom thou hast defied. This day will the Lord deliver thee into mine hand; and I will smite thee, and take thine head from thee; and I will give the carcases of the host of the Philistines this day to the fowls of the air, and to the wild beast of the earth; that all the earth may know that there is a God in Israel.*
>
> I Samuel 17: 42-46

Many leaders who attempt to handle the business affairs of the church according to the Holy bible are criticized and mocked, often with terrible disdain, and said to be outdated and old fashioned. In retaliation to your leadership being governed by the Lord, people will even threaten your life.

"AND I WILL GIVE THY FLESH TO THE FOWLS OF THE AIR!"

In our own modern vernacular, this statement is quite similar to that of saying; "I'm going to tell everybody everywhere! I'm going to BLACK-BALL your name across the country! I'm going to tell everybody that I know, not to show any respect for you in any manner, regarding your ministry!"

"AND TO THE BEAST OF THE FIELD!"

Here is Goliath's biggest mistake! He vowed by his own idle gods to destroy the name, the reputation, and the recognition of David in the earth among his peers and his enemies alike. He literally planned to take David out! He was determined to hurt David's family, to break the heart of his mother. The devil in Goliath, had a plan to annihilate the purpose of God over the life of David. The devil lied again!

Thank God; David never allowed fear to grip his heart causing him to back down from the uncircumsized challenge. David knew that he had been anointed with a divine purpose on his life, and he already knew the hand of the protection of the Lord, was over his life.

In David's response to the threat, I can hear him saying to Goliath; "MY LIFE IS HIDDEN IN THE HANDS OF THE LORD; IF YOU CAN GET IT AWAY FROM HIM THEN YOU CAN HAVE IT!" David took the responsibility to remember the purpose of the Lord over his life, knowing the there was no one else to depend on to cover him. He opened his own mouth and began to talk back to this demonically influenced rebel.

I like the fact that David did not have a mind to glorify himself in the presence of Goliath and the armies of the Philistines, rather he took action to glorify the God of his salvation.

And all this assembly shall know that the Lord saveth not by sword and spear: for the battle is the Lord's, and he will give you into our hands.

I Samuel 17:47

I am also impressed with the manner of which David included all of the armies of Israel and Judah in the victory of the battle. Stepping forward to do something that the others were never even ordained, neither anointed to do, would not be a reason to cast them aside, or to discount them as nothing or unimportant.

They had been fighting the battle all of the time prior to the confronting defeat of this Philistine giant. Somehow they caught a snag in their routine of successfully defeating this enemy, they were not equipped to remove Goliath themselves'. The armies of Israel and Judah were committed to keeping the safety of the camp for which they had been faithful to the charge.

David stepped up to the forefront with an urgency. He knew that now is the time to do away with this enemy before we suffer greater casualties in the battle. When the devil comes into your church, it is not good wisdom to just sit there and think that things will work itself out some way or another. If God wanted things to lead the church, you would have never been called and anointed to lead! Goliath; AINT bigger than God! Strengthen your back, and straighten up your posture in the CALLING that you have been called to walk in.

The church is in God's hands, but, He has entrusted you to lead the people, even the same people who often step out of line with the vision of the ministry of God. No matter how often Goliath shows up in the ministry of your church, more-so to the likes of giant sized challenges, it's your job as the shepherd of the sheep to knock him down and to take him out.

And it came to pass, when the Philistine arose, and came and drew nigh to meet David, that David hasted, and ran toward the army to meet the Philistine. And David put forth his hand in his bag, and took thense a stone, and slang it, an smote the

Philistine in his forehead, that the stone sunk into his forehead; and he fell upon his face to the earth. So David prevailed over the Philistine with a sling and with a stone, and slew him; but there was no sword in the hand of David. Therefore David ran, and stood upon the Philistine, and took his sword and drew it out of the sheath thereof, and slew him, and cut off his head therewith. And when the Philistines saw their champion was dead, they fled.

I Samuel 17: 48-51

"DAVID HASTED, AND RAN TOWARD THE ARMY TO MEET THE PHILISTINE."

Be mindful, that God and the things of God are always ahead of us moving forward in progression. Even when we have determined in our hearts to be victorious against the onslaught of the enemy, we must face the challenge head on. We must proceed on forward.

Here's Why: Anytime we choose to run in the opposite direction away from the challenge that is confronting us, we are most likely moving in a direction away from God. Always remember that God is forever in front of you. Only the curse of your past could ever be behind you!

What the men of the armies on both sides of the battlefield, and Goliath could not see, while David was running in the direction of Goliath; he was most assuredly running into the name of the Lord! Goliath was only a hindrance, and a potential stumbling block. David had to go THROUGH Goliath *TO GET TO* the safety of the name of Jesus. David realized that he needed to get in a hurry to get under the shelter of the name of the Lord.

David heard the name of Goliath very plainly as he also heard the voice of this great big evil giant making loud declarations towards the armies of Israel and Judah.

However, the name of the Lord did not just sound out loud in the ears of David, as did the name of Goliath; the name of the Lord rang deeply within the spirit and the soul of David, to the point that his convictions, and the righteous indignation of the Lord, was stirred to the maximum.

From the end of the earth will I cry unto thee, when my heart is over whelmed: lead me to the rock that is higher than I. For thou hast been a shelter for me, and a strong tower from the enemy.

Psalms 61: 2-3

I will say of the Lord, He is my refuge and my fortress: my God; in him will I trust.

Psalms 91: 2

But the Lord is my defense: and my God is the rock of my refuge. **Psalms 94: 22**

From the rising of the sun unto the going down of the same the Lord's name is to be praised.

Psalms 113: 3

The name of the Lord is a strong tower: the righteous runneth into it, and is safe. **Proverbs 18: 10**

I have become like David, in that if I have got to run through you to get to the praise of the name of my God, then so be it; Amen! David picked up five rocks, or smooth stones; but, he asked God to lead him to the rock that is higher. Shepherds, you have got to realize that God is bigger and greater than you, and He is higher than you. You can't find shelter under anything that is too small or too low-down to the ground to cover you.

David already had a revelation of the name of the Lord Jesus Christ. Jesus confirms the revelation of David's words concerning the rock.

And I say unto thee, that thou art peter, and upon this rock I will build my church; and the gates of

hell shall not prevail against it.
St. Matthew 16:18

And all did drink the same spiritual drink: for they drank of that spiritual rock that followed them: and that rock was Christ. ### I Corinthians 10:4

David was fighting for the establishment of the church of the Lord Jesus Christ, so that we that are standing in the stead of shepherding the sheep of God, would have the established power of the church to stand in spite of us, and in the behalf of us. The fight in David was bigger than all of the noise that Goliath was talking out on the battlefield. I believe that David knew that the gates of Hell could not be allowed to prevail against the church of God.

The rock that was indeed slung from the slingshot that David had in his hand was the establishment of the church of Jesus Christ being hurled right into the face of the devil citing the eternal defeat over Satan, both at that presence in that fight, and in the future. The rock sank into the forhead of Goliath, signifying the destruction of any demonic ideaology that should rule and govern the church. God struck down any devilish; demonic; Satanic and even humanistic thinking relative to the welfare of the church!

Therefore; the church prevailed before it ever manifested to the world. The very same power that pushed that rock, is the same power that raised Jesus from the grave. It was the power of the ressurection, set in motion through the word of God, to show the forefathers of the old covenant, that God's plan of salvation and redemption for all mankind, would never fail.

JESUS IS THAT ROCK! He lived among us; and went about doing good to all people. Jesus was crucified on the rocky; rugged hill called, Golgotha. Then very amazingly; the rock was nailed to a cross made from a tree. For millenniums now, people have wept over the cruelty of the crucifixion of Christ Jesus on the cross. Consider this: The nails placed in the body of Christ by man, were signification of the comprehensive imposition in the psycological blindness that would always blanket the minds of mere men.

> *But if our gospel be hid, it is hid to them that are lost: in whom the god of this world hath blinded the minds to them which believe not, lest the light of the glorious gospel of Christ, who is the image of God, should shine unto them.* **II Corinthians 4: 3-4**

The nails, would also signify that man would forever desire to determine the position and the only actual place for the church among the people of the earth. Don't you see how everything that is against the holiness of God, and the agenda of true Christianity, is often forcefully hurled in the direction of the church? For this reason alone preacher, you ought to be more responsible for what you allow to take place in the sanctuary of your church!

Jesus was taken down from the cross and buried in a borrowed tomb.

As a child I used to hear the senior pastors preaching about a rock in a rock; a rock around a rock; and a rock over a rock. To be honest with you, it was a hard saying to me, because, I could never get to the meat of the understanding in what they were trying to convey to us, other than the fact that Jesus was buried in a tomb made out of a rock, with a large rock covering the entrance, to shut up the grave.

I don't believe that they completely understood their message either?

I understand now more assuredly, what God was indeed saying through those patriarchal preachers of the faith. Many preachers who have gone on before us, preached the gospel of Jesus Christ, evidently with unimaginable, incomprehensible excellence! I say this because, as of these latter generations, preachers are fumbling over the message of the gospel, allowing the standards of holiness to fall, and even to be walked on by the people of the world, and the church.

When God spoke to Abraham, because he could sware by no other, because none was greater than He is; God said; "I sware by my own self!" Glory to God! Come on Let's Praise Him Right Now!

(Hebrews 6: 13)

Only natural substances of such as is rock, would be allowed to cover the rock of all the ages and our salvation. Jesus is that nail in a sure place; He's real; those things that are natural are authentic, they are real. The very solid Christ Jesus; was held in the sure place of the tomb which had been hewn out of the rock of the hill side.

Nothing was ever going to move the tomb nor the rock of our salvation in the grave, because it was already established, even before the foundation of the world.

> And I wept much, because no man was found worthy to open and to read the book, neither to look thereon. And one of the elders saith unto me, Weep not: behold the Lion of the tribe of Juda, the Root of David, hath prevailed to open the book, and to loose the seventh seal thereof. **Revelation 5: 3-4**

Make no mistake about it, we are in a battle everyday of our lives in this walk with the Lord. Though it may often appear that many people have lined up against you for whatever the cause, things are not always what they appear to be. It looked like the Philistines were winning the battle as long as Goliath was out on the battlefield destroying the men of Israel and Judah, one by one.

The very moment the stragedy of their win was alleviated, so was their courage to fight. They ran as if they had seen the Lord face to face, and they were running as if they were looking for a place to hide themselves. They now looked like cowards; while before, they were cheering and boasting their champion on. No matter which side of the situation you are standing on, your Goliath must die! He will come down!

What you fight with is always as important as the skill in which you use your weapon to fight. I have matured to the point now that I have the wisdom to choose Christ in the times of my battles! Many times before, whenever I had been faced with confronting challenges or challengers, my choices had not always been to pick Christ, through praising and worshipping Him as my weapon of choice. I have wanted to take matters into my own hands.

But, I realized that God allowed me to see the destruction of others who would not wait on the Lord, and whose decisions wrecked their families. So many times when I could have taken matters into my own hands to satisfy my anger and my distress, I would allow my own mind to reflect back on the mistakes of others who had been through what I was going through; that helped me to make sobering decisions.

Other people will always benefit from your righteous decisions, even those persons that were too afraid and sometimes too envious and jealous to help you conquer the challenges that was actually facing all of you. Though they entrenched themselves and hid their weapons underneath their bodies in the ditches, be advised and prepare your self for the celebration, because those persons that were really afraid, most of them, they are going to rejoice with you as if you all did it together.

What good is a victory anyway if there is no one to share in the celebration of the win with you? You might as well set yourself to praise the Lord, because after an obedient victory, God is going to speak a word to you being that He is pleased with you.

> *Awake, awake; put on thy strength, O Zion; put on thy beautiful garments, O Jerusalem, the holy city: for henceforth there shall no more come into thee the uncircumcised and the unclean. Shake thyself from the dust; arise, and sit down, O Jerusalem: loose thyself from the bands of thy neck, O captive daughter of Zion. For thus saith the Lord, ye have sold yourselves for nought; and ye shall be redeemed without money.* Isaiah 52: 1-3

Jesus redeemed us to advocate redemption to those who are yet sold away in slavery to sin and iniquity.

God is saying to the church, "COME TO YOURSELF AND REALIZE WHO YOU ARE!" I know that you have been through some things, but that does not define who you are, and neither does it determine what you can do as the church. Usually, the battle against the church is intense and very grievious, but the battle can never establish any dominating effect over the power of the church.

It is so awesome to me, how that God comes right back to the original plan from the beginning of the coming of the Lord. Satan can sidetrack people that are around the church, but, he can never sidetrack the God of the church!

God is so wonderously awesome, in that he doesn't ever need to focus, because there is never a time that God could ever be out of focus. God's vision can never be obscured. In the middle of any battle, it is imparative that we as the people of the church understand that God sees us in whatever state we are in.

Stop It; Let's Come Together In The Peace Of God!

I wonder when will we who are the "Big Guns" of the ministry of the church realize just how stupid and unnecessary it is to maintain, and to kindle, and to continuosly rekindle the wars that are destructively binding the intended repose of the church to reflect the power and the presence of God in the earth?

Battleships, tanks, and warplanes all carry the really big guns that are capable of major assaults against the enemy. The ammunition that is fired from these guns are much greater in diameter than those that are fired from an assault rifle or any gun. Bigger guns serve the purpose for much greater purposes. They are bigger for reasons that had already been preordained.

Every pastor doesn't have the same ranking among the brotherhood. This is not only so, relative to the length of time a person might have been in the ministry. But, it is relative to the level of definitive comprehension in the relationship that an indvidual has maintained with the Lord, and their calling.

Have you ever called out to a person while they were in the company of other people, and when they began moving in response to the direction of your call; so did the other people, as if you called them also? So it is with the calling of the ministry to pastor. The Lord called some indeed; while others took it upon themselves to just go in the same direction of them that were called, maybe even in the response to the call of someone other than the Lord calling them to step into the ministry.

A cruise ship is also a very huge vessel on the water, but it's size does not qualify it to be used in a battle as a certified battleship! The military even have ship vessels, that are hospitals on the water. Though there are beds, a kitchen and other facilities for the people on board, it would never be put in place to be used as a cruise ship, because internally, they have been constructed for very different purposes. There are things installed in the one vessel that were intentionally omitted from the construction of the other.

Cruise liners, are for recreation and vacationing to far away places from the norm of everyday living, and from the hustle and bustle of the stresses of society. Battleships, are exclusively produced for the business of fighting the war from the position of the sea, whereas only those persons who are inducted into the military are allowed on those ship vessels of war. Everything on board the ship is about the business of the battle. Although both vessels may have things installed that are intended to be used exactly, for same purposes, the two vessels on the water will never be exacted the same purposes.

HERE IS THE PROBLEM AMONG THE PASTORING BROTHERHOOD: The confusion lies within the individual that understand that they are called to be a battleship, but for some reason or another they struggle, questioning within themselves, if the Lord is OK with their decision to be a recreational Yatch, or a Cruise Liner. They see the battle and the warfare that confronts the church out on this sea of life on a consistent basis, but they would much rather haul a people that are just happy on their way to relaxation, with no intention to join in the fight of the battle against the enemy of the church of Jesus Christ.

Many pastors that have not been called to walk in the office of the Prophetic, are not often advocates of prophecy, rather they are usually adversaries to the prophets of their surroundings; both male and female alike. They teach the people of their congregations to shun prophets, and in some instances they even teach the people to reject prophecy altogether. Be careful about preaching prepared sermons against prophets and prophecy from the pulpits of your church. You need the prophet and the prophetess!

Prophets are to the likenesses of submarines; they can float on the surface of the water just like the other ships and floating vessels, but they can also submerge beneath the surface of sea and go very deeply underneath the ocean without imploding. They can withstand the depths, successfully traveling and moving close to the ocean floor with out being detected. When necessary they can shoot weapons and discharge explosives under the water, that approach the enemy from a very unexpected position of assault.

The Prophet and the Apostles are both anointed to help the pastor with the body, as they lead the people into salvation, deliverance, and healing. They are set in the body of Christ at large whether you like it or not! They are intentionally placed with abilities that others in the five fold ministry do not have. Being made differently does not make them an enemy to you, or to the people of your congregation!

I urge you to search the scripture again, to be informed

of what the Lord has to say about the prophets and the Apostles, relative to the body of Christ!

Pastors, I urge you also to stop embracing sin in the lives of the people of your congregation just because you feel it encourages them to cater to you. God is pulling the cover off of the foolishness in the ministry of the churches. If you will go ahead and live clean according to the word of God, and stop feeling guilty every time you come before the presence of God (if you ever do); you can stop thinking that other sinners should be allowed to go forth in the church of God without being delivered, as well.

Perhaps your purpose for embracing certain active sinners is for the reason of the fact that it is easier to hold them hostage to their active wayward lifestyles of sin, keeping them looking up to you and serving you, believing that you are the most well, spiritually put together person of your church. But God don't like ugly:

> For the time is come that judgment must begin at the house of God: and if it first begin at us, what shall the end be of them that obey not the gospel of God? And if the righteous scarcely be saved, where shall the sinner and the ungodly appear?

I Peter 4: 17-18

Pastors, Evangelist, Prophets, and Bishops are being judged all across the country for allowing disdain and a reproach against the church from an inward perspective. Pastor, whatever God hates, so do you! It shouldn't even matter if the society of your surrounding communities thinks that you are not loving or if they feel that you are too judgmental.

You belong to the Lord; that is the reason that most people will be shooting for you as a target. They are often determined to prove that you are not as connected to the Lord, as you are suppose to be. The worst decision that many pastors have made, was making their ministries more seeker sensitive, so that people could publicly come before the presence of the church any way that they choose to do so, and return to live anyway that choose to in their daily lifestyles.

You had better go back and redefine your position as the pastor of your church congregation before it's too late. Every soul that slips into hell underneath the leadership of your pastorage, you will give an account for them. Sadly, but you will have to stand before the Lord and explaine why you were determined to make friends so that everyone would like you, rather to make desciples, so that everybody would learn to love Jesus!

The driven wedge between men and the women in the ministry has been narrowed, but it has not been alleviated. It's bewildering to me how that most men in the ministry appear to believe that it's OK for a woman to do what's wrong around the church and sin with every man and any woman that will participate, but they feel that it is detestible for the woman to do what's right in that she has answered the masters call to the ministry?

It can't be right if the woman goes to hell for refusing to do what the Lord is calling her to do, but, wrong for the woman to work out her own salvation in the calling to which she has been called, regardless of what anybody else thinks of it.

I'm talking about a calling and not just some desired position in the body of Christ that she may have no business involving herself. Many men of the ministry still accuse women who preach of being lesbians, because of their calling to preach the word of God. However many of these same men have women in their congregations that are actively living the lives of lesbians that they will not even utter a peep to them about their lifestyles.

God never ordained you to consistently war against the women of the ministry. I would shut the door to my ministry if all there was were men and boys. Even the late R&B singer, James Brown wrote an sang a song that said; "This Is A Man's World; But, It Wouldn't Be Nothing Without A Woman Or A Girl!"

Many men in these latter times want to be the women of the church, but God forbid such foolishness be erected in the church as acceptable bofore the Lord. The church is God's; it does not belong to any community programs or social societies that promote lifestyles that are clearly in defiance to the word of God.

Though there have been men and women in the clergy, of the ministry of the church that practice homosexuality and lesbianism, who have hidden underneath the title of the leadership of their ministry; I want them to know;

YOU ARE NOT REALLY AS HIDDEN AS YOU MIGHT HAVE BEEN LED TO BELIEVE. GOD KNOWS WHO YOU ARE AND HE IS ABOUT TO PULL THE COVER OFF OF YOU. EVERY SOUL THAT IS DESTROYED THROUGH YOUR EXPOSURE, YOU WILL GIVE AN ACCOUNT FOR THEM.

So when they had dined, Jesus saith unto Simon Peter, Simon, son of Jonas, lovest thou me more than these? He saith unto him, yea Lord; thou knowest that I love thee. He saith unto him, Feed the lambs.

St. John 21: 15

Never in the history of time has it ever been the better judgment of good wisdom to feed the younger dependant ones whatever they want always, excluding the reality of their needs.

The saints have fought for many years to keep the partitions between the church's ordinances and the ways of the world installed, in order to maintain the position of the church. Whenever the young people of the society come looking for a change, or even for a church, they ought to find the church upright in it's place, holding fast to the word of God.

Growing up in the baptist church in our neighborhood, as young people we were always enticed to dance. Many of the young people our age could do all of the dances of that time. We spent the balance of our Saturday mornings watching "Soul-Train", and " American Band Stand." So as a result we were at least familiar with the dances of our times.

As Elementary school students, we would usually take a trip to the circus once a year. I can remember as if it were just yesterday, how that we were all so amused that a great big Elephant would move to the beat of the music under the tent. The elements of our surroundings always seemed to point into the direction of dancing to the music.

Whenever I came to the Church of God In Christ at the age of 14, I was intrigued and thoroughly impressed to see the people of the church dancing to the beat of a different drum, and an anointed drummer! What blessed me even the more was the fact that there was scripture to back up the activity of the saints in the sanctuary of the church. As the people of the Lord, we have a reason and a right to go forth in the dance before the Lord.

But, while dancing is appropriately appointed and approved for those who are victoriously change through the blood of Jesus, it is also to be governed and controled through the written word of God and the anointing. Having desires to dance in the church is not a brand new thing. The saints who taught us in the past, encouraged us to respect the fact that there is an anointed dance that reverences God, and a dance that excites the curiousity of the flesh. We never quit dancing, we only changed our partner and our dances. The Holy Ghost is our partner!

They send forth their little ones like a flock, and their children dance. They take the timbrel and harp, and rejoice at the sound of the organ. They spend their days in wealth, and in a moment go down to the grave. Therefore they say unto God, Depart from us; for we desire not the knowledge of thy ways. What is the almighty, that we should serve him? And what profit should we have, if we pray unto him? **Job 21: 11-15**

Any dance that doesn't reverence God, shouldn't be done in the atmosphere of the church! We come in to the church to be saved from our sinful lifestyles; not to be the same as we were whenever we came in! The same dances that are seen on the television, that have been reported to be the same dances that are being performed in nightclubs, are the same dances that are being seen in the aisles and on the platforms of the churches.

Nowadays, the young people of the churches are being allowed to do dance performances that call for rubbing and touching themselves in places that have nothing to do with being saved or giving reverence to God, at all! The average dancing young person in the church, can't even quote a single scripture that relates to dancing before the Lord in the sanctury, and neither can they give any spiritual reasons for dancing.

My point is that the young people are coming into the churches and they are expressing to the churches what they want to see in the church, instead of receiving what they need from the leadership of the church, they are being allowed to establish the atmosphere in the sanctuary.

I believe in the young people of the church, and I believe above all that they belong in the church with the rest of the saints. But, they are to be trained and instructed in the ways of the Lord, in effort to be the effective leaders whenever their time comes to be the heads the churches.

Though rebellion to the word of God is among many of the leaders of the churches of today, it is not the will of God for the younger generations of today to be taught to further rebel against the will of God for the church. In humble submission to the word of God, the young people are to be trained and influenced in the ways of the Lord.

Don't under-estimate the young people's ability to be taught effectively, how to lead the people of the Lord after your time as the leader of the church has expired. Every shepherd should desire to see the results of their teaching, in that a younger person have matured to show forth the teaching and training of their leader. I don't believe that your desire for the persons following your leadership, should be for them to take the helm only after you are dead and gone.

Not enough leaders of today are even living to see the effectiveness of their training. Perhaps your desire as the shepherd of the flock, should be to publically ordain and to endorse your successor, to carry on the work of God that you had been assigned and dedicated to for the time period that had been alloted to you. Pastor it's the only way that you will be at peace knowing that the work of your ministry will carry on in a manner that is pleasing to the Lord!

Too many pastors are fighting to hold on to the ministries of the churches that has outgrown their leadership! WOW! They are carrying on as if to suggest that they have been sentenced to the congregation where they are presently presiding. Many of the leaders might even live a lot longer if they would move around and refuse to be god in the eyes of the people. Thank God; I have determined through the word of God, that my only purpose is to point the people to the Lord, and then to teach them how to walk in His ways.

Preachers all over the country applaud the down-falls of other pastors who fall. Whenever a member of the body falls, the entire body is affected by the downfall of that individual.

> Brethren, if a man be overtaken in a fault, ye which are spiritual, restore such an one in the spirit of meekness; considering thyself, lest thou also be tempted. **Galatians 6: 1**

It is public knowledge that some of the leaders of the churches are so full of themselves that they will not even concede to being at fault even when they have been exposed, and even caught with their pants down around their ankles.

As a result, there is not even an initiation to the beginning of any restoration. It is forever impossible to help an individual that will not even admit to needing help. Those who are uplifted in pride, and are given to a very haughty spirit, make it easy for the other brotheren to point the finger to say; "I knew it!": or to say; "I Told You So!" People are more apt to allow an individual to complete a fall, if that individual carries themselves as if they are untouchable.

The pastors are so busy warring with each other, that they will watch the evening news consistently, as another clergyman goes down in flames, without even uttering a word of prayer for them.

The members of your congregation are spinning in their heads; their faith has been shattered, many of them; most have determined to leave the church of Jesus Christ altogether. While the war is in array among the leading clergy, I often wonder just who do these warring officials of church think is going to be responsible to restore the fallen ones of the church?

Many are often so preoccupied with the fight, that too much time is waisted before responding to the needs of the people who have been let down by their leader. Some of the people that have been allowed to leave the church while the fight is on, will never return! Many of the sheep won't even make it back to the safety of the fold. The predators of the wild will devour them before they will have a chance to find their way back.

The reality of this story is so prevalent that I have to search for a place to stop writing, so I will just say to you; come together as the body of Christ! NOW!

www.ingramcontent.com/pod-product-compliance
Lightning Source LLC
Chambersburg PA
CBHW062011090426
42811CB00005B/819